Gender and the Body in the Ancient Mediterranean

Gender and the Body in the Ancient Mediterranean

Edited by
Maria Wyke

BLACKWELL
Publishers

Copyright © Blackwell Publishers Ltd 1998

ISBN: 0-631-20524-1

First published in 1998

Blackwell Publishers Ltd
108 Cowley Road, Oxford OX4 1JF, UK

and
350 Main Street
Malden, MA 02148, USA

British Library Cataloguing in Publication Data
A catalogue record for this book is available
from the British Library

Library of Congress Cataloging-in-Publication Data
Applied for

This book is printed on acid-free paper

Gender and the Body in the Ancient Mediterranean

edited by Maria Wyke

CONTENTS

Abstracts   vii

Introduction
MARIA WYKE   1

Articles

The Essential Body: Mesopotamian Conceptions of the
Gendered Body
JULIA M. ASHER-GREVE   8

Auguries of Hegemony: The Sex Omens of Mesopotamia
ANN KESSLER GUINAN   38

With This Body I Thee Worship: Sacred Prostitution in Antiquity
MARY BEARD AND JOHN HENDERSON   56

Men Without Clothes: Heroic Nakedness and Greek Art
ROBIN OSBORNE   80

Women's Costume and Feminine Civic Morality in
Augustan Rome
JUDITH LYNN SEBESTA   105

The Ideology of the Eunuch Priest
LYNN E. ROLLER   118

Why Aren't Jewish Women Circumcised?
SHAYE J. D. COHEN   136

Creation, Virginity and Diet in Fourth-Century Christianity:
Basil of Ancyra's *On the True Purity of Virginity*
TERESA M. SHAW   155

Thematic Reviews

Engendering Egypt
LYNN MESKELL   173

Barbara Watterson, *Women in Ancient Egypt* (1991) Joyce Tyldesley, *Daughters of Isis: Women of Ancient Egypt* (1994) Gay Robins, *Women in Ancient Egypt* (1993) Dominic Montserrat, *Sex and Society in Graeco-Roman Egypt* (1996)

Re(ge)ndering Gender(ed) Studies
ALISON SHARROCK   179

Ian McAuslan and Peter Walcot (eds) *Women in Antiquity* (1996) Leonie J. Archer, Susan Fischler and Maria Wyke (eds) *Women in Ancient Societies: 'An Illusion of the Night'* (1994) Richard Hawley and Barbara Levick (eds) *Women in Antiquity: New Assessments* (1995) Amy Richlin (ed.) *Pornography and Representation in Greece and Rome* (1992) Nancy Sorkin Rabinowitz and Amy Richlin (eds) *Feminist Theory and the Classics* (1993) Ellen D. Reeder, *Pandora: Women in Classical Greece* (1995)

Manhood in the Graeco-Roman World
JONATHAN WALTERS   191

Maud W. Gleason, Making Men: Sophists and Self-Presentation in Ancient Rome (1995) Nicole Loraux, The Experiences of Tiresias: The Feminine and the Greek Man (1995)

Getting/After Foucault: Two Postantique Responses to Postmodern Challenges
PAUL CARTLEDGE   194

Simon Goldhill, *Foucault's Virginity: Ancient Erotic Fiction and the History of Sexuality* (1995) Linda Dowling, *Hellenism and Homosexuality in Victorian Oxford* (1994)

Reading the Female Body
HELEN KING   199

Joan Cadden, *The Meanings of Sex Difference in the Middle Ages: Medicine, Natural Philosophy, and Culture* (1993) Lesley Ann Dean-Jones, *Women's Bodies in Classical Greek Science* (1994) Nancy Demand, *Birth, Death, and Motherhood in Classical Greece* (1994)

Gendered Religions
GILLIAN CLARK   204

Bernadette Brooten, *Love Between Women: Early Christian Responses to Female Homoeroticism* (1996) Kate Cooper, *The Virgin and the Bride: Idealized Womanhood in Late Antiquity* (1996) Deborah F. Sawyer, *Women and Religion in the First Christian Centuries* (1996)

Gender and Sexuality on the Internet
JOHN G. YOUNGER   209

Notes on Contributors   214

Index   216

ABSTRACTS

Introduction

MARIA WYKE

How does the study of the ancient Mediterranean contribute to the writing of the history of gender? From the nineteenth century onwards, much modern theorizing about the origins, development and logic of marriage, the family, religion, property, class, subjectivity and sexuality grew out of analyses of ancient cultures. This Special Issue returns to a direct encounter with those ancient cultures, and the introduction offers an overview of its concerns and how they interact with and contribute to contemporary debates about gender, the body and history (both ancient and modern).

The Essential Body: Mesopotamian Conceptions of the Gendered Body

JULIA M. ASHER-GREVE

Linguistic, art historical, hermeneutic, gender and intercultural analyses clarify body and gender concepts in Sumerian and Akkadian mythology, literature and visual arts. The body was a fundamental point of reference in ancient Mesopotamia, metaphor for the total self, royal ideology, cities, humanity and deities. Humanity was created without gender; sex, gender and social status were subsequently inscribed on the body. Gender taxonomy tolerated ambiguity beyond the 'normative' masculine/feminine. Body and mind were an inseparable unity and denoted by the same Sumerian word. Mind/body and male/female dichotomy were unknown.

Auguries of Hegemony: The Sex Omens of Mesopotamia

ANN KESSLER GUINAN

Ancient Mesopotamian scholars examined problematic aspects of male erotic desire within the discourse of divination. They documented an array of sexual acts, reading each as an omen, a sign signifying an aspect of the future. Guinan shows that the omens are informed by a coherent perspective and, in general, are concerned with the impact of erotic desire on notions of male identity and expectations of gender hierarchy. The omens oppose masculine hegemony and male/female eroticism in such a way that the denial of one is the assertion of the other. In these omens, masculine power and agency are both expressed and preserved by the disavowal of erotic interactions with women.

With This Body I Thee Worship: Sacred Prostitution in Antiquity

MARY BEARD AND JOHN HENDERSON

Why do ancient writers tell us that sacred prostitutes massed on the citadel of ancient Corinth? What are we to make of Herodotus' famous account of the ancient customs of Babylon? Beard and Henderson examine the formation of the discourse of sacred, or cultic, prostitution both in classical texts and modern scholarship. They take a sceptical position on the existence, in Greece and the Near East, of institutions traditionally envisaged as 'sacred prostitution' and explore the uses which have been, and are still, found for such myth-making with the bodies of women, whether in the form of a 'marriage-market' or of various kinds of 'sacred prostitution'.

Men Without Clothes: Heroic Nakedness and Greek Art

ROBIN OSBORNE

The naked men of Greek art have been an excuse for male nakedness in more recent art, but the significance of male nakedness in classical art is debated. Osborne traces the history of the representation of the naked male body in Greek art and argues that although in early Greek art nakedness was unmarked, and clothing was used only to draw special attention to men, changes in visual rhetoric led artists to make increasingly detailed reference to the male body, causing a loss of semiotic innocence. Naked male bodies thus came to carry messages about sex as well as gender. The reinstatement of the naked male body in classical art followed the development of a highly artificial convention in which beardlessness was equated with sexual immaturity and held to render the male body asexual.

Women's Costume and Feminine Civic Morality in Augustan Rome

JUDITH LYNN SEBESTA

Augustus claimed that the moral decay of the Roman Republic was especially due to Roman women who had forsaken their traditional role of *custos domi* ('preserver of the house/hold'). In reforming feminine morality, Augustus created a new pictorial language that troped the feminine body as a 'moral sign' of civic morality and authorized a distinctive costume for women. Sebesta investigates the relationship between women's garments, the female body and the Roman concept of feminine civic morality.

The Ideology of the Eunuch Priest

LYNN E. ROLLER

Roller explores the evidence for eunuch priests who castrated themselves to honour the Great Mother Goddess Cybele. While the custom of sacred eunuchism originated in Phrygia (in central Turkey), such priests are best attested in Greek and Roman society, where they were viewed with disgust and loathing because of their asexual condition and because they adopted the dress, hairstyles and mannerisms of women. The negative reactions to the eunuch priest rest on an unspoken assumption of the superiority of masculine appearance and of the inviolability of appropriate gender roles for men and women.

Why Aren't Jewish Women Circumcised?

SHAYE J. D. COHEN

From Hellenistic to modern times, in the eyes of Jews and non-Jews alike, circumcision is a sign that marks the boundary between Jews and non-Jews. Jews are circumcised, gentiles are not. What, then, of Jewish women? Why are they not marked with a bodily sign attesting to their place within the covenant? Cohen argues that the Jews of antiquity seem not to have been bothered by this question probably because the fundamental Otherness of women was clear to them. Jewish women were Jewish by birth, but their Jewishness was assumed to be inferior to that of Jewish men. Jews and Christians, however, who opposed circumcision, used the non-circumcision of women as one of their supporting arguments.

Creation, Virginity and Diet in Fourth-Century Christianity: Basil of Ancyra's *On the True Purity of Virginity*

TERESA M. SHAW

Shaw explores the connections between dietary theory, Christian ascetic fasting, gender and the ideology of virginity in late antiquity, especially as represented in the fourth-century treatise on virginity by Basil of Ancyra. With its remarkable attention to the practicalities of embodiment and sexual renunciation, Basil's treatise is distinctive in its genre. After discussing Basil's treatise of creation, the nature of male and female sexual attraction and physiology, the control of bodily passions and the value of ascetic fasting for reducing desire, Shaw sets these topics in the context of ancient medical theory, gender and the theology of paradise.

Introduction

MARIA WYKE

How does study of the ancient Mediterranean contribute to the writing of the history of gender? As Mary Beard and John Henderson observe in this volume, from the nineteenth century onwards, much of the theorizing about the origins, development and logic of marriage, the family, religion, property, class, subjectivity and sexuality grew out of analyses of ancient cultures. From Frazer and Freud to Foucault, the ancient Mediterranean has been explored not just as the ruin of expired histories but as a site of supposedly 'originary' moments in the formation of Western culture.

In particular, the publication of Michel Foucault's three-volume *History of Sexuality* gave classics a significant purchase on the historiography of gender and sexuality which it has not lost over the intervening twenty years. In his second volume, published in English translation in 1985 as *The Use of Pleasure*, Foucault famously formulated sexuality as a culturally constructed discursive apparatus by charting the development of the desiring male subject in Athenian culture of the fifth and fourth centuries BCE.[1] Using the seeming alterity of ancient Greece, he attempted to challenge contemporary belief in the existence of universally fixed, naturally grounded sexual arrangements and behaviours. For Foucault, the study of ancient Greece and Rome helps us examine both the distance that separates us from and the proximity that binds us to past cultures in which we may think we see the origins of our own. The publication of Foucault's work was immediately followed by an explosion of interest among classical scholars in ancient sexual systems and ancient gender identities, and by a massive increase in the audience for such scholarship far beyond the students and teachers of classical studies.[2]

Scholarship on antiquity has thus informed the development of modern theory and been informed by it. Consequently, as the grand narratives of cultural history initiated in the nineteenth century become unravelled in our postmodern era, those of us who investigate the ancient cultures of the Mediterranean can contribute to their undoing by offering challenging rereadings of the privileged ancient sources on which such theories once relied. And, in the case of Foucault, we can expose the insufficiency of his understanding of ancient sexualities—for example, his notorious elision of

female desire—by offering new readings of ancient texts which were marginalized or entirely overlooked in his analyses.[3]

This volume returns us to a direct encounter with the ancient cultures of
the Mediterranean, and its otherwise disparate essays are unified by a central
concern with how ancient bodies are marked, represented, understood and
policed in terms of gender. As in most fields of historical inquiry, such
gender-sensitive[4] studies of the ancient Mediterranean have been preceded
by, and to some degree depend upon, the investigation of 'women in
antiquity', a mode of analysis which concentrates largely on three areas:
the realities, in so far as they can be reconstructed, of women's lives in
ancient societies; images of women in male-produced texts and artworks;
and the few surviving ancient works written by women. Such approaches
have been, and continue to be, crucial as correctives to the near-invisibility
of women in more traditional studies of the ancient Mediterranean. But the
evident shift in the 1980s to studies first of sexuality and then of gender has
been met with both approval and some apprehension.

In the thematic reviews contained in this volume, for example, Lynn
Meskell suggests that the 'women in antiquity' approach risks enstating
woman as a monolithic category that neglects such variable intersections
of difference as economic or marital status, age, nationality, ethnicity, or life
experience. Sex, she argues, cannot be isolated out as a structuring principle for the historiography of women nor, for that matter, can gender. Alison
Sharrock and Jonathan Walters both observe that, where gender studies
attempt to sustain a simple binary opposition between masculinity and
femininity, woman frequently becomes an Other—the carrier of gender
against which man is defined. While Sharrock advocates the continuation
of a woman's perspective (the exploration of women's lives, the recuperative
strategies of reading as a woman, a self-reflection on the status of women
in our academic institutions) and interdisciplinary scholarship (including
literary criticism) to counteract such tendencies, Walters commends recent
trends in scholarship which examine ancient constructions of masculinity
as complex and vulnerable, manifestly subject to slippages and contradictions, and fraught with considerable anxiety for the male elites who
wrote the vast majority of the ancient texts available for analysis.

The body has also become a central analytic tool in ancient Mediterranean studies. A continually growing corpus of critical literature has his-
toricized and theorized the body as a cultural construct, from, for example,
the sociological publications on the body of *Theory, Culture and Society* to
Judith Butler's concerns with discursive control over bodies and sexualities
in *Bodies that Matter: On the Discursive Limits of 'Sex'* (1993). Such studies
disclose that the body is a crucial site for the display of difference (including
gender difference), its investigation, and its transformation or containment
fundamental to a particular society's practices of power. As in the cultural
formation of sexuality and gender, so in the formation of the body, ancient
theories, social and cultural practices, and attendant readings of them have

contributed much. From the late 1980s, many works have appeared which both examine the historically constituted bodies of antiquity and interrogate their reception—the different ways in which various cultures have read the gendered bodies of their ancestors—in such varied domains as philosophy, medicine, religion, ethnography, politics, or the figurative arts.[5]

The body/gender axis of this book thus brings together two central trends in scholarship on the cultural construction of ancient subjects. The essays collected here investigate the ancient body as a peculiarly privileged site for the production, display and regimentation of gender identity and gender differentials, and as a visible, material locus for gender's complex intersection with other claims to identity in the communities of the ancient world. Although loosely chronological in arrangement, the essays do not pretend to construct some evolutionary tale of the ancient gendered body through the ages and are far too selective even to constitute representative scholarship on the geographical scope and huge chronological scale that together make up the heterogeneity of the 'ancient Mediterranean'. Instead the collection offers an archaeology of the gendered body, a far more fragmentary, contextual and multi-layered enterprise. For, as the contributors suggest, the gendered body of antiquity is never at any moment uniform, but is always multiple, always undergoing change, and always in a state of permanent contradiction. It is on the body, or in somatic metaphors, that cracks and fissures in the taxonomies of gender frequently emerge. In that, for us, lies its fascination.

Conventionally in Western philosophy from Plato to Descartes, women have been equated with the body, nature, emotion and the particular, men with mind, culture, reason and the universal, in a hierarchical organization of relations between the sexes. Julia Asher-Greve opens the volume provocatively with a broad dialectical survey of ancient Mesopotamian art and literature from c. 3000–1600 BCE that destabilizes such simple and familiar binary oppositions between masculinity and femininity. In Mesopotamian myth, the human body is a divine, genderless creation which only subsequently fragments into complementary anatomies required for procreation and upon which social gender is imposed. Furthermore,, Mesopotamian taxonomies of the body tolerate multiple or ambiguous genders, such as the castrated male or the sexless goddess. Emphasis on anatomical difference (on motherhood and male strength) and on binary oppositions between the sexes emerges, Asher-Greve argues, only with the increased militarism of Mesopotamian society and the consequent social and political marginalization of women.

After Asher-Greve's broad survey, Ann Guinan focuses in on a unique set of little-known texts from the late Mesopotamian culture of the first millennium BCE which offer an avenue on to the anxieties and erotic desires of embodied persons and their confrontation with socially instituted constructions of gender relations. How, she asks, did the male subject negotiate the interplay between his sexual and social desires? In Mesopotamian sex omens, an array of (especially non-procreative) sexual acts are read as signifying aspects of a man's future. Such acts are auspicious only where the male is the subject. Where the sexual partner is active and dominating, to that partner's behaviour is ascribed the power to destabilize the masculine self, to threaten a man's relations with his god, to weaken his social influence and to jeopardize his health and wealth. The logic of the sex omens constitutes a male subject who must constantly be vigilant over his physical passions and the vulnerable boundaries of his body, if he is not to surrender his fragile hold on a civically constituted masculinity.

Both in antiquity and in modern scholarship, bodies and gender have frequently been placed in the service of the formation of a Western myth about Eastern cultural exoticism. Ancient Near Eastern societies such as Mesopotamia have persistently been construed by Greeks and Romans (and by modern fans of their culture) as a primitive, feminized, sexually transgressive Other against which to set a civilized, masculine, moral and, by implication, superior West. Writers, both then and now, tell of unimaginably other dispositions of law and custom regarding the body, often repeating the story of 'sacred prostitution'. Mary Beard and John Henderson rigorously explore and carefully unpick the assembled testimonia for cultic prostitution in the cities of the Near East and Greece's own internal Other, Corinth. Western ethnographic narratives of temple prostitution operate, in their view, as an erotic fantasy of religious rite written upon the bodies and the women of other communities in a mixture of stereotyping and demonization. And, despite their total lack of foundation, such narratives have been so persuasive as to lie at the heart of nineteenth-century accounts of the origins of human civilization, marriage and the family and their discourses of 'ritual defloration' and 'temple harlots' continue to be difficult to erase.

Taking classical Greek art as their cultural reference point, modern discussions of the visual representation of nudity have until recently focused on the aesthetic structure and muscularity of the male and the sexuality and eroticism of the female body. But precisely how asexual was the naked male body in the sculpture and vase-painting of archaic and classical Greek art? Exploring the protocols for male fleshly display from the eighth to the fifth centuries BCE, Robin Osborne argues that in the course of the sixth and early fifth centuries the male body lost its semiotic innocence and became problematically sexualized. While nude male sculptures of the period began to permit their viewers a relationship of voyeuristic desire above that of identity, scenes of male nudity on vases (which were designed to be viewed in the context of elite male drinking-parties) became a troubled discourse about sex, and about the parameters of male sexual control and excess, while depictions of the penis became no mere index of the male gender but the marker of a sexual organ requiring restraint. Only a very fragile artistic convention could rescue men without clothes from their sexual charge. Correspondingly, Judith Sebesta could be said to ask how apolitical was the clothed female body in the iconography, rhetoric and rituals of dress of the Augustan regime at Rome in the first century BCE? While woman's immorality was read as an assault on the virility of the Roman male and the Roman body politic, her chastity was associated with the preservation of her husband's household and, by extension, the Augustan state. The regimentation of the Roman wife's body and sexuality, through legislation, monumental iconography, moral discourses and the claimed 'restoration' of her distinctive and confining dress, worked to close down the boundaries of Romanness thought to be at risk from the invasive corruption of the East. Troped as the husband's house and the Roman body politic, bearing the burden of civic morality and ethnic identity, the ideally conceived body of the Roman wife had to undergo careful rituals of costuming to preserve it from literal and symbolic invasion.

Lynn Roller returns us to a persistent theme of this volume—the dynamic interplay between gendered bodies and the formation of ethnic definitions of Self and Other—and further links the essays on the Near Eastern Mediterranean with those concerning Greece and Rome. In the western regions of the Mediterranean, the display of the mutilated bodies of the eunuch priests of Cybele (the Great Mother whose worship orginated in the Near East) forced a direct confrontation, in Roller's view, with ancient definitions of what it meant to be masculine or feminine, to be Greek/ Roman or foreign. While the Great Mother was fairly readily accommodated into the pantheons of Greek and Roman religion and into state ceremonial, the bodily appearance, dress, mannerisms and sexual behaviours of her priests were obsessively and contemptuously described and variously conceptualized as un-male, feminine, spuriously female, or effeminate, but always Other. In the literature of Republican and imperial Rome, in particular, the mutilated bodies and ambiguous gender of men who had relinquished their testicles could be used by male authors as a sustained metaphor through which to reflect on sensations of estrangement and alienation from civic communities in which gender identity was clearly circumscribed and masculinity policed.

Mutilation of the body and questions about membership of a community also figure in Shaye Cohen's essay on classical rabbinic Judaism. Here the circumcision of the eight-day-old baby boy operates as a bodily sign of inclusion in the community of Jews (a fleshly sign of the covenant between God and Israel) and as a boundary marker between Jew and gentile. Yet there is no embodied representation of women's Jewish identity. How, Cohen asks, did the Jews of antiquity explain this anomalous treatment of male and female bodies? He explores the various debates concerning this practice, debates that circulated widely within the Jewish community, and between Jews and Christians, from the first to the mid-fifth centuries CE. Supporting arguments ranged from the theological to the physiological and psychological—circumcision serves to check male lust which is stronger than that of females and to check male pride in their greater contribution to procreation—but otherwise, argues Cohen, the rabbis were largely unconcerned with the apparent discrepancy. As in the civic communities of Greece and Rome, so in the religious and ethnic communities of Judaism, women belonged only in a peculiar sense (as mothers, wives, sisters and daughters who produced, educated and served the real male members). The fundamental inferiority of women, their marginality and Otherness seemed so self-evident that rabbis were largely untroubled by women's lack of a bodily sign of Jewish identity.

Christian theology, the ritual of baptism and the practices of asceticism or bodily denial and virginity, might at first appear to offer greater accommodation for women in the faith communities of the late ancient Mediterranean. In the concluding essay of this collection, however, Teresa Shaw argues against such a view through a close reading of a physiologically and socially gendered treatise on virginity which circulated in Christian communities of the fourth century CE. In contrast to the opening account of the genderless or ambiguous bodies of ancient Mesopotamia, Shaw draws attention to the female of Christian doctrine as inherently grounded in the perceived weaknesses of the flesh. To achieve salvation, the Christian virgin must deny her body-oriented female nature and identity through a strict physical and social regime of fasting, segregation and camouflage. A constant attempt must be made to strip away the heavy garment of the female body (fertile, procreative, dangerous and pleasurable) and replace it with a more masculine bodily image and demeanour, but female gender is here so deeply inscribed into the body that success can be only limited. In the present life, her female flesh will always make the Christian virgin defective in terms of spiritual equality with her male counterparts.

This volume also includes a survey of materials available on the Internet to readers interested in the historical construction of gender and sexuality. The numerous e-mail discussion groups and web sites concerned specifically with antiquity that John Younger catalogues in his review are further testimony to the centrality of the ancient Mediterranean in the writing of the history of gender. When the call for papers to appear in this volume was originally distributed by Edith Hall (for whose substantial work on the initial stages of the project I would like to express my great thanks), the overwhelming response led to the preparation of a sister volume on *Parchments of Gender: Deciphering the Bodies of Antiquity*, which will be published by Oxford University Press in 1998.

Notes

1. It has become a recognized convention among scholars of antiquity to substitute Before the Common Era (BCE) or the Common Era (CE) for Before Christ (BC) or *Anno Domini* (AD), and it will be adhered to throughout this Special Issue.

2. In 1990 alone, three book-length essay collections and one special issue of a non-classical journal were published on the subject of ancient gender and sexuality: John J. Winkler's *The Constraints of Desire: The Anthropology of Sex and Gender in Ancient Greece* (Routledge, London, 1990); David Halperin's *One Hundred Years of Homosexuality* (Routledge, London, 1990); *Before Sexuality: The Construction of Erotic Experience in Ancient Greece*, ed. David Halperin, John J. Winkler and Froma Zeitlin (Princeton University Press, Princeton, NJ, 1990); *differences*, 2.1 (1990), guest-edited by David Konstan and Martha Nussbaum under the title 'Sexuality in Greek and Roman Society'. For convenient surveys of the substantial literature on ancient genders and sexualities, see further the reviews in this volume.

3. See, for example, the thematic review by Paul Cartledge, 'Getting/After Foucault'.

4. See the review by Alison Sharrock, 'Re(ge)ndering Gender(ed) Studies', for the use of this term.

5. See, most recently, *Changing Bodies, Changing Meanings: Studies on the Human Body in Antiquity*, ed. Dominic Montserrat (Routledge, London, 1997) and *Constructions of the Classical Body*, ed. James I. Porter (Michigan Press, Michigan, 1998). On medicine and religion, see also the reviews by, respectively, Helen King and Gillian Clark.

The Essential Body: Mesopotamian Conceptions of the Gendered Body

JULIA M. ASHER-GREVE

Researching the body in ancient Mesopotamian art and literature reveals how essential the body was considered in Mesopotamian thought. Western philosophical tradition denies the body a function in reason and spiritual meaning, but the ancient Mesopotamians may have had quite different structures of understanding. 'Objectivism' has been criticized for not giving consideration to the body as a component of rationality and understanding. Some philosophers have proposed that we need a theory of meaning and rationality that puts 'the body back into the mind'.[1] In ancient Mesopotamia the mind was still in the body, mind and body were inseparable, meaning and understanding were, to use Mark Johnson's term, 'embodied'.[2] This article focuses on how early Mesopotamian (c. 3000–1600 BCE) concepts of the body differ from subsequent Western views and on the analysis and meaning of selected Sumerian and Akkadian[3] terminology as well as textual and visual evidence of how the body was marked, represented and understood.

The Graeco-European tradition inscribes the mind/body dichotomy with two binary gender categories assumed to be universal: male mind versus female body. The spate of recent publications on the body has been influenced firstly by the mind/body dichotomy and the long Western tradition from Plato to Descartes which denigrates the body, and thus women, and secondly by contemporary discourse on postmodern, feminist and gender theories.[4] Caroline Bynum's article, 'Why All the Fuss About the Body', surveys the literature recently published about 'the Body'.[5] The literature reveals that the term is used as a synonym for senses, sex, gender, sexuality, gestures, corporeal functions, disease, physical activities, the corpse, or even for the person and the self. Bynum remarks that the usage of 'body' is confusing and contradictory. While dualistic ontology need not necessarily imply something negative, feminism has exposed the fact that dualism in the Western philosophical tradition has unfortunately always included Plato's misogyny and his denigration of the body, with women designated as body-directed beings. Since Plato, nature, body, emotion and the particular have been equated with women and negative values, whereas culture, mind, reason and the universal have been equated with men and positive values.[6]

Platonic and Cartesian tradition contrasts body as anatomical, material, spatial, temporal and fallible to mind as mental, spiritual, eternal, universal and infallible. The views expressed in Sumerian and Babylonian sources, however, demonstrate that mind/body, mind/matter or spiritual/material dualisms are not at all 'universal', nor do they include a denigrating view of women.[7]

The Sumerian language[8] offers several terms for body, addressing the different contexts in which the body is set:

—**su** and **su-bar** (in the Akkadian language *zumru)*[9] refers to the external body, and often stands for people, groups and society *per se*. It is used in phrases such as 'body of a deity', 'body of the king', 'body of a city', 'body of Sumer' or 'body of the land'.[10] The term **su** (in Akkadian *erû)*[11] can also mean naked, and it is a synonym for image.
—**ša₃** (in Akkadian *karšu* and *libbu)*[12] includes the external and internal body. The original meaning is heart. That **ša₃** came to mean the total body—not only individual organs such as heart, stomach, belly, womb but also mind, thought, plan, desire—indicates that the heart was perceived as the central core of the self. Knowing and feeling were located in the body.
—(**me-**) **dim₂** (in Akkadian *binâtu* and *binûtu)*[13] is written with an abstract sign whose original meaning is not known. It primarily means limbs but also creation and creature. The verb **dim₂** (in Akkadian *banû)*[14] refers to the form and shape of the body and means 'to create, to form, to fashion'. It is also used for the fashioning of objects, such as statues and steles.[15] In creation myths it can be applied to the creation of humanity by deities. The body is humanity, the object of creation.[16]

A hymn for King Išmedagan of Isin (1953–1935 BCE), a song celebrating the city of Nippur, juxtaposes two Sumerian words for body, **su** and **ša₃**:

City [= Nippur] your centre [**ša₃**] is sacred,
your appearance [**bar**] is lustrous,
your body [**su-bar**] exhibits awe-inspiring radiance [**melam**].[17]

The city of Nippur is compared with a divine body. The term **su-bar** is used metaphorically for the entire city as a larger body, meaning external, visible body and appearance. The body of the city emanates, like a deity, awe-inspiring radiance (**melam**).[18] Nippur's main temple, which constitutes the centre of the city and makes Nippur holy, is the main temple of the god Enlil, the highest deity in the Sumerian and Old Babylonian pantheon before Hammurapi (1792–1750 BCE); **ša₃** is used for this sacred centre; the core is equally 'heart, mind and body'. Such a passage could also describe a deity by simply substituting for the city a deity's name.

There is no specific Sumerian term for mind or human brain. A connection between the brain and thinking was not made. The Sumerian word for intelligence, understanding and sense, **geštu₂**, is written with the sign for ear, which indicates that these faculties were acquired by listening. The term **geštu₂** is a frequently mentioned quality of kings.[19] There is no evidence, however, that intelligence or reason (another translation for **geštu₂**) is conceptualized in opposition to the body. This is not unique to Sumerians. In his study *Foundations of Primitive Thought*, Christopher Hallpike notices that in many cultures understanding, thinking and knowing are associated with hearing.[20]

The Sumerian term **ša₃** ('body' and 'heart') implies the same meaning as that in ancient Egypt, where the heart was considered the seat of will, thought and feeling, had power over the limbs and was open to the influence of the gods. Locating psychological processes in physical organs is also known in other cultures.[21] In ancient Mesopotamia deities choose kings with their hearts. The heart is not only the core of the body, but heart, body and mind as the same word is a holistic concept.[22] Thus conceptually there is no dichotomy between mind and body. This holism is also confirmed by Sumerian creation myths: humanity is formed in one process, it is complete, mother- and birth-goddesses are guarantors for the wholeness and perfection of creation.[23] This may be one of the reasons that kings (who are described as ideal humans) claim goddesses as their symbolic mothers,[24] and why for the fashioning of some statues the metaphor 'born' (**alan mu-tud**) is used.[25] Physical perfection and imperfection are related to social position.[26]

Conventions for representing the body in Mesopotamian culture are equally significant. From the late fourth millennium onwards written and pictorial documents represent the human body as:

—sexed, with anatomical and physiological sex markers such as genitals, breasts, or beards (Figures 6, 7, 9–13).
—gendered, marked by socio-cultural gender elements such as masculine or feminine clothing or hairstyle, or baldness for men, and adornment, attributes, context and occupation (Figures 1, 2, 3, 6).
—or ambiguous and asexual, showing neither unequivocal anatomical sex markers nor gender-specific markers (Figures 1, 3–6, 10).

lu₂ = person    **nita** = man   **munus** = woman

Diagram I

The Sumerian signs are equally distinctive for human being, man and woman: the sign for human being (**lu₂**) is the pictograph of an ambiguous human body,[27] the sign for man (**nita**) is the penis and the sign for woman

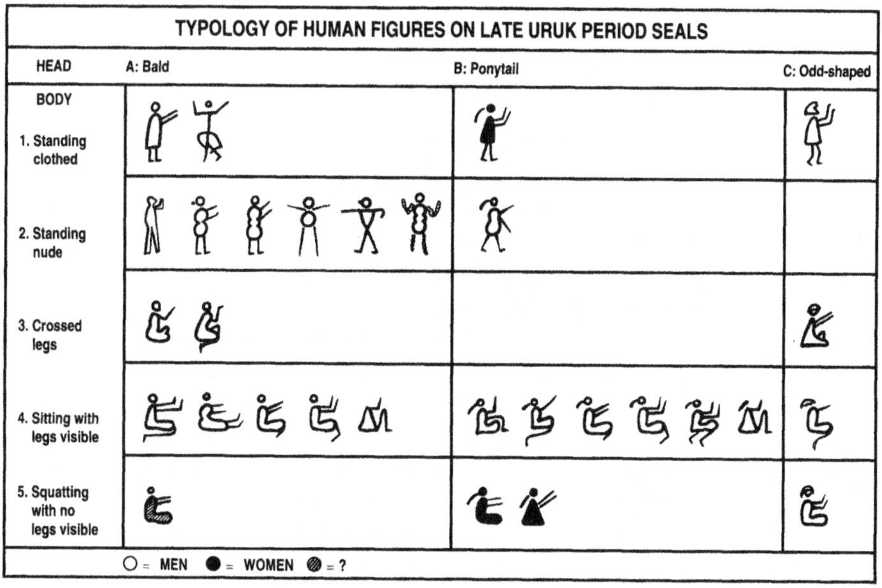

TYPOLOGY OF HUMAN FIGURES ON LATE URUK PERIOD SEALS			
HEAD	A: Bald	B: Ponytail	C: Odd-shaped
BODY 1. Standing clothed	*[pictographs]*	*[pictograph]*	*[pictograph]*
2. Standing nude	*[pictographs]*	*[pictograph]*	
3. Crossed legs	*[pictographs]*		*[pictograph]*
4. Sitting with legs visible	*[pictographs]*	*[pictographs]*	*[pictograph]*
5. Squatting with no legs visible	*[pictograph]*	*[pictographs]*	*[pictograph]*
O = MEN ● = WOMEN ⊘ = ?			

Figure 1: Typology of human figures on Uruk period cylinder seals, *c*. 3200–2900 BCE. From J. M. Asher-Greve, 'Gender and Seals within the Bureaucracy of the Late Uruk Period' (in preparation).

(**munus**) the vulva.[28] The pictograph for body is chosen for writing person, and the pictographs for genitals for writing woman and man. It is an ambiguous human body that signifies person, thus the general is not sexed, but the specific is. This confronts scholars with many problems. Because the Sumerian language has no grammatical gender, it is often not clear which gender is addressed. Nevertheless, Sumerologists tend to prefer the masculine gender in their translations. For instance, the Sumerian word for person or persons, **lu₂**, is generally translated man or men. But the word is gender-neutral, and should be translated person(s) or people.

The ambiguity of the archaic sign for person can be compared with that of human figures depicted on cylinder seals (Figure 1). The so-called 'simple pattern' style differentiates between women and men, who are gendered by clothing, male nudity and hairstyles and who, on some seals, are engaged in gender-specific work, such as weaving or animal herding. On some seals persons (**lu₂**) are engaged in a task that was not gender-specific (e.g. handling pots or animals). These figures often lack gender markers such as hair and/or distinct clothes.[29]

In the visual arts, gender ambiguity is often evident in European figurative art, such as in the depiction of angels and saints.[30] Hieronymus Bosch orchestrates sometimes more, sometimes less sexed bodies. In contemporary art the sex of bodies is often elusive, implying that humankind is androgynous.[31]

Figure 2: Statute of a woman. Early Dynastic period, *c.* 2500 BCE; calcite; h: 30 cm. London, British Museum 90929. Courtesy, Hirmer Fotoarchiv, München.

Figure 3: Votive plaque with inscription of King Urnanše of Lagaš. Early Dynastic period, *c.* 2494–2465 BCE; calcite; h: 40 cm, w: 47cm. From Tello. Paris, Louvre AO 2344. Courtesy, Hirmer Fotoarchiv, München.

Whether a representation appears ambiguous or androgynous may also depend on the viewer's knowledge of implicit culturally determined gender signifiers and markers and/or accompanying titles or text.[32] Visual statements on humanity in European art seem to fluctuate between giving particular prominence to the male, as in Michelangelo's *Creation* in the Sistine Chapel, or simply depicting sexless or ambiguous bodies.[33]

Decoding gender in the visual arts of ancient societies poses comparable problems. Not all codes are self-evident or understood by modern scholars. Two examples may illustrate the problem (Figures 3 and 4). On the so-called 'family relief' (Figure 3) of King Urnanše of Lagash (2494–2465 BCE), the king and his sons (**dumu**, 'child') are easily identifiable by skirts worn only by men,[34] bare chests and shaven heads. But one figure wears a dress covering the right shoulder and has long hair, both of which are gender-neutral. Name and designation as 'Abda, child [**dumu**] of Urnanše' do not specify the gender of the person, who has been identified as either prince or princess.[35] Circumstantial evidence, however, indicates a priestess: this figure's combination of dress and hairstyle is typical for women (Figure 2) but not for men, her height is superior to that of the crown prince Akurgal standing behind her, and there is also the ritual context. As high priestess Abda can head a procession, and her asexual appearance may be linked to her priestly status.[36]

The statue of another Urnanše (Figure 4), a leading singer (**nar-maḫ**) in the city of Mari, possesses a name and wears a type of skirt which are both masculine markers. Yet it also exhibits features primarily coded as feminine, such as an effeminate face and bulging breasts.[37] These features may reflect castration.[38] Effeminate or masculine traits in sculpture remain enigmatic; women are often flat-chested (Figure 2), men occasionally have effeminate breasts, such as some foundation figurines assumed to represent kings (Figure 5).[39] Considering the emphasis on masculine strength and heroism in royal ideology these figurines are difficult to integrate into the royal imagery. Perhaps they represent demiurgic creatures whose gender is not clearly defined, or perhaps asexuality and sexual ambiguity are associated with priestly functions.

There were more than two gender categories in Mesopotamia;[40] the third was castrated men (**amar-TUD**), the same term also applying to castrated animals.[41] These men were the sons of female weavers and women of low social status; they were castrated at a young age, worked in groups and are often listed as fugitives. In the Ur-III period (2112–2004 BCE) their status is at the lowest end of society. In the creation myth known as 'Enki and Ninmaḫ' a fourth gender is also introduced.[42] The goddess Ninmaḫ forms (**dim$_2$**) a human being that is neither male nor female; her brother Enki finds a role in society for this creature at the royal court.[43] This person is described as 'neither having penis nor vulva in its body', it is thus sexless. All the persons Ninmaḫ creates are adults, and it is therefore remarkable that the lack of female breasts is not mentioned. Apparently breasts were not conceived of as a primary distinction between the sexes. Breasts, however, are emphasized in visual representations of nude women (Figures 12 and 13), but not always indicated in clothed females (Figure 2). Many clothed women are portrayed flat-chested, which makes it difficult to distinguish them from men (Figures 2, 3, 6, 10). In the literature emphasis is placed on the vulva and the womb rather than breasts.[44] Perhaps because breasts developed in puberty and therefore were not considered primary sexual organs, women were essentially defined by the vulva and the womb. This may be why, in narrative imagery, women often represent a gendered category (garments and hairstyle; Figures 2 and 6), whereas men are more often characterized by sexual markers such as beard or nakedness (Figures 7–9).

Gender categories as described above are already operational at the beginning of the third millennium BCE on the oldest known monumental narrative, the 'Uruk vase' (Figure 6).[45] The narrative mirrors Sumerian economic and cultic activities: water standing for irrigation (on the bottom), plants and pairs of ram and sheep for cultivation symbolizing prosperity and fertility of the land. In the third register (from the bottom) a group of

Figure 4: Statute of the singer Urnanše. Early Dynastic period, *c.* 2400 BCE; alabaster; h: 12.6 cm. From Mari. Aleppo Museum. Courtesy, Hirmer Fotoarchiv, München.

Figure 5: Foundation figurine with inscription mentioning Kudur Mabuk and his son King Rimsîn of Larsa. Old Babylonian, *c.* 1770 BCE; bronze; h: 26cm; Berlin, Vorderasiatisches Museum, VA 3025. Courtesy of Staatliche Museen zu Berlin, Preussischer Kulturbesitz.

Figure 6: Drawing of relief on alabaster vase from Uruk. Late Uruk period, *c.* 3000– 2900 BCE; h: 105cm. Baghdad, Iraq Museum. Reproduced from Elke Lindemeyer and Martin Lutz *Uruk: Kleinfunde III* (1993): Plate 25.

nine naked men moves left carrying vessels and baskets with produce. The men are sexed by genitals and gendered by baldness, meaning that their bodies are inscribed with two gender signifiers: anatomical—the male genitals; and socio-cultural—baldness. These strong, young men might well represent **guruš**, the Sumerian term for young, unmarried men. According to later textual evidence **guruš** were at least occasionally referred to as being virginal.[46] A striking feature of the lower and middle registers is the isocephalic composition—heads and the tops of plants are on the same level. This plus the repetition and the structuring in rows emphasizes uniformity and order, displaying the young nude men as a group, not as individuals.

In the top register the uniformity of repetition, isocephaly and unidirectional rows is broken: although the direction of the procession continues with the three-figure group facing right (one mostly missing, with just one foot and parts of the skirt preserved), it comes to a halt as the naked bearer holds his basket of offerings in front of the theme's central figure. The space is divided into human and divine (or sacred) spheres by the central axis which separates the main actors from the symbols and objects. Just behind the central figure facing left are two reed poles with streamers, the symbol and sign of the goddess Inanna.[47] The divine sphere (right) contains three Inanna symbols, large and small offering vessels, votive objects, a sacrificial male ram and two small figures on pedestals (dressed in skirts and having long hair) of ambiguous gender.

To the left, in the human sphere, stands a priestess in front of the gate or temple of Inanna. The priestess receives a group of three men consisting of a nude offering bearer, the En of Uruk (identifiable by the fragment of net-skirt, a garment only worn by the En on other images, where he is always bearded),[48] and his servant who carries the trail of his skirt. Remarkable in the treatment of bodies is that only the subordinate offering bearer is sexed, the En as in other representations is marked sexually (beard) and socio-culturally (netskirt). His servant, however, exhibits the same gender ambiguity as the two persons in the divine sphere, only his short skirt marks him as male.[49]

Identification of the main figure as a woman is based on her dress, and the iconographic pattern that men always wear either short skirts or long skirts plus beard. The bodies are inscribed with a gender role which also encompasses social, religious and gender identity. Clothing determines gender and social status.

The visual representation of the nude body is also instructive for the analysis of gender in Mesopotamian culture. Nude men in ritualized action are a recurrent motif in Mesopotamian art; more common than groups are single men, assumed to be priests performing a ritual act such as libation.[50] Apart from an occasional dancer or musician, women in ritual and cult always wear garments (Figures 3 and 6). Sumerian and Akkadian texts do not explain the nudity of men in ritual and cult, but it is mentioned in several Hittite texts.[51] Cross-cultural comparison provides further explanations. As mentioned, at least some young men (**guruš-tur**) were virginal. Naked, young, virginal men might thus signify purity, possibly a prerequisite for the participation in certain rituals and cults. Further, a nude person is believed to be more receptive to divine influence. According to Philo of Alexandria:

> The High Priest shall not enter the Holy of Holies in his robe, but laying aside the garment of opinions and impressions of the soul, and leaving it behind for those that love outward things and value semblance, shall enter naked ...[52]

It is possible that the concept of purity expressed through nudity extends to the so-called nude hero (Figure 7). Contrary to the nude young men in ritual context, the hero is depicted as an adult, bearded man.

Figure 7: Impression of cylinder seal with contest scene of bearded nude men with lions and bull. Akkadian period, *c.* 2300–2250 BCE; 4.1 × 2.7 cm. Chicago, Oriental Institute Museum, A 30923. Courtesy, The Oriental Institute, University of Chicago.

The motif of the nude heroic man combating wild animals appears during the Early Dynastic period (*c.* 2800–2350 BCE) and develops into the most popular motif on cylinder seals of the later Early Dynastic and especially in the Akkadian period (*c.* 2350–2150 BCE).[53] The emergence of this motif occurs at a time when the concept of rulership began to change, suggesting a connection between the nude hero and royal ideology.[54] The nudity of the combatants is the key to further interpretation. There is a connection between the portrayal of heroic combatants as nude and the nudity of gods depicted in the 'battle of the gods' (Figure 8), a mythological motif in the 'flood myth' (Atraḥasis).[55] The divine battle is the only context in which gods are portrayed in the nude. The heroic deed is accomplished naked, which emphasizes and enhances the magnitude of the feat. There is no protection, victory is accomplished by pure physical prowess and superiority, the hero fighting lions or bulls against all odds (Figure 7).

Figure 8: Impression of cylinder seal with 'battle of the gods'. Akkadian period, *c.* 2270–2150 BCE; 2.6 × 1.5 cm. Berlin, Vorderasiatisches Museum VA 686. Courtesy, Hirmer Fotoarchiv, München.

The nude hero celebrates male physical power, a theme well attested throughout antiquity, and he develops into an icon of masculinity based on physical strength.[56] The Sumerian word for young man (**guruš**) reflects this concept, written with the sign for 'strong' (**kala**). One of the most common royal epithets is 'strong man' (**nita kala-ga**).[57] In a copy of a statue inscription the king Išme-Dagan of Isin (1953–1955 BCE) is described as follows:

> Išme-Dagan, the strong young man with muscles and the body of a lion, mighty youth, who possesses fearsome splendour.[58]

The king's strong body is a sign of his perfection, superiority and godlike appearance. Due to his physical might he can perform heroic deeds, he is the hero.[59] Image and text convey the glorification of masculine strength and heroism, thus the nude male hero is a royal allegory which also links the king's heroic battle with the divine battle through the notation of nudity. The hero—the king—resembles a god physically. This places him in proximity to the gods, insinuating powers customarily attributed to the divine.

Nakedness, however, can also signify deprivation, humiliation and social dispossession, as well as what a Sumerian poem describes as pre-civilization:

> And there was no cloth to wear …
> The people of the distant days,
> They knew no bread to eat;
> They knew not cloth to wear;
> The people went about naked.[60]

Dead or captured enemies about to be killed, blinded or castrated, are stripped of all clothes (Figure 9). Fallen or captured enemies who are depicted naked are always men.[61] Women were also captured and led into slavery, but they do not appear in visual imagery until the first millennium BCE on Assyrian wall reliefs (Figure 10), where they are depicted as sexless, and are often hard to distinguish from men; the presence of children sometimes indicates that the captured persons are women (Figure 10).[62] In the context of war and captivity the bodies of enemies convey the message of victory and subjugation. Whereas enemies can be portrayed as fierce soldiers in order to emphasize the heroic victor, the gender of women and possibly male civilians seems irrelevant and they are represented as a mass of conquered bodies.

Male nudity signals either purity and heroism, or enslavement and death, whereas female nudity is linked primarily to sexual activity and eroticism.[63] Nude women and goddesses are numerous in Mesopotamian art (Figures 11 and 12). Scholars have struggled with their interpretation because insight into their meaning cannot be derived from textual sources.[64] In the broader analysis of the body and gender roles, it becomes evident that the nude female—both divine and mortal—is a symbol of erotic power. Bodily appearance is perceived as a powerful force, just as with the hero-king.[65]

Figure 9: Fragment of stele with prisoners of war. Akkadian period, *c.* 2250–2160 BCE; alabaster; h: 29 cm; w: 21 cm. Baghdad, Iraq Museum. Courtesy, Hirmer Fotoarchiv, München.

Figure 10: Fragment from wall relief of King Sennacherib's palace in Ninive. Neo-Assyrian period, 704–681 BCE; gypsum, h: 26 in. Charles Amos Cummings Bequest Fund (60.133). Courtesy, Museum of Fine Arts, Boston.

An inscription on the back of a nude female stone torso found near the Ishtar temple in Niniveh (Figure 11) states that this statue is the property of the palace of the Assyrian king Assurbelkala (1073–1056 BCE), and that Assurbelkala 'made these sculptures in the provinces, cities and garrisons for titillation'.[66] It is a puzzling inscription, inviting our speculation as to who had to be titillated and why. But one fact is obvious: female nudity was erotic and nude female statues were intended to stimulate the libido of men. Numerous statuettes and terracottas—popular art forms—convey the image of nude women as sexually alluring.[67] How such images relate to the concept of the perfect female body as sexually pure is enigmatic. Female sexuality was strictly controlled by men. Violations of the female body such as defloration, rape, pre- and extra-marital sex, natural or intentional abortion were treated in the Sumerian and Akkadian collections of laws.[68] In literary texts, however, the female body is described in sexual and erotic terms.[69] Such descriptions and nude depictions apparently were not perceived as contradictory to the laws. Perhaps most of these representations were not in public spaces. They might have been related to private erotic stimulation and lovemaking. Yet some nude female statues clearly were installed in public spaces.

In literary texts and votive inscriptions, many goddesses have the epithet 'beautiful women' (**munus-ša₆-ga**), but it is not made explicit what beauty entails. In fact, there is a startling contrast between descriptions of bodily pleasures and the more general concept of beauty. Metaphors of beauty seem to be primarily agricultural; the attractiveness of women, for instance, is compared with that of grain, palm tree or cow.[70] Erotic pleasure was one of the divine powers, called **me** in Sumerian.[71] Sumerian love-literature focuses on the body, in particular the vulva, the lap and thighs, and human love was portrayed as bodily pleasure with the anticipated result of procreation.[72]

In ancient Greece the ideal form of the human figure was presented as nude.[73] This may be an ancient Near Eastern pattern, traceable to prehistoric nude female figurines (Figure 13). If the nude male hero alludes to divine proximity, the nude female can be similarly understood, especially since many terracotta figurines exhibit ambiguity concerning divine or mortal female identity. The only goddesses depicted nude or partially dressed are Inanna-Ishtar—goddess of love, sexuality, eroticism and war—and various goddesses associated with her.[74]

The body's life starts with birth and, according to Freud, the first ego is the body-ego. This is still generally accepted psychoanalytic theory based on studies of infant behaviour.[75] Mesopotamians conceptualized the body as the agent of thinking, feeling, experiencing and knowing. The body was the essential ego/being. In the absence of a specific concept of mind the corporeal body was representative of the totality of the individual.

Creation narratives support this interpretation. The creation passage in *Atraḥasis*, also known as the 'Flood Myth', contains wordplay between *tēmu* ('intelligence and understanding') and *etemmu* ('spirit and ghost') both integral to the human being.[76] The body and thus humanity is created from the blood and flesh of a slain god mixed with clay and shaped by the goddess Nintu.[77] The spirit-ghost comes from the god's flesh, intelligence from his blood.[78] That the spirit was thought to have corporeal shape is implied in Early Dynastic economic texts that list offerings of clothes for the statues and spirits of male and female ancestors.[79] The spirit survives the postmortem decomposition of the flesh, yet remains bound to the body in the form of its bones. The Akkadian word **šīru** covers a meaning as broad as the Sumerian **su** and **ša₃**, that is, ranging from 'flesh' and 'kin' to a metonymic use for 'body', 'person' and 'self'.[80] Perhaps the flesh from the god stands for his total body including the bones. This would better explain why the spirit does not totally transcend the body but stays linked to its bones. The body was conceived as the essence of humanity and survived in a form still reminiscent of the body.

Thinking, feeling, knowing and afterlife were located in or linked to the body. Here, as in the Sumerian concept, intelligence (**gestu₂**) is inseparable

Figure 11: Fragmentary statue of a nude woman with inscription on back from Ninive. Middle Assyrian period, 1073–1056 BCE; h: 94 cm. London, The British Museum, WA 124 963. Courtesy, The British Museum, London.

Figure 12: Nude female terracotta plaque from Ishchali. Old Babylonia period, *c.* 1950–1750 BCE; h: *c.* 13 cm. Chicago, Oriental Institute Museum, A 17 672. Courtesy, The Oriental Institute, University of Chicago.

Figure 13: Painted female terracotta figurine from Tell Halaf. *c.* 6th/5th millennium BCE; h: 5.8 cm. Berlin, Vorderasiatische Museum, VA 12 517. Courtesy, Staatliche Museen zu Berlin, Preussischer Kulturbesitz.

from the body. Transferred to humanity through the blood of the god, it might be expected that intelligence is extinguished with death. Tzvi Abusch claims that *tēmu* ('intelligence') represents the link between life and after-life, because it is phonetically present in the word *etemmu.*[81] In fact, only *etemmu*, the 'spirit' (in Sumerian **gidim**), survives death, it is the spirit of the dead.[82] It has been suggested that *etemmu* is the ghost not the spirit, because the word is used only in conjunction with the dead.[83] But *etemmu* is conceptualized as being integral to the whole body beginning with creation. The spirit is the 'form-giving' element, and at death this form survives. Intelligence, however, is never mentioned in conjunction with the spirit-ghost of the dead.

The self is located in the inseparable unity of body and spirit. Because the self could be re-created and actually be present in an image, Mesopotamian visual representations possessed a form of reality which is difficult to com-prehend for modern scholars. This form of reality becomes clearer when we consider that many monuments are inscribed with curses invoking mal-edictions and punishment for those who destroy or mutilate the monu-ment, symbolically equivalent to the destruction of the image or the actual killing of a person. One of the most severe curses was the deprivation of progeny which meant that no ancestor cult could be performed and the referent spirit became a nameless wandering demon.

Further evidence for the importance of corporeal presence in visual depictions of the body can be obtained from literary references to abductions of divine statues from temples and cities.[84] Such abduction represented a major catastrophe for the Babylonians, because the absence of the deity ensured that the cult was discontinued until the statue was returned. It was believed that the deity had turned against the city and abandoned it.[85] Only the return of the divine statue could reverse such a fate. Statues of humans also had life, serving as an *alter ego*: the statues of King Gudea of Lagash (2141–2122 BCE) are his proxies, perpetually placed in the presence of, and in communication with, the deities.[86] Thus the statue is believed to be more than an inanimate image, it is a corporeal being.

The early Mesopotamian conception of the body seems to be that of a self, comprising body and spirit, which can replicate itself in other mani-festations such as statues or monuments which are more than symbolic proxies but less than distinct duplicates. The spirit, not a replica but a unique entity, can apparently inhabit several objects simultaneously. In a sort of reciprocal interaction the deity bestows life not only on the human individ-ual but also on all its subsequent images (such as statues or monuments) and these in turn can independently and eternally converse or negotiate with the deity. This conception differs from that of Platonic idealism which regards phenomenal bodies as replicas of an ideal or metaphysical form of the human figure. Mesopotamian statues are placed in the path of the deity whose life-giving glance (**igi nam-ti-la**) animates them. That removal or destruction of statues causes death or lack of progeny may be interpreted as meaning that both they and the individual they represent are removed from the divine glance (**igi-zi**).[87]

In closing this analysis of gender and the body in Mesopotamian culture, I want to note that studying texts and images from a feminist and gender perspective opens new avenues of interpretation. As I have shown, in early Mesopotamia the mind/body dichotomy was absent. Ancient Mesopotamians did not develop a system of binary gender equating male with positive and female with negative values. The Mesopotamian holistic concept of the human being was based on a physical system, with the body as fundamental point of reference. The body was the total self, the essence of humanity, equally matter and spirit, emotion and reason, both temporal and eternal. Gender was the interpretation of anatomical differences and imperfections. The inscription of gender on the body was one option to structure society.

The human body was a divine, genderless creation. As humanity was created in one process prior to sex or gender, it can be presumed that the body, as metaphor for humanity, contained within itself all possible gender. This is corroborated by the archaic sign for person (the plural also means humanity), a genderless body. The secondary creation of the two 'normative' sexes, male and female, in the Atraḫasis myth was understood as requiring a complementary anatomy for procreation, upon which social gender was imposed. But gender categories extended beyond the binary concept to multiple gender and social status for persons of ambiguous, or no, sex and castrated men. Gender differentiation followed the nature of physical differences: those born with sex anomalies (certain singers and courtiers) were integrated into society; those, however, whose sex was artificially altered (castrates) were marginalized. Although in historical periods (beginning *c.* 2600 BCE) men generally held a higher status than women and other genders, neither the female gender nor persons of no, or naturally ambiguous, sex were denigrated or assumed to lack culture, mind and reason because they were still considered divine creations.

The visual arts provide evidence of the mode of gender inscription on the body: anatomy signifies the ideal image of masculine and feminine. The absence or presence of sex markers plus various combinations and types of clothes and hairstyles are employed to signify different gender groups. But these codes do not always suffice for unequivocal gender identification. Either we lack the information required to decipher all codes and combinations, or the borders between gender groups are fluid. The coexistence of female and male images with ambiguous gender images in the same genres (sculpture, relief, seals), sometimes juxtaposed in narrative images, can be explained by the existence of multiple, fluid gender categories.

In a thought system where the body is perceived as a fusion of the spiritual, emotional and physical, anatomical differences have another significance than in Western dualistic ontology because spiritual and emotional qualities are equally and evenly present in all genders. Thus in the earliest Sumerian pantheon goddesses dominated. Goddesses and women and certain persons of ambiguous gender still held prominent positions in the Early Dynastic period.[88] The demotion of goddesses and the deterioration of the status of women in later periods is paralleled by a rising emphasis on anatomical properties of male and female bodies (images of nude heroes and women), on motherhood and on male strength. The roots of this development reach back to the Early Dynastic period when royal ideology changed and wars were more frequent, resulting in Mesopotamian society becoming more militaristic. According to Amélie Kuhrt, women's exclusion from warfare is reflected in their social marginalization.[89] Increasing militarization of Mesopotamia is probably the major reason for the change of gender status which is reflected in the regulations of women's bodies in the law codes, but also in increasingly numerous representations of nude females in Ur III and Old Babylonian art (c. 2150–1600 BCE).

Notes

This article was written during the academic year 1995/96 while I taught and conducted research at the Harvard Divinity School. In two lectures, at Harvard University and the University of Chicago, I presented my arguments. I also discussed many points with my husband, friends and colleagues: Tzvi Abusch, Lawrence Asher, Robert Biggs, Constance Buchanan, Miguel Civil, Maureen Fitzgerald, David Gimbel, Brigitte Groneberg, Dinghwa Evelyn Hsieh, Brenda Meehan, Leslie Pierce, Piotr Steinkeller, Claudia Suter, Stephanie Tayengco, Irene Winter and Jenai Wu. My deep thanks to all of them.

For help with the photographs I wish to thank Rita Freed (The Museum of Fine Arts, Boston), Karen Wilson (The Oriental Institute Museum, Chicago), and Evelyn Klengel-Brandt (Vorderasiatische Museum, Berlin).

Throughout this article Sumerian words are shown in **bold** and Akkadian words in *italic*.

1. E.g. Mark Johnson, *The Body in the Mind: The Bodily Basis of Meaning, Imagination and Reasoning* (University of Chicago Press, Chicago and London, 1987); for quote, see p. XIV.

2. Johnson, *The Body in the Mind*, p. XIV.

3. Sumerian and Akkadian are the languages of ancient Mesopotamia written in cuneiform script. Sumerian does not belong to any known group of languages, Akkadian is a Semitic language; cf. Marie-Louise Thomsen, *The Sumerian Language: An Introduction to its History and Grammatical Structure*, Mesopotamia 10 (Academic Press, Copenhagen, 1984), pp. 15–33; Richard Caplice, *Introduction to Akkadian*, Studia Pohl: Series Maior 9 (Biblical Institute Press, Rome, 3rd edn, 1988), pp. 1–13; C. B. F. Walker, *Reading the Past: Cuneiform* (British Museum Publications, London, 1987); D. O. Edzard, 'The Sumerian Language', in *Civilizations of the Ancient Near East*, ed. Jack M. Sasson (Charles Scribner's Sons, New York, 1995; hereafter *CANE*), pp. 2107–16; John Huehnergard, 'Semitic Languages', in *CANE*, pp. 2117–34.

4. E.g. Michel Foucault, *Volenté de savoir* (Editions Gallimard, Paris, 1976), published in English as *The History of Sexuality*, vol. I (Allen Lane, London, 1979); Susan

R. Suleiman (ed.) *The Female Body in Western Culture* (Harvard University Press, Cambridge, MA and London, 1986); M. Feher (ed.) with R. Naddaff and N. Tazi, *Fragments for a History of the Human Body,* Part One–Part Three, ZONE 3–ZONE 5 (Urzone Inc., New York, 1989), includes a comprehensive bibliography and topical index; Alison M. Jaggar and Susan R. Bordo (eds) *Gender/Body/Knowledge: Feminist Reconstructions of Being and Knowing* (Rutgers University Press, New Brunswick, NJ, 1989); Thomas Laqueur, *Making Sex: Body and Gender from the Greeks to Freud* (Harvard University Press, Cambridge, MA and London, 1990); Elizabeth Grosz, *Volatile Bodies: Towards a Corporeal Feminism* (Indiana University Press, Bloomington and Indianapolis, 1994); Caroline Bynum, 'Why All the Fuss About the Body? A Medievalist's Perspective', *Critical Inquiry,* 22 (1995), pp. 1–33.

5. Bynum, 'Why All the Fuss?', pp. 2–12.

6. Elizabeth V. Spelman, 'Woman as Body: Ancient and Contemporary Views', *Feminist Studies,* 8 (1982), pp. 109–31: Elizabeth V. Spelman, *Inessential Woman: Problems of Exclusion in Feminist Thought* (Beacon Press, Boston, MA, 1988), pp. 37–56; see also Monique Canto, 'The Politics of Women's Bodies: Reflections on Plato', in Suleiman, *The Female Body,* pp. 339–53.

7. Jerrold S. Cooper, 'Gendered Sexuality in Sumerian Love Poetry', in *Sumerian Gods and Their Representations,* ed. I. L. Finkel and M. J. Geller, Cuneiform Monographs 7 (Styx Publications, Groningen, 1997), p. 89.

8. Cf. note 3 above.

9. *The Assyrian Dictionary of the Oriental Institute of the University of Chicago* (The Oriental Institute and J. J. Augustine, Chicago and Glückstadt, 1956–), vol. Z, pp. 157–60 (hereafter CAD).

10. It is a common topos in early Old Babylonian royal hymns, but not in Ur III hymns.

11. CAD E, pp. 320–21.

12. CAD K, pp. 223–5; CAD L, pp. 164–75.

13. CAD B, pp. 237, 243–4.

14. CAD B, pp. 83–90 (*banû* A).

15. For the creation of statues the verb **tud** ('to be born') can be employed; see Agnès Spycket, *Les statues de culte dans les textes Mésopotamiens des origines à la 1re dynastie de Babylone,* Cahiers de la Revue Biblique 9 (J. Gabalda et Cie, Paris, 1968), pp. 37–8, 54, 58, 61; Elena Cassin, 'Le mort: valeur et représentation en Mésopotamie ancien', in *La mort, les morts dans les sociétés anciennes,* ed. G. Gnoli and J. P. Vernant (Cambridge University Press, Cambridge, UK and Editions de la Maison des Sciences de l'Homme, Paris, 1982), p. 356 (reprinted in E. Cassin, *Le semblable et le différent: Symbolismes du pouvoir dans le Proche-Orient ancien* [Editions la Découverte, Paris, 1987], pp. 236–57.

16. Another verb that is used for the creation of humanity as well as statues is **tud** ('to give birth'). In the 'Enki and Ninmaḫ' myth, **tud** is connected with the birth of the deities and humanity, and **dim**$_2$ ('to form', 'to create') with the creation of handicapped humans; cf. Carlos A. Benito, *Enki and Ninmah and Enki and the Worldorder* (University Microfilms no. 70–16; Ann Arbor, MI, 1969), pp. 21–44. A more detailed analysis was presented by this author at the meeting of the American Oriental Society in Philadelphia on 20 March 1996 ('From Nidaba to Nabû: What Happened to the Goddesses'); the publication is in preparation.

17. Marie-Christine Ludwig, *Untersuchungen zu den Hymnen des Išme-Dagan von Isin,* SANTAG 2 (Otto Harrassowitz, Wiesbaden, 1990), pp. 97–102: IšD Wa, lines 57–61.

18. CAD M/II, pp. 9–12; cf. Irene J. Winter, 'Aesthetics in Ancient Mesopotamian Art', in *CANE*, p. 2575, for interpretation of **melam** as an aesthetic and emotional quality of art and architecture.

19. M.-J. Seux, *Epithètes royales Akkadiennes et Sumériennes* (Letouzey et Ané, Paris, 1967), pp. 407–8.

20. Cf. Christopher R. Hallpike, *The Foundations of Primitive Thought* (Clarendon Press, Oxford, 1979), pp. 390, 404–9. Hallpike argues that in many primitive languages to 'understand' is the same word as to 'hear', and that 'the distinction between the mind in its cognitive aspects ... and the body ... would not be drawn nearly as distinctly in primitive cultures and that, correspondingly, there would be a fusion between the physical and the psychical'. He cites A. R. Johnson, *The Vitality of the Individual in the Thought of Ancient Israel* (University of Wales Press, Cardiff, 1964), who states that in ancient Israel there is no clear distinction between mental and physical function, that 'man is conceived, not so much in dual fashion as "body" and "soul", but synthetically as a unit of vital power'. (cited in Hallpike, p. 404).

21. Cf. Hallpike, *The Foundations of Primitive Thought*.

22. In this context Hallpike's conclusion are of interest for ancient Mesopotamia (see *The Foundations of Primitive Thought*, p. 408): '... we find that the person is comprehended not as mind/body duality but rather synthetically, as a fusion of the psychical and the physical, such that organs and members of the body have psychical attributes, and the result is a physiological psychology'.

Hallpike further observed a 'general absence of an awareness of the cognitive function of the mind as the translator and mediator of experience'. If this is also valid for the Mesopotamians, it would merit a study.

23. It was inconceivable to the ancient Mesopotamians for a goddess *to give birth* to handicapped, imperfect people. That is why in the 'Enki and Ninmaḫ' myth two different verbs are used; cf. note 16 above. For an overview of creation myth see Gwendolyn Leick, *A Dictionary of Ancient Near Eastern Mythology* (Routledge, London and New York, 1991), pp. 25–8, 42–3, 52–5, 63–6, 108–9, 119–21.

24. Seux, *Epithètes*, pp. 160, 392–5; Jacob Klein, *Three Šulgi Hymns: Sumerian Royal Hymns Glorifying King Šulgi of Ur*, Bar-Ilan Studies in Near Eastern Languages and Culture (Bar-Ilan University Press, Ramat Gan, 1981), Shulgi A, D and X (hereafter 'Šulgi'); Werner R. Mayer, 'Ein Mythos von der Erschaffung des Menschen und des Königs', *Orientalia, NS* 56 (1987), pp. 55–68, lines 15', 33'–6', 40'.

25. See above, note 15.

26. Benito, *Enki and Ninmah*, pp. 21–44, Thorkild Jacobsen, *The Harp That Once ... Sumerian Poetry in Translation* (Yale University Press, New Haven, CT and London, 1987), pp. 151–66.

27. M. W. Green and H. J. Nissen, *Zeichenliste der archaischen Texte aus Uruk*, Ausgrabungen der Deutschen Forschungsgemeinschaft in Uruk-Warka, Band 11 (Gebr. Mann Verlag, Berlin, 1987), sign no. 332.

28. Green and Nissen, *Zeichenliste*, signs nos. 604 and 443.

29. This is elaborated in a forthcoming article by this author: 'Gender and Seals Within the Bureaucracy of the Late Uruk Period'; cf. Julia M. Asher-Greve, *Frauen in altsumerischer Zeit*, Bibliotheca Mesopotamica 18 (Undena Publications, Malibu, CA, 1985), pp. 2, 11–12, 38. Figures having no distinct gender are also depicted in many banquet scenes on cylinder seals; for instance, Dominique Collon, *First Impressions: Cylinder Seals in the Ancient Near East* (British Museum Publications, London, 1987), p. 30, nos. 91–3; p. 34, no. 109.

30. E.g. Margaret R. Miles, *Carnal Knowledge: Female Nakedness and Religious Meaning in the Christian West* (Beacon Press, Boston, MA, 1989), pp. 35–6; Ursula Prinz (ed.) *Androgyn: Sehnsucht nach der Vollkommenheit* (Neuer Berliner Kunstverein, Reimer Verlag, Berlin, 1987), pp. 38, 46 (illustrations). Although there are new studies on androgyny in art, recent art historical studies of the asexuality of many saints and angels are lacking.

31. E.g. Prinz, *Androgyn*.

32. For art from other cultures, see e.g. Islamic or Japanese art: Alexandre Papadopoulo, *Islamische Kunst* (Herder Verlag, Freiburg, Basel and Wien, 1977), pls 20, 26, 34, 38, 41, 51, 55, 60, 63; original French edition as *L'Islam et l'art Muselman* (1977); Danielle and Vadime Elisseeff, *Japan, Kunst und Kultur* (Herder Verlag, Freiburg, Basel and Wien, 1981), pls 44–6, 62, 63; original French edition as *L'Art de ancien Japon* (1980).

33. Cf. Prinz, *Androgyn*, pp. 144–83, 206–17.

34. Women wear dresses covering most of the chest part.

35. Horst Steible, *Die altsumerischen Bau- und Weihinschriften,* Teil I: *Inschriften aus Lagaš,* Freiburger Altorientalische Studien, Band 5 (Franz Steiner Verlag, Wiesbaden, 1982), pp. 82–4 (Urnanše 20); Jerrold S. Cooper, *Sumerian and Akkadian Inscriptions,* vol. I: *Presargonic Inscriptions* (The American Oriental Society, New Haven, CT, 1986), p. 22 (La 1.2); Asher-Greve, *Frauen*, pp. 91–2; Eva A. Braun-Holzinger, *Mesopotamische Weihgaben der frühdynastischen bis altbabylonischen Zeit*, Heidelberger Studien zum Alten Orient, Band 3 (Heidelberger Orientverlag, Heidelberg, 1990, p. 308 (W 1).

36. Cf. Asher-Greve, *Frauen*, pp. 86–97.

37. André Parrot, *Les temples d'Ishtarat et de Ninni-Zaza,* Mission Archéologique de Mari III, Institut français d'archéologie de Beyrouth, Bibliothèque d'Archéologique et Historique (Paul Geuthner, Paris, 1967), pp. 89–96 (no. 68), 377, pls 45–6; Braun-Holzinger, *Weihgaben*, p. 249. The controversy goes back to Parrot, who first published this statue; the last contribution is by Karl Oberhuber, 'Sänger/Musiker oder Sängerin/Musikerin? Zu einer Streitfrage der altmesopotamischen Bildkunst und Epigraphik', in *Musica Privata: Die Rolle der Musik im privaten Leben, Festschrift zum 65. Geburtstag von Walter Salmen,* ed. M. Fink, R. Gstrein and G. Mössmer (Edition Helbling, Innsbruck, 1991), pp. 339–43. Parrot already mentioned the possibility that a castrato is depicted (p. 95). Other biological causes could be imputed such as hormonal or chromosomal (XO) disorders or ingrown testes. The singer's association with the temple of ᵈMUŠ.ZA.ZA, the Semitic Aštar (later Ištar, a bisexual deity), may also serve as a clue to Urnanše's gender, because the statue is dedicated to her (cf. W. G. Lambert, 'The Pantheon of Mari', *Mari Annales de Recherches Interdisciplinaires* [hereafter *MARI*], 4 [1985], p. 537 and Alfonso Archi, 'Išḫara et Ištar à Ebla', *MARI,* 7 [1993], p. 76). Oberhuber's argument concerning the reading of the name 'Urnanše' is obsolete, because names composed with **ur** are masculine names. Oberhuber mentions an anthropologist who identified this statue as very likely representing a woman. What is typical of this debate is the reduction to an either-or categorization. The statue's ambiguous nature points to other possibilities: multiple gender categories. Even if we exclude castration (for which the earliest documents are from the Ur III period), other possibilities should have been taken into account, as, for instance, hermaphroditism, chromosome or hormonal disorders that result in 'effeminate' features. Cf. Gwendolyn Leick, *Sex and Eroticism in Mesopotamian Literature* (Routledge, London and New York, 1994), pp. 157–62, 167–8.

38. On castration, see Stanley Sadie (ed.) *The New Grove Dictionary of Opera*, vol. I (Macmillan Press, London, 1992), pp. 766–8; Angus Heriot, *The Castrati in Opera* (Martin Secker & Warburg, London, 1956), pp. 44–5. Heriot mentions (p. 10) that

apparently in Constantinople eunuchs were constantly used as singers. This might be an old Near Eastern tradition. For eunuchs in Byzantium see Kathryn M. Ringrose, 'Living in the Shadows: Eunuchs and Gender in Byzantium', in G. Herdt (ed.) *Third Sex, Third Gender: Beyond Sexual Dimorphism in Culture and History* (Zone Books, New York, 1994), pp. 85–109.

39. Subhi Anwar Rashid, *Gründungsfiguren im Iraq,* Prähistorische Bronzefunde, Abteilung I, Band 2 (C. H. Becksche Verlagsbuchhandlung, München, 1983). Rashid refers only to 'modelled chests' and never doubts these are images of kings.

40. Some societies recognize more than two gender categories, although usually no more than three or four; Sue-Ellen Jabobs and Christine Roberts, 'Sex, Sexuality, Gender, and Gender Variance', in *Gender and Anthropology,* ed. S. Morgan (American Anthropological Society, Washington, DC, 1989); see also Herdt, *Third Sex.*

41. Kazuya Maekawa, 'Animal and Human Castration in Sumer, Part II: Human Castration in the Ur III Period', *ZINBUN, Memoirs of the Research Institute for Humanistic Studies* (Kyoto University, Kyoto, 1980), pp. 1–55; cf. Leick, *Sex,* pp. 157–62. Leick does not mention the Ur III evidence for castration.

42. Benito, *Enki and Ninmah,* pp. 21–44 (lines 75–8). For another translation, see Jacobsen, *Harp,* pp. 151–66; cf. also Leick, *Sex,* p. 159.

43. Eunuchs were almost always castrated either in childhood or for crimes committed. The practice of keeping eunuchs at the courts might be because they could not procreate and thus could not establish a new dynasty. Placing a sexless person at the royal court could thus be understood as an etymology of the later attested eunuchs in royal service. Perhaps the practice was much older but originally relied on persons born with a sexual abnormality.

44. Bendt Alster, 'Sumerian Love Songs', *Revue d'Assyriologie et d'Archéologie Orientale,* 79 (1985), pp. 127–59; Bendt Alster, 'Marriage and Love in the Sumerian Love Songs', in *The Tablet and the Scroll: Near Eastern Studies in Honor of William W. Hallo,* ed. M. E. Cohen, D. C. Snell and B. Weisberg (CDL Press, Bethesda, MD, 1993), pp. 15–27; Elena Cassin, 'Virginité et stratégie du sexe', in *La première fois, ou le roman de la virginité perdue à travers les siècles et les continents,* ed. J.-P. Bardet and E. Cassin (Ramsay, Paris, 1981), pp. 241–58 (reprinted in Cassin, *Semblable,* pp. 338–57; Leick, *Sex*; see also Joan G. Westenholz, 'Love Lyrics from the Ancient Near East', in *CANE,* pp. 2471–84 (with bibliography).

45. Eva Strommenger and Max Hirmer, *Fünf Jahrtausende Mesopotamien* (Hirmer Verlag, München, 1962), pp. 55–6, pls 19–22 (in English as *5000 Years of the Art of Mesopotamia* [1964]; Elke Lindemeyer and Martin Lutz, *Uruk: Kleinfunde III,* Ausgrabungen in Uruk-Warka, Endberichte, Band 9, herausgegeben von R. M. Boehmer (Verlag Philipp von Zabern, Mainz, 1993), p. 81, pls 19–25.

46. **guruš-tur** = *batūlu*: MSL XII (*Materials for the Sumerian Lexicon XII: The Series lú = ša and Related Texts,* ed. Miguel Civil (Pontificium Institutum Biblicum, Roma, 1969), p. 105 (Lu excerpt II, line 31); CAD B/2, p. 174. See also Cassin, 'Virginité', pp. 338–57. For **guruš** = *etlu,* see CAD E, pp. 407–11.

47. Green and Nissen, *Zeichenliste,* sign no. 374.

48. Pierre Amiet, *La glyptique Mésopotamienne archaïque* (Editions du Centre National de la Recherche Scientifique, Paris, 1980²), pls 43–6, nos. 636B–43, 645–51, 655; Strommenger and Hirmer, *Mesopotamien,* pls 16–17.

49. Amiet, *Glyptique,* pl. 44, nos. 639–43.

50. Cf. Zainab Bahrani, 'The Iconography of the Nude in Mesopotamia', *Source,* 12 (1993), pp. 13–14.

51. Stefano de Martino, 'Nudità rituale e senso del pudore nella letteratura Ittita', *Oriens Antiquus*, 24 (1985), pp. 253–62. For the possibility of prostitutes being naked see Alster, 'Marriage'.

52. Philo of Alexandria, *Legum allegoria* 2.56 (Loeb Classical Library, 1929), p. 259, cited by Mario Perniola, 'Between Clothing and Nudity', in Feher, *Fragments*, p. 239.

53. Collon, *First Impressions*, p. 27 (figs 77, 80–4), pp. 193–7.

54. For the political history, see Piotr Steinkeller, 'Early Political Development in Mesopotamia and the Origins of the Sargonic Empire', in *Akkad, The First World Empire: Structure, Ideology, Traditions,* ed. M. Liverani, History of the Ancient Near East, Studies V (Sargon srl, Padova, 1993), pp. 107–29; Piotr Steinkeller, 'On Rulers, Priests and Sacred Marriage: Tracing the Evolution of Sumerian Kingship', in *Priests and Officials in the Ancient Near East,* Papers of the Second Colloquium on the Ancient Near East in the Middle Eastern Culture Center 2 (Universitätsverlag C. Winter, Heidelberg, CDL Press 1997; in press).

55. Collon, *First Impressions*, pp. 178–81; W. G. Lambert and A. R. Millard, *Atra-ḫasis: The Babylonian Story of the Flood* (Clarendon Press, Oxford, 1969); for other translations, see Stephanie Dalley, *Myths from Mesopotamia: Creation, the Flood, Gilgamesh and Others* (Oxford University Press, Oxford and New York, 1989); Benjamin R. Foster, *From Distant Days: Myths, Tales, and Poetry of Ancient Mesopotamia* (Bethesda, MD, 1995.

56. The importance of physical strength and heroism for rulers is evident in royal hymns. E.g., in the hymns of King Shulgi of Ur (see Klein, *Šulgi*, Shulgi A, D and X), the king's fate is described in this sequence: first heroism, followed by 'en'-ship (priestly duties) and kingship. The hymn describes Shulgi's qualities in that order: strength, heroism, courage on the battlefield, intelligence and understanding, physical achievement (runner) and provision of prosperity. In Shulgi's hymn A, heroism and strength also precede wisdom; his (superior) strength is repeatedly mentioned. Further, Shulgi's physical perfection is ideally suited for the task of king (Shulgi X, lines 59–70). For a different interpretation of a ruler's physical qualities cf. Irene J. Winter, 'Sex Rhetoric, and the Public Monument: The Alluring Body of Naramsîn of Agade', in *Sexuality in Ancient Art: Near East, Egypt, Greece, and Italy,* ed. B. Kampen (Cambridge University Press, Cambridge, UK and New York), pp. 16–26.

57. Seux, *Epithètes*, pp. 429–30.

58. Douglas Frayne, *The Royal Inscriptions of Mesopotamia, Early Periods,* vol. 4: *Old Babylonian Period (2003–1595 BC)* (University of Toronto Press, Toronto, Buffalo and London, 1990), p. 36–7 (no. 8, line 5).

59. Many royal hymns contain similar descriptions of the king's body: e.g. Seux, *Epithètes*, p. 436 (**pirig**, 'lion'), p. 459 (**ur-sag**, 'hero'); see also Klein, *Šulgi*.

60. From the 'Disputation between Ewe and Wheat'. The translation of line 23 is based on Miguel Civil's reading (as Civil communicated to me personally): **un giš-gi-na su-bi mu-un-du**. Cf. Bendt Alster and Herman Vanstiphout, 'Lahar and Ashnan: Presentation and Analysis of a Sumerian Disputation', *Acta Sumeriologica* (Japan), 9 (1987), pp. 16–17, lines 16–20.

61. Bahrani, 'Iconography', pp. 15–16.

62. See, e.g., the illustrations in Giovanni B. Lanfranchi and Simo Parpola, *The Correspondence of Sargon II,* Part II: *Letters from the Northern and Northeastern Provinces,* State Archives of Assyria, vol. V (Helsinki University Press, Helsinki, 1990), p. 65, fig. 16; p. 118, fig. 25; p. 170, fig. 33; p. 174, fig. 34.

63. Alster, 'Marriage'; Bahrani, 'Iconography'; Leick, *Sex*, plates.

64. E.g. Marie-Therèse Barrelet, *Figurines et reliefs en terre cuite de la Mésopotamie antique*, Bibliothèque Archéologique et Historique, Tome LXXXV (Paul Geuthner, Paris, 1968); Felix Blocher, *Untersuchungen zum Motiv der nackten Frau in der altbabylonischen Zeit*, Münchner Vorderasiatische Studien, Band IV, Münchner Universitäts-Schriften, Phil. Fakultät 12 (Profil Verlag, München,1987); Bahrani, 'Iconography', p. 15; Jeremy Black and Anthony Green, *Gods, Demons and Symbols of Ancient Mesopotamia* (British Museum Press, London, 1992), p. 144.

65. See Johnson, *The Body in the Mind,* pp. 7–12, 65–74 on the metaphoric meaning of physical appearance.

66. Kirk A. Grayson, *The Royal Inscriptions of Mesopotamia, Assyrian Periods,* vol. 2: *Assyrian Rulers of the Early First Millennium BC (1114–859)* (University of Toronto Press, Toronto, Buffalo and London, 1991), p. 108; Cooper, 'Gendered Sexuality', p. 87 with n. 12.

67. E.g. Bahrani, 'Iconography'; Leick, *Sex,* plates; for further illustration, see Barrelet, *Figurines.*

68. Martha T. Roth, *Law Collections from Mesopotamia and Asia Minor,* Writings from the Ancient World, vol. 6, Society of Biblical Literature (Scholars Press, Atlanta, GA, 1995); see also Leick, *Sex,* p. 47.

69. Leick, *Sex,* pp. 90–6.

70. Leick, *Sex,* pp. 111–29; Alster, 'Love Songs'; Westenholz, 'Love Lyrics'; Joan G. Westenholz, 'Metaphorical Language in the Poetry of Love in the Ancient Near East', in *La circulation des biens, des personnes et des idées dans le Proche-Orient ancien,* Actes de la XXXVIIIe Rencontre Assyriologique Internationale (Paris, 8–10 juillet 1991), ed. D. Charpin and F. Joannès (Editions Recherche sur les Civilisations, Paris, 1992), pp. 381–7.

71. Gertrud Farber-Flügge, *Der Mythos 'Inanna und Enki' unter besonderer Berücksichtigung der Liste der* me, Studia Pohl 10 (Biblical Institute Press, Roma, 1973), pp. 107–8.

72. Irving Finkel, 'The Crescent Fertile', *Archiv für Orientforschung,* 27 (1980), pp. 37–51; Leick, *Sex,* pp. 26, 45–6; Westenholz, 'Love Lyrics'. The link between sexuality and procreation is evident in myths and other literary texts. But this is not the case in, e.g., the sex omens; cf. Ann Guinan's article in this volume.

73. Perniola, 'Clothing and Nudity', p. 238.

74. Ursula Seidl, 'Inanna/Ištar', *Reallexikon der Assyriologie und Vorderasiatischen Archäologie,* Band 5 (Walter de Gruyter, Berlin and New York, 1976–80), pp. 87–9; Bahrani, 'Iconography'.

75. For a recent study on psychological and psychoanalytic views of the body, see Grosz, *Volatile Bodies,* pp. 27–61; see also Laqueur's analysis of the history of body 'models' in *Making Sex.*

76. Cf. Brigitte Groneberg, 'Zu den mesopotamischen Unterweltsvorstellungen: Das Jenseits als Fortsetzung des Diesseits', *Altorientalische Forschungen* 17 (1990), pp. 250–7 (with bibliography); Tzvi Abusch, 'Etemmu', in *Dictionary of Deities and Demons in the Bible,* ed. K. van der Toorn, B. Becking and P. W. van der Horst (E. J. Brill, Leiden, New York and Köln, 1995), pp. 588–93 (with bibliography). A new study will be published by Abusch, who presented his interpretation at the American Oriental Society meeting in Philadelphia in March 1996: 'Ghost and God: Some Observations on a Babylonian Understanding of Human Nature' NUHEN, Supplement 1997 (in press). My interpretation owes a lot to Abusch, although we do not agree on all points.

77. For the text, see Lambert and Millard, *Atra-ḫasis,* pp. 56–9; for other translations, see Dalley, *Myths,* pp. 115–16; Foster, *Distant Days,* pp. 58–9.

78. See above, note 76.

79. Josef Bauer, 'Zum Totenkult im altsumerischen Lagash', *Zeitschrift der Deutschen Morgenländischen Gesellschaft*, Supplement 1 (1969), pp. 107–14; Philippe Tallon, 'A propos d'une graphie présargonique de ŠL 577 (GIDIM)', *Revue d'Assyriologie et d'Archéologie Orientale*, 68 (1974), pp. 167–8; cf. also Piotr Michalowski, 'The Death of Šulgi', *Orientalia*, NS 46 (1977), pp. 220–5.

80. CAD Š/III, pp. 113–22.

81. See above, note 76.

82. Groneberg, 'Unterweltsvorstellungen'; Abusch, 'Etemmu'.

83. Jerrold S. Cooper, 'The Fate of Mankind: Death and Afterlife in Ancient Meso-potamia', in *Death and Afterlife: Perspectives of World Religions*, ed. H. Obayashi, Contributions to the Study of Religion, 33 (1992), pp. 19–33.

84. J. Renger, 'Kultbild', in *Reallexikon der Assyriologie*, Band 6 (Walter de Gruyter, Berlin and New York, 1980–3), pp. 313–14; Thorkild Jacobsen, 'The Graven Image', in *Ancient Israelite Religion: Essays in Honor of Frank Moore Cross*, ed. P. D. Miller, P. D. Hanson and S. D. McBride (Fortress Press, Philadelphia, PA, 1987), pp. 15–32; Samuel N. Kramer, 'Lamentation over the Destruction of Nippur', *Acta Sumeriologica* (Japan), 13 (1991), pp. 1–26; Piotr Michalowski, *The Lamentation Over the Destruction of Sumer and Ur*, Mesopotamian Civilizations 1 (Eisenbrauns, Winona Lake, 1989), esp. pp. 45–7.

85. Jerrold S. Cooper, *The Curse of Agade*, Johns Hopkins Near Eastern Studies (Johns Hopkins University Press, Baltimore, MD and London, 1983), pp. 52–53 (lines 60–64).

86. E.g. Gudea's statue B: Horst Steible, *Die neusumerischen Bau- und Weihinschriften*, Teil I: *Inschriften der II. Dynastie von Lagaš*, Freiburger Altorientalische Studien, Band 9, 1 (Franz Steiner Verlag, Wiesbaden, 1991), pp. 170–3 (7: 7–48).

87. Life comes through birth (**tud**) or for statues through the glance (**igi-zi**) of a deity.

88. Cf. Steinkeller, 'Early Political Development' and 'On Rulers, Priests and Sacred Marriage', and Julia Asher-Greve, forthcoming article 'From Nidaba to Nabû: What Happened to the Goddesses' (cf. note 23 above); cf. also Asher-Greve, *Frauen*.

89. Amélie Kuhrt, 'Women and War in the Ancient World' (lecture given at the sym-posium Gender Studies in den Altorientalischen Wissenschaften, Basel, 15 June 1996); a summary is published in the '40ème lettre circulaire' by the Schweizerische Gesell-schaft für Orientalische Altertumskunde (Fribourg, 1997), pp. 6–7.

Auguries of Hegemony:
The Sex Omens of Mesopotamia

ANN KESSLER GUINAN

Ancient Mesopotamian scholars studied human erotic diversity within the discourse of divination. They documented an array of individual behaviors, reading each as an omen, a sign signifying an aspect of the future. When scribes recorded an omen they expressed it as a conditional sentence: the protasis specifying the ominous sign and the apodosis its divinatory meaning. Each sentence was inscribed on a tablet as a single entry in a series of topically related omens. The protasis of each sex omen presents a single act, habit, or event; the apodosis specifies a future physical, emotional, economic, or social condition. The omens address a range of erotic activity: choice of partners, positions and locales. A few of the omens refer to sexual behavior in terms of its reproductive potential, but more often they mention non-procreative acts such as ejaculation without intromission, masturbation, or anal intercourse.

The sex omens are contained on two tablets of the large first-millennium BCE omen compendium, *šumma ālu*.[1] Both texts deal with variable patterns of individual erotic behavior. Tablet 103 has thirty-two omens and deals exclusively with heterosexual intercourse. Tablet 104 is separated by a dividing line into two sections.[2] The first thirty-eight omens document a broad spectrum of sexual behavior. The second section of text contains thirty-five omens detailing the miseries that threaten a man in the aftermath of a divorce and as a result of marital abuse.

They reflect the ancient scholar's understanding that the variables of human erotic behavior are linked to the vagaries of individual fortune. The orientation of the material is male. Behavior initiated by a woman has meaning in terms of male fortunes. The sex omens have much to tell us about the meaning and emotion attached to male erotic desires and the way they were located in a discourse of masculine hegemony.

The implications of the omens stretch in many directions and suggest provocative avenues of inquiry. How was erotic desire experienced and how was the male body observed, inscribed and endowed with meaning? In what way was the body considered vulnerable and to what end could the body be used?

These are very large questions to put to a limited assortment of odd omens. We need to assess the potential of these texts as a source and develop a strategy for utilizing them. The task is immeasurably aided by the development over the last twenty years of a rich discourse on gender and sexuality within institutions of hierarchy and power.[3] Omen texts engage sexual topics and codify meanings in a way that is very different from other written genres or cultural institutions in general, and from the other constructions of Mesopotamian sexuality, in particular.[4]

What is lacking, however, is a theoretical framework for understanding the meanings that spin out from this specific mode of discourse. The result has been that even those Mesopotamian sex omens that are relatively free of philological difficulties have been difficult to understand and interpret. In order that these omens may be situated in relation to other Mesopotamian discourses on sexuality and gender and be made available for other studies of ancient sexuality, they have to be analyzed within the context of divinatory inquiry.

This alien genre affords a frame for modern interpretation. The place where the ancient scholar locates his inquiry—where human erotic behavior and the scholarship of omens converge—can help us understand one of the ways in which a Mesopotamian man perceived his desires and negotiated the interplay of sexual and social motives.

Divination is a two-part process. First, divination establishes a connection with a source of knowledge that lies outside human vision, intellect, or control. Secondly, it is the human mind alone which receives or recognizes a divinatory message and interprets and applies its meaning. The first process that ends in the production of a divinatory message needs to be distinguished from this second, overlapping process that begins once the message is received and is completed when the message is interpreted, understood and applied.

Unlike other forms of divination (i.e. meaning voiced in the mouth of a medium or deliberately requested by a special technique), the observation of an omen requires the observer to be alert to the possibility of a sign and to recognize one when it appears. The phenomenon is abstracted, attributed to an external agency, and endowed by the observer with uncanny power to supply meaning.

The two-part structure of divination requires a two-part interpretive strategy for reading omen texts. When the conceptual structure of the protasis of an omen is allowed to define the erotic logic of the text a complex intellectual construct is revealed. The omens cast man both as a divinatory object and as a sexual subject. When the passions of the body become a source of omens, the intersections of human and divine, material and linguistic, spill out of our conceptual categories and flow together into thought that we are hardly able to describe. The predicted meanings, however, fall entirely in the human domain of experience. Thus, when one turns one's focus to consider how the behavior in the protasis is connected to the broader aspect of life in the apodosis, the complexity raised by the formulation of the omens disappears.

Using this two-part structure of divination, I deal initially with the resolution of the sex omen's meaning as it is determined from the connection between the protasis and the apodosis. Then I consider the omens that deal with sex between males. These omens are significant because they relate to two Middle Assyrian laws and by extension to other Mesopotamian sources. They suggest the possibility of broader historical and theoretical analysis and they demonstrate the difficulties encountered when the omens are compared with other sources. I then turn to the protasis and consider the more difficult conceptual problem of omen formation and its implications for reading the body as an omen.

An Akkadian omen text collects related omens, organizes them into topical groups and designates each omen to be either auspicious or inauspicious. This structure generates a straightforward methodology. It is often difficult to understand the connection between any single ominous act and its signified prediction but when individual and small groups of omens are contrasted and compared, systematic patterns of positive and negative meaning emerge. Omens which may initially elude interpretation become meaningful when incorporated into an expanding semantic structure.

The binary structure of the omen genre imposes a resolution that is dialectical and relentlessly grounded in gender asymmetry. A common perspective emerges from the resolution of auspicious and inauspicious meanings. The omens oppose the male public persona and male/female eroticism in such a way that the denial of one is the assertion of the other. When a woman directs sexual action toward a man it is inauspicious for him. Conversely, it is auspicious when a man turns his sexual energy away from a woman and invests in enlarging his public position. Asymmetries of gender derive from dominant institutions and they are held in place by the logic of binary symbolism. Binary classifications of hierarchy (domination/subordination), sex (male/female), gender (masculinity/femininity) and sexuality (penetration/receptivity) become conflated and the resulting conceptual structure does not distinguish between the various components. As a result the social and political world becomes suffused with gender and sexual meanings. As long as this conflation is institutionalized by culture it appears natural and inevitable. Nevertheless, unexpressed contradictions reverberate uneasily across social and sexual domains and emerge on the body as somatic metaphors.

Human sexuality is imbued with liminal meaning. Exchanges, openings, penetrations and permeable boundaries are an inherent part of human erotic life. Ambiguous or anomalous phenomena appear in the cracks and spaces in taxonomies and cultural classifications. Liminal phenomena are displacements deriving from contradictions and challenges to social structure; at the same time that they define structural lines, they challenge their integrity. These phenomena are perceived to be powerful, disgusting, uncanny, or dangerous. As Mary Douglas says:

> Any structure of ideas is vulnerable at its margins. We would expect the orifices of the body to symbolize its specially vulnerable points. Matter issuing from them is marginal stuff of the most obvious kind. Spittle, blood, milk, urine, feces or tears by simply issuing forth have traversed the boundary of the body. Each culture has its risks and problems. To which particular bodily margins its beliefs attribute power depends on what situation the body is mirroring.[5]

If human sexuality is experienced as liminal, then the omens that consider occasions of sexual marginality can be considered doubly liminal. These body-related sex omens represent liminalities of two types. They deal with sexual interactions that take place on the boundaries of male and female bodies (omens 2, 3, 4, 12) and with the ominous import of body emissions (omens 6, 7, 8, 11(?), 17). The asymmetries of power and the binary construction of gender electrify the boundary between male and female bodies and constrain the way the erotic body is experienced and deployed.

The omens 1, 2, 3 and 5 project apprehension on the marginal points where male and female bodies meet. In these omens the woman has an active rather than a passive role. The woman, not the man, is the agent of the action of omens 1, 3 and 5. In order to preserve the male subject the text distorts the normal Akkadian word order.[6]

As omen 1 states:

> 1. If a man, a woman mounts him, that woman will take his vigor; for one month he will not have a personal god.

A woman who is allowed to take a sexually dominant position is able to rob a man of his physical power. The sexual inversion of gender hierarchy deprives him of his vigor and his personal god, in essence, his drive to pursue his proper place in the world.

> 2. If a man causes a woman to repeatedly take hold of his penis, he is not pure; the god will not accept his prayer.
> 3. If, when a man is facing his woman, she handles her vagina, that man is not pure; for the rest of (his) days his hand will tremble.

Omens 2 and 3 depict a woman touching either a man's genitals or her own. In both cases the act causes the man to be impure. In the text of Tablet 104, omen 2 follows an omen which also specifies impurity and cultic offense in the case of repeated ejaculations. These are the only three circumstances in Tablets 103 and 104 in which a man becomes impure as the consequence of a sexual act. In omen 2 the man is specifically said to have encouraged the woman to repeatedly take hold of his penis. The omen may imply that he desires sexual outlet through her manual stimulation, but it is not stated. It is not clear whether this impurity is derived from her touch, from his desire for it, or from the forces of desire her actions arouse. Omen 3 stems from a woman handling her own genitals (probably during or immediately after intercourse). Again it is not clear whether impurity is the product of just her touch or her contact with the liminal area where both bodies meet. Her action directed toward herself permeates the man's body and provokes a reciprocal reaction—his hand will tremble.[7]

Omens 4 and 5 turn on the understanding that 'seeing' is an act of taking. Power is wielded by the subject who looks at another. To be the object of a look makes one vulnerable and exposed.

> 4. If a man repeatedly stares at his woman's vagina, his health will be good; he will lay his hands on whatever is not his.
> 5. If a man is with a woman (and) while facing him she repeatedly stares at his penis, whatever he finds will not be secure in his house.

In the context of a society that kept things of value hidden, scrutinizing observation could be a breach of boundary.[8] The man's act of seizing with his eyes corresponds to grabbing goods that are not his. However, what he seizes is not some other woman but his own. Thus, the meaning of the apodosis when he reaches out for things that are not his, helps define the dynamics of male and female interaction. The female body lies over the same boundary that separates 'what is mine' from 'what is not mine'. The man's looking is an obtrusive act. It is based on the proper relationship between male subject and female object and is auspicious. His bold looking designates a man who reaches out and takes. But with appropriation comes the threat of loss. Her look turns the man into an object. In the apodosis of omen 4 things are seized and brought under the man's control. Omen 5 presents a contrasting situation, but the apodosis can also be read as a continuation of the events of the previous omen: the things he took are threatened and his control over them is undermined. The unusual connection between the apodoses of omens 4 and 5 demonstrates the dynamics that are brought into play when the man's position switches from subject to object. The woman's look is penetrating and undermines his mastery and control.

The Mesopotamian sex omens pay marked attention to the meaning of semen when ejaculated outside the vagina or ejaculated in excess. Semen has an economic corollary—it is a man's capital which can be squandered or well spent.[9]

> 6. If a man has sexual relations and then, in the same night, he ejaculates, that man will experience heavy expenses.
> 7. If a man ejaculates in his dream and is spattered with his semen, that man will find riches; he will have financial gain.

8. If a man has sexual relations with a woman and then ejaculates and is spattered with his semen, it is good; that man will have financial gain.
9. If a man persistently (has sexual relations) with a woman and always ejaculates repeatedly, he will die in his prime.

A nocturnal emission that follows a sexual encounter is expressed in financial terms as a heavy depletion of resources (omen 6). Omen 9 describes a man who always ejaculates again and again.[10] The man will die in his prime, depleted of the source of his vitality and strength. This omen may refer to persistent premature ejaculation, but it appears to be the excess discharge that makes the omen so malefic. A second omen from Tablet 104 also depicts a man who 'always ejaculates again and again'. In this omen the behavior is described as a great sin and creates cultic impurity.[11]

Omens link the expenditure of semen to financial profit. Assets that are squandered are contrasted to assets that are invested. Wasteful is opposed to profitable spending. In omen 7 the financial theme is doubly expressed —a single nocturnal emission signifies finding riches and financial gain. Omen 8, like omen 6, deals with ejaculation that is subsequent to an initial act: 'If a man has sexual relations with a woman and then ejaculates … it is good; that man will have financial gain.' It is unclear whether the ominous ejaculation occurs at the approach or after withdrawal. The word for sexual relations, ṭehû, is literally 'to come near' and, thus, is inchoative in its original meaning. Here it is used as a euphemism and is not specific about the beginning or end of the act in question. The omens do not consider the reproductive value of semen. In fact omen 8 positively values an act that withholds semen from a woman.

When a woman takes an active role and asserts her sexuality it threatens a man's relations with his god, jeopardizes his health and puts whatever competitive advantage he might have at risk. While it is not surprising that this reversal of gender hierarchy is considered to be unfavorable, it is more unusual that sexual domination of women has a negative value. According to the omens, both rape (omen 10) and marital abuse are inauspicious.[12] It is the outward vector of sexual energy that produces the positive meanings. In this text masculine power expresses itself as disavowal and withdrawal from erotic interactions with women.

Nevertheless, sexuality can be propitiously deployed. According to omen 12:

12. If a man talks with a woman on a bed and then he rises from the bed and makes manhood [i.e. masturbates], that man will have happiness and jubilation bestowed upon him; wherever he goes all will be agreeable; he will always achieve goal.

The positive predictions of omen 12 extend to all the significant areas of human life. This act alone produces happiness and joy, harmonious social relations and personal success. The verb *dabābu* may have a sexual mean-ing beyond the translation 'talks', but the exact nuance is relatively unim-portant. The omen makes the sexual context clear and evidently coitus does not take place. The meaning of the omen turns on our understanding of what is meant by the term *zikarūtu* translated here as 'manhood' and only attested in the sex omens of Tablet 104. I understand the word to denote an act of masturbation. Omen 12 which deals with the benefits resulting from the making of *zikarūtu* should be compared with omen 11 where *zikarūtu* is denied the man.[13] He relinquishes the woman and achieves satisfaction on his own. The import of omen 12 echoes omen 8 which positively values the withholding of semen during heterosexual intercourse. Omen 12, however, is the most auspicious omen of either Tablet 103 or 104. In texts that are more concerned with the balances of profit and loss and the possibility of affliction, the prediction goes beyond happiness to exhilaration and beyond success to triumph. A man who turns from a woman and literally 'makes manhood' thereby expands his scope of social achievement.

In the predictions of omens 2, 3, 4, 5 and 12 the introduction of the binary ideology of social hierarchy cuts short the mutuality of touching, looking, talking. Erotic reciprocity is replaced by images of domination and subjugation, endangered borders and loss of power. Questions of power, gender and sexuality become questions of masculine agency and social identity. As a structuring device the binary opposition of gender categories defines a symbolic boundary. The need of the masculine social body to claim a masculine social space conflicts with essential features of physical sexuality which requires that boundaries be crossed. When masculine identity is defined in these terms, not only must the boundary be firmly drawn, it must be fortified. Woman is seen as what man is not. Socially constructed notions of personhood organized by such oppositions are vulnerable from within and without—the behavior of others has the power to intervene and disrupt the way personal identity is conceived and presented.

The four omens that deal with sex between males also demonstrate that sexual energy can be directed out for non-sexual gain. These omens eroticize social categories and value those sexual acts and objects that extend the domain of social influence. Erotic interactions in the male social arena are measures of position, power and prestige.[14] The late John Winkler's often quoted characterization of Greek sexuality appears similarly applicable in this Mesopotamian context:

> Of all the meanings and facets of sexual behavior that might be singled out for special attention the Greeks insistently focused on dominance and sub-mission, as constituted by phallic penetration ... Sex, so understood, was basically a way for men to establish their social identities in the intensely competitive, zero-sum formats of public culture.[15]

In the historical constructions of Greece and Rome, the sexual position of the male partner conformed to social status. A proper and licit but passive partner was lower in status. The Mesopotamian sex omens are also conceived in terms of social role, but the conclusions reached are different.[16]

> 13. If a man has sexual relations with an *assinnu*, hardships will be unleashed from him.
> 14. If a man has sexual relations with a *girsequ*, for an entire year the deprivations which beset him will be kept away.
> 15. If a man has sexual relations with a male house(-born) slave, hardship will seize him.

Omens 13, 14 and 15 occur together as a group. The two auspicious omens are contrasted with a single inauspicious one. Both the *assinnu* and the *girsequ* function in some official capacity in the public arena. An *assinnu*, a character who appears in a variety of Mesopotamian sources, is a performer in an Ištar cult and is distinguished by dress, hairstyle, and female accoutrements. Variously a transvestite, a hermaphrodite, or eunuch, the *assinnu* is a transgressive figure of ambiguous or, perhaps, even mutable gender and overt sexual display.[17] A *girsequ* has domestic duties associated with the palace or temple.[18] Sexual relations with these partners represent dominance and gaining of power. The male house-born slave is also a domestic, but he is the antithesis of a *girsequ* because he belongs to the house. Sexual relations with a slave born of the house are a type of encounter that is, perhaps, too close to home and this sexual involvement does not have a place in the social arena.[19]

Another omen to be considered is one that deals with sex between male equals:

> 16. If a man has sex *per anum* with his social peer, that man will become foremost among his brothers and colleagues.

The term *meḫru* (peer) refers to parity of status. The omen turns on the switch of positions from 'behind' to 'in front' and on the paronomastic relationship between the words *qinnatu* ('anus') and *kinātu* ('colleagues'). Thus, one can put oneself ahead of one's peers in the community by penetrating one of them from behind. The possibility that collegiate relations could also be sexual is underscored by the telling pun.

This omen can be compared to two Middle Assyrian Laws (MAL) which is significant because it opens the omens to comparisons with other Mesopotamian sources and to the possibility of broader historical analysis.[20] The first comparable law, MAL 19, deals with slander: a man says of his *tappû*, ('comrade'), either furtively, by rumor, or in a quarrel in front of other men, 'Everyone always penetrates you' but is unable to prove it. The transitive verb *nâku*, here translated 'penetrates', refers to illicit sex. When referring to male/female relationships the man is always the active agent with the woman as the object (or passive subject). The word *tappû*, variously translated ('comrade', 'friend', 'neighbor'), refers to a close associate who can share business ventures, danger, or adjacent property. The slanderer has defined a member of his fraternal community as the receptive partner. The iterative form of the verb has been understood to refer to promiscuity, but it seems more likely to be a reference to a stigmatized sexual preference—a male penetrated by choice.[21]

The second law, MAL 20, concerns the act: a man penetrates his comrade. The penalty is significant. If the charges are proved and he is found guilty, he is penetrated and then he is turned into a eunuch. Both the placement of these laws in the context of legislation on adultery and the punishment required by MAL 20 indicate the gendered nature of the offenses. Reflecting a general principle of Mesopotamian legal composition, the two laws represent polar cases which are juxtaposed to form a legal statement and maximally varied in order to define the outer boundaries of a legal situation.[22] The meaning encompassed by the juxtaposition is a matter of interpretation.[23] One line of reasoning understands these laws as a prohibition against consensual sexual acts between those who share a *tappû* relationship. According to a second line of reasoning, however, these laws are not to be read as a general condemnation of sex between males. Thus it has been argued by Bottéro and Petchow that MAL 19 is a prohibition against male prostitution and MAL 20 refers to rape. The fact that anal penetration is the specified punishment supports this interpretation of MAL 20. Force is not entailed in the basic meaning of the verb *nâku*. Even so, it seems unlikely that consensual acts fall within the scope of this legal statement. There are no penalties for the comrade; in both MAL 19 and 20 he is the victim, the object of the offense.[24] If the laws refer to consensual acts which could be kept private, what would be the circumstances of discovery or complaint? By either word or deed one close associate has feminized and subordinated another—it is an infringement of masculine position and agency in a community of men who share the prerogatives of power. In one case the victim has been publicly defined as someone known to be the passive partner, and in the polar case he has been placed in the same position through active violation. But it also cannot be claimed that consensual sex between male equals is by implication licit. That issue is left unaddressed.

The two MAL laws protect the *tappû* relationship. They safeguard male agency and identity against attack from inside boundaries that mark off prerogatives and entitlements of social space. The punishment, an example of a penalty fitting the crime, is a gendered and sexual assertion of hierarchy. What the perpetrator did to a comrade, the community does to him. By castration he is permanently reduced to the role he imposed on his victim and his body is violently reconfigured to conform to his new gender position.

How can the discursive space between the omens and the laws be mapped? If sexual acts between male equals, including those who prefer the passive position, were licit and proper, then male/male sexual relations are constructed in a way that is significantly different from the cultures of Greece and Rome.[25] One could argue that there is some aspect of closeness to the *tappû*-relationship that does not extend to the *meḫru* (a social peer). Even if that is the case, the omen seems to authorize an act that is either equivalent to or not markedly different from the one the law prohibits.

Omen 16 and MAL 19 and 20 have opposing orientations, but are mobilized by the same underlying conception—the penetrating male gains position and agency which the receptive male loses. Where the laws in general articulate social boundaries and prohibitions applicable to all, divination operates on a case-by-case basis to deal with specific situations. The omens take the individual's point of view and determine whether he is positively or negatively positioned in relation to the social whole. The omens express aspects of culture generally left unaddressed. The auspicious omens exploit hidden possibilities and the inauspicious ones reveal unexpected peril. Both the penalties of the laws and the resolution of omen 16 are gender-based assertions of hierarchy.

Omen 16 reveals a hidden line of hierarchy. It distinguishes an unseen category that divides a class of equals. The omen refers to a *meḫru* ('a peer'), to *aḫḫū* ('brothers') and *kinātu* ('colleagues'), but seemingly avoids *tappû* ('a comrade'). Omens 13, 14 and 15 deal with three types of lower-status males who when grouped together form a category of possible passive partners. The contrast between the two auspicious and the one inauspicious omen defines a finer category distinction.

Just as every man can be a penetrator, he can also be penetrated. The binary structures of gender asymmetry are located on the same male body. A male equal who chooses to be penetrated makes the somatic contradictions inherent in the logic of gender asymmetry all too close to becoming visible. His act threatens the logic of binary gender and undermines the terms of gender hierarchy on which social organization is predicated. Sex between male equals, which opens the possibility of reversible positions and the symmetrical deployment of the body, is a double annihilation of hierarchy.

The resolution of the connections between protasis and apodosis in the Mesopotamian sex omens generates interpretations grounded in binary opposition and sealed within the textual universe. When interpretation is approached from the perspective of the protasis alone, the body is a divinatory vehicle, desire is an ominous signifier and, at the same time, the male subject is constituted in a divinatory system of signification.

In the protasis of an omen, the numinous, unseen forces that inhabit the Mesopotamian universe send messages into the sensory world embodied in natural phenomena. An omen may be something out of place, it may cross one's path, fall nearby, manifest itself suddenly. The phenomena that are construed as omens stand out from the non-signifying background of everyday life—they deviate in some way from the norm. The human body and, more significantly, human behavior take their place along with the behavior of animals, the configurations of the viscera of sacrificial animals, meteorological phenomena and the movement of the stars—as sites of inscription and objects that can be activated by divine forces and turned into language.

Yet, omens derived from human behavior stand out from other forms of Mesopotamian omens. It is hard to understand how behavior that one chooses or that is defined by law can be construed as an omen. Behavior can function as an omen only as long as the observer has no knowledge of what it foretells. If the meaning is known and behavior altered in response, it can no longer be read as an omen. If the inauspicious omens signify behavior to be avoided, do the auspicious omens indicate behavior that is permissible, or even, going further, should auspicious behavior be sought out to bring about a favorable outcome? In other words, can a man bolster his future by seeking out penetrative intercourse with his peer? If a ritual can be used to avert the adversity portended by an act, does prior knowledge of the ritual mean the act could be repeated without adverse results?

A paradox derives from the subject position constructed within the two-part structure of divinatory inquiry and would not be present if the omens dealt only with the external view of the scribe. The short apotropaic rituals which are appended to a number of the omens, and intended to ward off the evil threatened by the prediction, suggest that the two points of view (that of the scribe who produces the omen text and that of the observer constructed inside the text) can be distinguished:

> 17. If a man is with his wife in a tavern and he urinates, he will not prosper.
>   So that this [i.e. the evil] does not approach: he should sprinkle his urine to the right and the left of the door jamb of the tavern and then he will prosper.

In omen 17 the malefic prediction, 'he will not prosper', derives from the inappropriate transgression of body margins. By urinating on the threshold of the tavern, a man can protect himself and turn the prediction around.[26] The rituals are contiguous operations made to prevent the evil from emerging. The omens followed by rituals present a subject who, if he knows the ritual, also must know the significance of the act at the moment he engages in it. The magical logic of contiguous transfer presupposes an awareness that moves seamlessly from event to remedy.

The subject in the first part of the omen observes his behavior as a external sign but when he turns, in the second part, to interpret the sign and formulate a response, he appears to be the agent of the behavior. The subject constituted in the first part of the divinatory structure is uneasily situated at the intersection of several domains.

Divination deals with edges where no guidelines are provided by other structures. On the one hand, divination provides an individual with social validation for acts that involve conflicting choices, sexual desires, or special risks. It can allow someone to exploit the cracks in and contradictions of a social system. On the other hand, it provides a social context for evaluating individual misfortune. Although culture provides models of normative behavior and creates the forms and constraints of collective life, erotic desire is often roused against the grain of those constraints. The acts, positions, partners and locales that allow an individual to produce, sustain and gratify desire are variable. Erotic life provides experiences of disjuncture and a basis for self-interpretation where desire can be measured against a perception of the social norm.

An omen embodies ambiguity. It exists in the immediate world but derives its signifying force from outside that world. The omen is charged with the conflict of competing aims, desires and possible courses of action. Every omen contains *in ovo* two possibilities. When an omen forms, it demands resolution and anticipates meaning. The displaced tensions of contradictory demands are directed to the boundaries of the body and emerge as omens. The tension dissipates once the meaning is located.

The two-part structure of divination and the resolution of the omens into binary categories expose paradoxes, contradictions and liminalities bisected into their component parts. For example, sexual desire can be transformed in an omen into non-sexual meaning and positively deployed for social gain. Positive resolution discriminates between and sustains finer lines of gender hierarchy, while negative resolution erects sexual body boundaries and abnegates desires that call those boundaries into question.

Selected Sex Omens[27]

1. If a man, a woman mounts him, that woman will take his vigor; for one month he will not have a personal god.[28]
2. If a man causes a woman to repeatedly take hold of his penis, he is not pure; the god will not accept his prayer.[29]
3. If, when a man is facing his woman, she handles her vagina, that man is not pure; for the rest of (his) days his hand will tremble.[30]
4. If a man repeatedly stares at his woman's vagina, his health will be good; he will lay his hands on whatever is not his.[31]
5. If a man is with a woman (and) while facing him she repeatedly stares at his penis, whatever he finds will not be secure in his house.[32]
6. If a man has sexual relations and then, in the same night, he ejaculates, that man will experience heavy expenses.[33]
7. If a man ejaculates in his dream and is spattered with his semen, that man will find riches; he will have financial gain.[34]

8. If a man has sexual relations with a woman and then ejaculates and is spattered with his semen, it is good; that man will have financial gain.[35]
9. If a man persistently [has sexual relations] with a woman and always ejaculates repeatedly, he will die in his prime.[36]
10. If a man seizes a woman in the crossroad and has sexual relations [with her], that man will not prosper; either the hand of the god or the hand of the king will catch him.[37]
11. If a man excites himself to 'manhood' in captivity but, when erect, the rise of the emission (?) of 'manhood' is denied him, that man will experience one-time misfortune.[38]
12. If a man talks with a woman on a bed and then he rises from the bed and makes manhood [i.e. masturbates], that man will have happiness and jubilation bestowed upon him; wherever he goes all will be agreeable; he will always achieve his goal.[39]
13. If a man has sexual relations with an *assinnu*, hardships will be unleashed from him.[40]
14. If a man has sexual relations with a *girseqû*, for an entire year the deprivations which beset him will be kept away.[41]
15. If a man has sexual relations with a male house[-born] slave, hardship will seize him.[42]
16. If a man has sex *per anum* with his social peer, that man will become foremost among his brothers and colleagues.[43]
17. If a man is with his wife in a tavern and he urinates, he will not prosper.
    So that this [i.e. the evil] does not approach: he should sprinkle his urine to the right and the left of the door jamb of the tavern and then he will prosper.[44]

Notes

Abbreviations:
  CAD   *The Assyrian Dictionary* (The Oriental Institute, Chicago and J. J. Augustin, Glückstadt)
  CT   *Cuneiform Texts from Babylonian Tablets in the British Museum*, vol. 39, plates 44–6 (British Museum Publications, London, 1925–31)
  MAL   Middle Assyrian Laws
  [ ]   restored word
  ( )   supplied word

I would like to thank Drs. Beth Jewell and Tikva Frymer-Kensky for help that has been invaluable at all stages of this work and also Julia Mantle for insightful and careful editing.
  1. The omen series *šumma ālu* is a collection of terrestrial omens observed against the background of the human environment. For a general introduction to the series, see Sally Moren, 'The Omen Series *šumma ālu*: A Preliminary Investigation' (PhD diss.,

University of Pennsylvania, 1978). The previous text edition is F. Nötscher, 'Die Omen-Serie šumma âlu ina mêlê šakin (CT 38–40)', *Orientalia*, 31 (1928–30), pp. 38–42, 51–4, *Orientalia*, n.s. 3 (1933) pp. 177–95. Copies of the cuneiform tablets have been published by C. J. Gadd, *Cuneiform Texts from Babylonian Tablets in the British Museum*, vol. 39, plates 44–6 (British Museum Publications, London, 1925–31); hereafter CT. The interpretations discussed in the present article were developed during my analysis of the text which forms part of my doctoral research. Further discussion and the relevant documentation will be found in Ann Kessler Guinan, forthcoming doctoral dissertation, an examination of the sex omens within a theory of divination, and tentatively titled, 'Mesopotamian Erotomancy: The Sex Omens of *šumma ālu*' (University of Pennsylvania).

2. See pp. 473–4 for a sequential translation of omens discussed in this article. For previous translations of selected sex omens see A. K. Grayson and Donald Redford (eds) *Papyrus and Reed* (Englewood Cliffs, NJ, Prentice-Hall, 1973), pp. 148–9; A. K. Guinan, 'De houding ten aanzien van sexualiteit in Mesopotamië. Akkadische gedragsomina', *Phoenix*, 25 (1980), pp. 68–81; J. C. Pangas, 'Aspectos de la Sexualidad en la Antigua Mesopotamia', *Aula Orientalis*, 6 (1988), pp. 211–26; the most recent treatment of Tablet 104 omens is Wilfred G. Lambert's discussion of omens that deal with male sex partners: 'Prostitution', in *Aussenseiter und Randgruppen, Xenia*, heft 32 (Universitätsverlag Konstanz, 1993), pp. 145–6, 151; Gwendolyn Leick, *Sex and Eroticism in Mesopotamian Literature* (Routledge, London and New York, 1994), pp. 217–18.

3. See, for example, David M. Halperin, John J. Winkler and Froma I. Zeitlin (eds) *Before Sexuality: The Construction of Erotic Experience in the Ancient Greek World* (Princeton University Press, Princeton, NJ, 1980); John J. Winkler, *The Constraints of Desire: The Anthropology of Sex and Gender in Ancient Greece* (Routledge, London, 1990); Michel Foucault, *The History of Sexuality*, vols 1–3, tr. R. Hurley (Random House, New York, 1978–86); R. A. Padung, 'Sexual Matters: On Conceptualizing Sexuality in History', *Radical History Review*, 20 (1979), pp. 3–23; Judith P. Butler, *Gender Trouble: Feminism and the Subversion of Female Identity* (Routledge, New York and London, 1990); Naomi Schor and Elizabeth Weeds (eds) 'More Gender Trouble: Feminism Meets Queer Theory', *differences: A Journal of Feminist Cultural Studies*, 6 (1994), pp. 1–315; Henrietta L. Moore, *A Passion for Difference: Essays in Anthropology and Gender* (Indiana University Press, Bloomington and Indianapolis, 1994).

4. The sources that deal with Mesopotamian gender and sexuality span three millennia and several subcultures and languages. They encompass a variety of literary genres, iconographic material and archeological evidence. The omen series *šumma ālu* was compiled at the end of the second or the beginning of the first millennium. The sex omens are the products of the first millennium and reflect sensibilities of the last period of Mesopotamian history. The *Reallexikon der Assyriologie und vorderasiastischen Archäologie* (Walter der Gruyter, Berlin, 1933–1937) contains entries that give the cuneiform sources for a variety of sexual topics. See, for example, J. Cooper's article on erotic plaques and seals, 'Heilige Hochzeit. B. Archäologisch', in *Reallexikon der Assyriologie und vorderasiastischen Archäologie*, 4 (1975), pp. 259–69. The laws that deal with sex offenses, in particular the Middle Assyrian laws, provide evidence for social norms. For a general discussion see Gwendolyn Leick, *Sex and Eroticism in Mesopotamian Literature* (Routledge, London and New York, 1994).

5. Mary Douglas, *Purity and Danger* (Routledge & Kegan Paul, London, 1966), p. 121.

6. The language of the omens reveals a number of distortions, ambiguities and gaps related to the expression of female subjectivity. This subject is treated in my doctoral thesis (see above, note 1).

7. The complex issue of purity and impurity needs to be carefully studied. Initially see K. van der Toorn, 'Sin and Sanction in Israel and Mesopotamia: A Comparative Study', *Studia Semitica Neerlandica*, 22 (1985), pp. 27–8.

8. The house omens of *šumma ālu* (CT 38 10–18) reflect the same cultural values as are embodied in the structure of the typical Mesopotamian courtyard house. See Ann Guinan, 'Social constructions and private designs: the house omens of *šumma ālu*', in *Houses and Households in Ancient Mesopotamia*, ed. K. R. Veenhof (Nederlands Historisch Archaeologisch Instituut, Istanbul, 1996), pp. 61–8.

9. There is a large anthropological and historical literature on the meaning of semen in various cultures and histories. The economic metaphor is very common: it is usually based on the management of a finite resource and marked by parsimony. Most recently, see Gilbert Herdt and Robert J. Stoller, *Intimate Communications: Erotics and the Study of Culture* (Columbia University Press, New York, 1990).

10. Pangas, 'Aspectos de la Sexualidad', p. 219, points out that this situation, out of all the acts in Tablet 104, is the only one that predicts death.

11. Note the significantly different interpretation of similar acts in the biblical sources; see, for example, Leviticus 15. If read in the context of the other sex omens dealing with ejaculatory acts, it is not the fact but the excess of the emission that makes this act defiling.

12. Different types of marital abuse occur in the second part of Tablet 104 (CT 39 45–6)—all are inauspicious.

13. For a discussion of the term *zikarūtu* in omen 11 see note 38.

14. According to Tablet 104 (CT 39 44:8), it is auspicious to have sex with another man's wife. This omen clearly has to be understood not as a positive interaction with a woman, but rather as getting the best of another man.

15. Winkler, *The Constraints of Desire*, p.11.

16. David Greenberg, *The Construction of Homosexuality* (University of Chicago Press, Chicago and London, 1988), pp. 141–60; Amy Richlin, 'Not Before Homosexuality', *Journal of the History of Sexuality*, 3 (1993), pp. 523–73.

17. For the texts relating to the *assinnu* see Richard A. Henshaw, *Female and Male: The Cultic Personnel—The Bible and the Rest of the Ancient Near East* (Pickwick Press, Allison Park, PA, 1993); for a general discussion see Leick, *Sex and Eroticism*, pp. 157–61; see also Brigitte Gronenberg, 'ḫabābu—ṣabāru', *Revue d'assyriologie et d'archéologie orientale*, 80 (1986), pp. 188–90; for a recent discussion of the history, origin and possible modern survivals of similar cults, see Rabun Taylor, 'Two Pathic Subcultures in Ancient Rome', *Journal of the History of Sexuality*, 7 (1997), pp. 328–37.

18. For a *girsequ* as a sexual partner see Greenberg, *The Construction of Homosexuality*, pp. 114–15.

19. Contrast this with Artemidorus of Daldis in the second century CE: to dream of 'having intercourse with one's servant, whether male or female, is good; for slaves are the possession of the dreamer, so that they signify, quite naturally, that the dreamer will derive pleasure from his possessions'; *The Interpretation of Dreams*, tr. R. J. White (Noyes Press, Park Ridge, NJ, 1975), p. 59. The relationship between sex omens of *šumma ālu* and the Mesopotamian omens based on erotic dreams, on the one hand, and the other erotic dreams treated by Artemidoros, on the other hand, warrants an extended discussion. For Akkadian omens see A. L. Oppenheim, *The Interpretation of*

Dreams in the Ancient Near East, Transactions of the American Philosophical Society, n.s. 46 (Philadelphia, 1956), p. 290–1. Note UM = *teḫû* 'to approach sexually'.

20. A translation of the laws can be found in Martha T. Roth, *Law Collections from Mesopotamia and Asia Minor* (Scholars Press, Atlanta, GA, 1995), p. 159.

21. Richlin, 'Not Before Homosexuality', pp. 523–73.

22. The principle of polar cases and maximal variation is elucidated by B. L. Eichler, 'Literary Structure in the Laws of Eshnunna', in *Language, Literature, and History: Philological and Historical Studies Presented to Erica Reiner*, ed. Francesca Rochberg-Halton (American Oriental Society, New Haven, CT, 1987), pp. 71–84.

23. G. R. Driver and J. C. Miles, *The Assyrian Laws* (Oxford University Press, Oxford, 1935), pp. 66–8; G. Cardascia, *Les lois assyriens* (Les Éditions du Cerf, Paris, 1969), pp. 68, 134–5; Lambert, 'Prostitution', pp. 146–7; J. Bottéro and H. Petschow, 'Homosexualität', *Reallexikon der Assyriologie und vorderasiastischen Archäologie*, 4 (Walter Gruyter, Berlin, 1975), pp. 460–1.

24. According to Saul M. Olyan, Leviticus 18:22 and 20:13 in their present form should be considered a general prohibition against anal intercourse applying to males of all social classes. The language, however, indicates that at an earlier stage of formulation these laws, like MAL 19/20, applied only to the penetrating partner. Olyan suggests that the receptive partner is the legal equivalent of a woman. Women were not excluded as juridical subjects. It seems more likely that the receptive partner was the discursive rather than the legal equivalent of a woman. Saul M. Olyan, ' "And with a Male You Shall Not Lie the Lying Down of a Woman": On the Meaning and Significance of Leviticus 18:22 and 20:13', *Journal of the History of Sexuality*, 5 (1994), pp. 179–206.

25. Omen 16 and MAL 19 and 20 can also be read in light of a number of historically and theoretically oriented studies of sodomy. The issues addressed and the concerns of the Mesopotamian sources both overlap and diverge in ways that are suggestive and compelling. Among such studies are Olyan, ' "And with a Male You Shall Not Lie the Lying Down of a Woman" '; Richlin, 'Not Before Homosexuality'; Alan Bray, 'Homosexuality and the Signs of Male Friendship in Elizabethan England', *History Workshop Journal*, 19 (1990), pp. 1–19; Eve Kosofsky Sedgewick, *Epistemology of the Closet* (University of California Press, Berkeley and Los Angeles, 1990); Jonathan Goldberg, *Sodmetries: Renaissance Texts, Modern Sexualities* (Stanford University Press, Stanford, CA, 1992).

26. In Mesopotamia the tavern constitutes a sexual and ritual context; Tzvi Abusch, 'Gilgamesh's Request and Siduri's Denial', in *The Tablet and the Scroll: Near Eastern Studies in Honor of William W. Hallo*, ed. Mark E. Cohen, Daniel C. Snell and David B. Weisberg (CDL Press, Bethesda, MD, 1993), p. 7, n. 29.

27. The cuneiform copy of Tablet 104 is published in CT 39 44–6; a small fragment of Tablet 103 (K.3134) can be found in CT 39 43. Although the material has the potential to be a valuable resource for scholars in a number of fields, it is largely unknown. The lack of modern text editions makes these seventy omens of Tablet 103 and 104 almost inaccessible to Assyriologists and certainly to scholars outside the field. Tablet 103, although now reconstructed from published and unpublished fragments, is to date, unpublished. Tablet 104, on the other hand, is one of the best preserved of the *šumma ālu* tablets and one of the earliest cuneiform texts to be identified and published. Even though Tablet 104 is well known and widely read by Assyriologists, little about it has appeared in print. Originally it was ignored because of its subject-matter: now the enduring obstacles are mainly philological. Rare logograms, unusual orthography and uncommon Akkadian words make the texts difficult for modern scholars to

understand and to translate. The difficulties derive from the use of sexual terminology unattested elsewhere, as well as from the cryptic nature of divinatory language.

28. DIŠ NA MI₂ *ir-kab-šu₂* MI₂.BI UR.BI *i-leq-qe₂* ITU.1.KAM₂ DINGIR NU TUK-*ši* (CT 39 44:17).

29. DIŠ NA GIŠ₃-*šu₂* MI₂ *uš-ta-na-aṣ-bat* NU EL ZI ŠU-*šu₂* DINGIR NU TUK-*ši* (CT 39 45:28).

30. DIŠ NA UD-*ma* KI MI₂-*šu₂* <*šu*>-*ta-tu-u₂* GAL₄.LA-*ša₂* *ina* ŠU.II-*ša₂* TAG.MEŠ NA.BI NU EL *ana* EGIR UD-*mi* ŠU-*su* *i-ra-'-ub* (CT 39 45:36). The orthography of the first clause of the protasis, which is identical in both manuscripts, is problematic. The CAD restores a *šu* and reads *šumma amēlu enūma sinništišu* <*šu*>-*ta-tu-u₂* (A/II s.v. *atû*). I understand the verb to be a stative, third person singular, subjunctive. The singular of *šutâtû* constructed with *itti* takes an accusative object. Therefore, the woman is the object of the action in the dependent clause, but she is clearly the subject of TAG.MEŠ in the independent clause, with MEŠ standing for plurality of action (see CAD s.v. *lapātu*).

31. DIŠ NA GAL₄.LA MI₂-*šu₂* *it-ta-nap-la-as* UZU.BI DUG₃.GA *mim+ma la šu-a-tum* ŠU-*su* KUR-*ad₂* (CT 39 44:19).

32. DIŠ NA KI MI₂ *ina šu-ta-ti-šu₂* GIŠ₃-*šu₂* *it-ta-nap-la-as mim+ma ma-la ut-tu-u₂ ina* E₂-*šu₂* NU GI.NA (CT 39 45:20). The basic meaning of the verb *šutâtû* is 'to face one another, to meet'. It also occurs in omen 3 (see n. 22) and in a sexual context in omen 5 of Tablet 103 (Guinan, unpublished manuscript, K.8268+, 10–11). The three attestations in the sex omens suggest that the verb has a more specific sexual meaning or nuance. W. Lambert points out that *šutâtû* (from *atû*) is 'used of a blow in a bilingual passage: **sig₃-sig₃-ga ri-a-ba** = *ša mi-ḫi-is-su šu-ta-tu-u₂*, IV R 24 1 36f. "When (his) blow had struck" can be used in the sense of "a blow aimed at something". The common meanings of the root [i.e. *atû*] "find", "select", are well suited for a blow aimed at something …'. W. Lambert, 'The Babylonian "Man and His God"', in *Language, Literature, and History: Philological and Historical Studies Presented to Erica Reiner*, ed. Francesca Rochberg-Halton (American Oriental Society, New Haven, CT, 1987), p. 197. This discussion suggests that in a sexual context, the verb may refer to the thrusting motion of intercourse and a suggested translation might therefore be 'to hammer'. My translation understands the woman to be the subject of the verb *ittanaplas* and the entire omen to be the antithesis of omen 4.

33. DIŠ NA TE-*ma* u *ina* GI₆-*šu₂* *ig-lut* NA.BI ZI.GA DUGUD IGI-*mar* (CT 39 45:25).

34. DIŠ NA *ina* MAŠ.GI₆-*šu₂* II(=*ig-lut*)-*ma ni-il-šu₂ bul-lul* (+) NA.BI NIG₂.SIG₅ *ut-tu₂* A₂.TUK TUK-*ši* (CT 39 45:26).

35. DIŠ NA *ana* MI₂ TE-*ma ig-lut-ma* II (=*ni-il-šu bul-lul*) SIG₅ NA.BI A₂.TUK TUK-*ši* (CT 39 44:10).

36. DIŠ NA *ana* MI₂ *la-za-zu u gi-na-a ig-da-na-lut ina la-li-šu₂* UG₇ (CT 39 44:11). A second exemplar, British Museum tablet K.126, preserves a variant reading of this omen: DIŠ NA *ana* MI₂ *la za-ku-ti gi-na-a ig-da-na-lut ina la-*<*li*>-*šu₂* BA.UG₇, 'If a man [has sexual relations] with an unclean woman and always ejaculates repeatedly.'

37. DIŠ NA *ina* SILA.LIMMU₂ MI₂ DIB-*ma* TE NA.BI NU SI.SA₂ (CT 39 45:29).

38. DIŠ NA *ana zi-ka-ru-ti ina ki-li uš-tak-ti-it-ma u ina* ZI-*e/ ni-iš na-aq zi-ka-ru-ta ḫu-uš-šu-uḫ-šu i-na pi₂-qi₂* ḪUL IGI (CT 39 44:15).

All the previous translations of this omen have followed the CAD Ḫ s.v. *ḫašāḫu* and have been based on reading the first six signs on the second line of Gadd's copy (CT 39 44:15): *aṣ₃-se₂-e-ni-iš* (like an *assinnu*). The major problem with this reading is that the copy is based on British Museum tablet K.1994, one of the four exemplars that preserve this line. A second exemplar, British Museum tablet K.126, divides the signs into two words written on separate lines. This division, which cannot be discerned in Gadd's copy and is not mentioned in his notes, strongly argues against interpreting the signs as a single word. Of course, it is possible that the scribe of this second exemplar (K.126) did not understand the omen and divided *as$_3$-se$_2$-e-ni-iš* into two words. The interpretation of *nak/q zikarūta ḫuššuḫšu* requires the phrase be understood as a genitival construct despite the ungrammatical form. The word *nak/q* may be derived from *nâku* ('to have illicit sexual intercourse'), hence Grayson's 'mating with men' (p. 149) and Lambert's 'fails to achieve a sexual climax during intercourse', (p. 151). Jacobsen (in private communication) derives the word from *naqû* ('to pour out', 'to libate'). My translation is based on this last suggestion.

39. DIŠ NA KI MI$_2$ *ina* UGU GIŠ.NA$_2$ *id-bu-um-ma* TA UGU GIŠ.NA$_2$ ZI-ma*zi-ka-ru-tam* DU$_3$-*uš* NA.BI ŠA$_3$-*bi* DUG$_3$.GA$_3$ *u ri-ša$_2$-a-tum* GAR.ME-*šu$_2$* KI DU-*ku ka-liš* ŠE.GA *ir-ni-ta-šu$_2$ ik-ta-na-šad* (CT 39 44:18).

40. DIŠ NA ⌈*a-na*⌉ *as-sin-ni* TE *da-na-tu* DU$_8$-*su* (CT 39 45:32).

41. DIŠ NA *a-na* GIR$_3$.SI$_3$.GA TE *ka-la* MU.1.KAM$_2$ *tam-ṭa-a-tum ša$_2$* GAR.MEŠ-*šu$_2$ ip-pa-ra-sa* (CT 39 45:33).

42. DIŠ NA *ana du-uš-mi-šu$_2$* TE KI.KAL DIB-*su* (CT 39 45:34).

43. DIŠ NA *ana* GU.DU *me-eḫ-ri-šu$_2$* TE NA.BI *ina* ŠEŠ.ME[-*šu$_2$*] *u$_3$ ki-na-ti-šu$_2$, a-ša$_2$-re-du-tam* DU-*ak* (CT 39 44:13).

44. DIŠ NA KI DAM-*šu$_2$, ina* E$_2$.EŠ$_2$.DAM KAŠ$_3$.MEŠ-*šu$_2$ iz-zi* NU SI.SA$_2$ *ana* NU TE ZAG.DU$_8$ E$_2$.EŠ$_2$.DAM KAŠ$_3$-*šu$_2$,* XV *u* GUB$_3$ *i-sal-la-aḫ-ma* SI.SA$_2$.MEŠ (CT 39 45:22). For urine in dreams see Jean Bottéro, *Mesopotamia: Writing, Reading, and the Gods*, tr. Zainab Bahrani and Marc Van De Mieroop (University of Chicago Press, Chicago, 1992), pp. 115–16; for the protecting power of urine, see *A Dictionary of Superstitions*, ed. Iona Opie and Moira Tatem (Oxford University Press, Oxford, 1989), p. 417.

With This Body I Thee Worship: Sacred Prostitution in Antiquity

MARY BEARD AND JOHN HENDERSON

> The whole citadel was sacred to Aphrodite, the charms of whose worship brought untold wealth to her shrine. Crowds of courtesans took part in the services of the goddess. Strabo tells us that it actually owned more than a thousand such *hierodouloi*, whom both men and women had dedicated to Aphrodite's service. When private persons made vows to her they promised that in thanksgiving for an answer to their prayers they would bring courtesans to the temple. 'And therefore it was', says Strabo, 'that because of these women there was always a crowd in the city and it grew rich.'[1]

In the course of his encyclopaedic *Geography* of the Mediterranean, the Greek writer Strabo (philosopher, geographical theorist and subject of the Roman Empire under its first emperor Augustus) lingered on the peculiar habits of Corinth (8. 6. 20). It is an unusual and surprising report about one of the leading cities of Greece, which has prompted, and prompts, a range of very different responses. Some standard accounts of the history of Corinth choose to stay silent (or as close to silent as they can manage) on the presence through the centuries of a large-scale sacred brothel at the heart of the city—on, or in close association with, the acropolis.[2] Alternatively, this strikingly unhellenic-sounding institution has been conveniently defused, 'safely' reinterpreted as an elaborately dressed up red-light district synonymous with any port, any place, any time: such cults of Aphrodite flourished wherever 'sex-hungry' sailors thronged, and what Strabo honours with the title 'sacred slaves' were in fact just regular 'whores' in rich supply—no more, no less (*hierodoulous ... hetairas*).[3]

In a quite different mood, Strabo's bizarre picture can instead be embraced, polemically, as a defining feature of Greek religion and cult that traditional scholars have wilfully refused to acknowledge. Lay the blame where you will: at the feet of 'Victorian divines and classical scholars' or 'scholars of our own time' whose 'resistance' has comprehensively obscured Corinthian sexualities;[4] or with their ancient predecessors, who have also misled us with their reticence ('Herodotus expresses strong disapproval of temple prostitution ... He may have thought it better to be silent about

Corinth.').[5] But those critics prepared to shed their scholarly 'embarrass-ment' can bring the institution back into our picture of the classical world[6] and can easily be supplied with a variety of corroborations in other pieces of information about Corinth to set alongside Strabo's story. In particular, the salacious after-dinner badinage that Athenaeus presents in his third century CE parody of sophists' talk features a string of saucy anecdotes that weave quotations from classical literary texts into an account of Corinth as a paradise of sacred sex.[7] It is here that we find a crucial story about Pindar's production back in the early fifth century BCE of an ode in honour of a victor who dedicated a hundred sacred prostitutes to Aphrodite,[8] and a report of an epigram of Simonides commemorating the prayer of the prostitutes of Corinth on behalf of the salvation of the Greeks from the invading Persians—again back in the early fifth century BCE.[9] According to B. MacLachlan, Athenaeus' account offers 'dramatic evidence for the way in which all of Greece "took seriously" the temple-prostitutes of Corinth'.[10] Out of the wreckage of classical literature, its silences and occlusions, the inheritance of temple prostitution still remains to be discovered for those prepared to see: 'the evidence, once it is assembled, is simply over-whelming'.[11]

These debates, their claims and counter-claims, must prompt us in turn to reflect on the status of Corinth and its central role in the imaging, and image-making, of Greece and Greek culture. Not only *the* port-city (with its multicultural society of get-rich-quick traders, sailors and hangers-on); but a city caught between Athens and Sparta, straddling West and East. There was of course economic advantage here—*wealthy* Corinth, poised to grow rich out of its ideal location as the crossroads for trade by land and sea.[12] But inevitably the political destiny of Corinth was to act as the third man of Greek politics, both calling on its likeness to its neighbours, and always claiming an intrinsic difference from them both. The rest of Greece saw Corinth as a foreign city within their midst, an Orientalizing Other. Corinthians embraced this image, not merely colluding in but celebrating their city's image as Greece's internal Other.[13] As Aphrodite's city, Corinth could not fail to exploit the lure of sexuality always associated with the love goddesses of the erotic East. Here is a prime myth of cultural exoticism acted out on the bodies of women ...

In what follows, we shall be exploring these different responses, both the classical 'testimonia' and its modern commentary; we shall be interro-gating the certainties and uncertainties of the different accounts of sacred prostitution in the Greek world, which may or may not count as 'evidence' for the practice either in Greece or the Near East; examining its role in our own myth of the Orient *and* in a distinctively nineteenth-century version of the origins of human civilization. Temple prostitution remains a multicul-turalist's scandal, writing obedience to law and proper conduct of religion on to gender and sexuality in a(n) (un)comfortable mix of stereotyping and demonization. How could we understand the *body* within such a duty of service?

At the centre of all the different responses to the idea of a crowd of religious sex slaves in ancient Corinth is the effect of the label 'sacred prostitutes' (within the institution of *temple, cult,* or *sacred prostitution*). Each of those names carries its own particular set of associations within their common oxymoron: for our culture 'prostitution is, after all, the most debased form of sex, and sex is the activity which is furthest removed from the lofty and pure realm of the sacred'.[14] But, whichever label we choose, the important point is that none of the ancient evidence offers a *narrative* of any encounter within the institution that it envisages; nor are the modern discussions concerned to provide one. What story would fit the supposed negotiation between customer and hierodule? Was sex with a sacred prostitute a mystic union with divinity? The best a man can get? Or was it just a commercial commodity, the sex-aid of the Isthmus—the girls performing 'the hectic task of satisfying the desires of numerous ordinary Corinthians and others',[15] with all profits going to the goddess? Just how routinized must this priestly trade have been? How are we to imagine the infrastructure and services required by a full-scale temple brothel? Could the Acropolis of Corinth physically accommodate the bodies of a thousand whores? Or if they were always down-town, outworkers of the temple's trade, then how different from the other working girls could they ever have seemed? How precarious was cultic sacrality?

The aura attached to any of the formulae (*sacred prostitute, temple prostitution* ...) turns attention away from just these questions—pointing instead to a destination much further east. In almost every modern account, understanding the prostitutes of Corinth is *not* part of our understanding of classical Greek sexualities; not one of a loaded set of variants on the norms governing the exchange of sex, money and civic space in the classic(al) *polis* ('city-state'). Instead, Corinth figures in a wider arena of similarly labelled practices and institutions among the cultures of the Near East. The prostitutes of Corinth, in fact, are one component of a story about the service of women's bodies that leads ultimately to the origins of human culture itself.

The primal scene in this story is Herodotus' Babylon, the account of the metropolitan customs of sixth-century neo-Babylonia—with which the historian winds up his first book. It is part of the pre-history of the Great War between Greece and Persia, the story of the Persian conquest of Assyria under King Cyrus, in the narrative of the expansion of the Persian Empire. At the start of the next book, Herodotus launches equally far from Greek experience, into the Egyptian empire conquered by Cyrus' heir. According to Herodotus' account of Babylonian customs:

> The most shameful custom the Babylonians have is this: every native woman
> must go sit in the temple of Aphrodite, once in her life, and have sex with an

adult male stranger. Many of them disdain to mix with the rest, on the high horse of wealth, and so drive to the temple on covered carriages, taking their stand with a large retinue following behind them. But many many more do as follows: they sit in the sanctuary of Aphrodite, these many women, their heads crowned with a band of bow-string. Some arrive while others depart. Roped-off thoroughfares give all manner of routes through the women and the strangers pass along them as they make their choice. Once a woman sits down there, she doesn't return home until a stranger drops money in her lap and has sex with her outside the temple. When he drops it he has to say 'I call on the goddess Mylitta'. Assyrians call Aphrodite Mylitta. The money can be any value at all—it is not to be refused, for that is forbidden, for this money becomes sacred. She follows the first one who drops money and rejects none. When she has had sex, she has performed her religious dues to the goddess and goes home; and from that time on you will never make her a big enough gift to have her. All those who have looks and presence quickly get it over with, all those of them who have no looks wait for a long time unable to fulfil the law—some of them wait for a three- or four-year spell. In some regions of Cyprus there is a custom similar to this. (*Histories* 1. 199)

This account has provoked widely divergent reactions, from frank disbelief that Herodotus knew anything about Babylon to no-nonsense insistence that we face, and face up to, human diversity.

The commonest tactic for crediting Herodotus' account is to take it for granted that such customs were generally prevalent in the Near East; in the Orient we should not be surprised to find that all great cities featured temple complexes on a huge scale, complete with resident prostitutes sacred to a Love (or Mother) Goddess—often subsumed in modern accounts under the one name, Ishtar.[16] This is one of the classic differences posited between 'our' West and the 'alien' East. 'The temple in Babylon was probably … near the city wall' outside the city centre, 'to make more convenient the concourse of women who there assembled to be chosen by strangers for indiscriminate adultery. This dark and immoral feature of the Ishtar cult is all too well confirmed by the inscriptions.'[17] According to J. G. Frazer in *The Golden Bough: A Study in Magic and Religion*:

> Similar customs prevailed in many parts of Western Asia. Whatever its motive, the practice was clearly regarded not as an orgy of lust, but as a solemn religious duty performed in the service of that great Mother Goddess of Western Asia whose name varied, while her type remained constant, from place to place. Thus at Babylon every woman … had … to submit to the embraces of a stranger at the temple of Mylitta … At Heliopolis or Baalbec in Syria … the custom … required that every maiden should prostitute herself to a stranger at the temple of Astarte … In Phoenician temples women prostituted themselves for hire in the service of religion … At Byblus … women who refused to sacrifice their hair had to give themselves up to strangers on a certain day … In Armenia … damsels acted as prostitutes for a long time before they were given in marriage … Again, the goddess Ma was served by a multitude of sacred harlots at Comana in Pontus.[18]

Herodotus brackets his story of Mylitta and the compulsory 'prostitution' of women together with another distinctive custom. This was the first he reported for Babylon and he picked it out as 'in my opinion the wisest of all':

> I'm told that among Illyrians the Enetoi also practise it. In each of the several villages this was done once a year: whichever nubile virgins [*parthenoi*] were ready for marriage they rounded up *en masse* in one spot, to get them all together; a crowd of men stood around them, and the crier stood them up one by one and auctioned them, in first place the best-looking of them all; thereafter, when she had found a big price and was sold, he would put up another, the one best-looking after her. They were sold for marriage. As many Babylonian males as were rich and marriageable outbid each other to buy the loveliest ones, while all the marriageable men of the people, they had no need for good looks, and they would get money along with the uglier girls. For once the crier had got through selling the best-looking of the girls, he would put up the worst-looking one, or any of them that was disabled, and offer her up for whomever would take her to wife for the smallest sum, until she was handed to the one who would take the least. The money would come from the good-looking girls, and so the best-looking gave dowries for those without looks and disabled. (*Histories* 1. 196)

It was in the attempt to fit these two customs together (as Herodotus prompts us to do) that much of modern theorizing about the origins, development and logic of marriage, religion and so ultimately of all human culture was born.

J. G. Frazer's collection of evidence was one, particularly influential, account among a redoubtable array of late nineteenth-century pioneering essays in anthropology which, more than writing a history of the West and the East, sought to trace the original nature of social groups such as the family, the power of religious institutions such as the temple, the first functions of property, exchange and money, and the origins of human hierarchies of class, caste and status (such as serfdom and slavery).[19] Eastern culture— the cradle of civilization—was construed as preserving authentic vestiges of earlier phases in human development, and would provide the foundation for a single grand narrative of cultural history.[20] The pull of Herodotus' twin accounts of the disposition of women in Babylon cannot be underestimated: here, explicitly and paraded by the father of history, were found two blank assertions that struck right to the heart of the project: brides were once sold; women's bodies were once sexually shared.

How could these customs *not* cry out for attention? Did they attest an original communism of wives? Was virginity in some sense devoted to the gods? Had prototypical kings commanded the sexual services of their subjects? Was culture founded on the heterosexuality enshrined in the exchange of women? Under the slogan 'promiscuity', for example, a fierce (patriarchal) debate wondered if the original condition of man· had been one of indiscriminate lust, and so the point of culture had been to police and reticulate desire, male desire; was prostitution, then, one of the options deployed by early civilization precisely to bring order to sex? What contracts could be sealed with women's bodies?[21]

The prostitution of Herodotus' Babylonians proffered crucial, but inevitably contested, evidence for any such postulations; it had to be the missing link between civilization and its pre-history. In particular, the scandalous notion that marriage may have been a late-comer to humanity was both read *into* and read *out of* the scene. One influential theorist, for example, drawing general conclusions from an analysis 'Concerning the Rite at the Temple of Mylitta', declared: 'Prostitution is not a primitive practice; it is a product of civilization.'[22] But he was emphatically *not* accepting that prostitution helped tame the wildness of primitive promiscuity; he was arguing instead that we should understand the customs at Babylon as a complex of maturation or pre-marriage ritual—and at the same time discounting 'prostitution' (in our terms) as an unrelated or debased institution which does not touch the core of 'sacred, or cult prostitution'. In Babylon, so the argument ran, we should recognize the devotional traits that hallow (however strangely to our eyes) the sanctity of the bride-to-be's dedication of her virginity to the goddess who will prosper her forthcoming marriage. At first we may be just as shocked as Herodotus, but then learn how to see it better—as a decayed remnant of an alien, but well-meaning, assurance that marriage had from the first been a holy estate.

The flurry of interpretative activity created for the discussion of such phenomena a language that still retains much of its power: 'ritual defloration', '*ius primae noctis*' ('the right of the first night'), 'sacrifice of virginity', 'temple harlots' ... This discourse about the body is very likely ineradicable, even if in future it may be mentioned only as a discard. In the first two editions of the *Oxford Classical Dictionary*, for example, the entry under 'Prostitution, sacred' (there is no entry in these editions for any other kind), presented 'two forms. (I) The defloration of virgins before marriage ... originally a threshold rite', with some customs as 'constituting a half-way step to (2) regular temple Prostitution'. The third edition has a fine new article on 'Prostitution, sacred', which roundly punctures 'the modern view that their professional activities were ritually significant', before identifying 'a quite distinct institution, reported only from the margins of the Greek world ... the practice of pre-marital sex with strangers, the *locus classicus* being Herodotus' often hilarious description of Babylon (1. 199, not confirmed but not contradicted by cuneiform sources). This is a one-off rite, compulsory for all, in the service of the goddess Mylitta ... the act itself ... involving a strictly religious obligation.' But this revisionary iconoclasm is followed at once by a (remarkably brief) entry on 'Prostitution, secular' which begins: 'the prostitution of women ... may have arisen in Greece out of contact with earlier Near Eastern manifestations of so-called sacred prostitution (see preceding entry); this may have been "temple prostitution", "prostitution" in order to gain a dowry, or both.'[23] How many readers will indeed 'see preceding entry', and there pick up the tales without picking up their cancellation? The present essay, too, may well do more to spread the myth of sacred prostitution than scotch it.

Seminal works such as A. Van Gennep's *Rites of Passage* will continue to make 'sacred prostitution' canonical; Frazer's stores of information remain a constant reference-point for all manner of scholarship.[24] Within biblical scholarship, in particular, with its huge reach beyond academic frontiers into the lives of the general public, sacred prostitution has a strong hold; and wherever anthropological theorizing threatens to deny the presence of the 'institution', a new strain of speculation always promises to fill the void. So, for example, it is one thing to be able to admit that 'in recent years ... the widely accepted hypothesis of cultic prostitution [in ancient Israel] has been seriously challenged. Various scholars have argued that the current view rests on unwarranted assumptions, doubtful anthropological premises, and very little evidence.' But the very same writer can simultaneously find reassurance only just around the corner with a subtly different hypothesis: 'among Israelites, the custom of paying vows by means of prostitution was a known phenomenon ... Until the Deuteronomic reform it seems to have been tolerated by the official religion, which preferred the resulting votive gifts over an ethical rigorism ... There is no need to postulate the existence of sacred prostitution in the service of a fertility cult.'[25] Traditional interpretations of biblical passages that find 'cultic prostitution lurking behind scenes of sexual promiscuity on ritual occasions' must be scotched over and over again, and yet refutations of this and of other themes not only shadow the cancelled mythology but themselves amplify the mystification afresh—moving inexorably through dubitation over evidence from Mesopotamia, to home on the inevitable 'famous passage of the *Histories*, 1. 199 ... Assyriologists disagree about the accuracy of this information. Supposing Herodotus was right, one cannot make him say that the women did so as part of a fertility rite ... We may even wonder whether Herodotus might not have mistaken the prostitution in payment on a vow for a general, once-in-a-lifetime duty.'[26] The myth exerts its fascination through its every abomination.

Undeterred by unwanted scholarly scepticism, devotees will hotly embrace the 'sacred sexuality' of Ishtar as an alternative vision of humanity; and with it they will rewrite a wilder, would-be empowering, universal myth for women, envisioning (somehow) liberationist empowerment through bodily celebration.[27] The myth of sacred prostitution is not *just* a relic of expired history, whether the history of civilization or of its theorizing, but a model for alternative humanities paraded by our archives, available for new living, for different lives.

As they looked east, the Victorian theorists of culture strove for categorial clarity, aware of the pitfalls that lay between their scattered testimonia and

Figure 1: Edwin Long, *The Babylonian Marriage-Market*, 1875. Courtesy of Royal Holloway and Bedford New College, London.

recovery of the lost archetype(s): 'one of the most fertile sources of error in the interpretation of custom is the fatal tendency of rites distinct, or even altogether different in origin and intention, but similar in expression, to converge'; 'one rite might easily pass into the other'.[28] In broad agreement, they recognized three patterns of temple service for women: 'a class of holy women ... the daughters of good families dedicated by their fathers to religion ... not to be identified with the temple-prostitutes of Babylon or Erech, who excited the wonder and often the reprobation of the later Greek world'; 'from these two institutions we must distinguish that other, for which Herodotus is our earliest authority', viz. the one-off obligation of the Babylonian women to Mylitta.[29] But at the same time there was a tremend-ous incentive to bring together Herodotus' 'sex customs of the Babylonians' into a single frame. The right of Mylitta was spliced with Herodotus' other custom of bride-auction (immortalized in Edwin Long's *The Marriage Market* [1875], shown in Figure 1: 'one of the most popular [high-priced] pictures of its day'[30]), to be interpreted as 'the consecration to the goddess of the first-fruits of the women's virginity before marriage'. Here some neat temporal logic might have to be introduced. If all the virgins originally were sold into marriage, but all the women must at some point in their lives sell sex to a stranger, surely this must mean they were supposed to visit Mylitta in the interval between the marriage contract and the wedding? Surely Herodotus must 'vouch for' this defloration ritual, 'though [he] does not explicitly say [so]'?[31] It requires strong will to resist this inter-articulation, despite the fact that Herodotus *excludes* it by describing the 'women' who visit Mylitta as 'women/wives' (*gunaikes*), whereas the bids at the auction were for 'marriageable virgins' (*parthenoi*).[32]

But there are further difficulties in reading Herodotus' account of the two Babylonian customs as two sides of the same institution. Today we are less likely to miss the explicit chronological disjunction in Herodotus' narrative for these two, best and worst, practices: 'Mylitta' characterizes Babylon in the present tense; but the auction is a lost virtue of the Babylonian *past*— 'This *was* their finest custom, but it has not continued in existence to the present. They have thought up another practice ... since they were conquered, they have suffered and been ruined, so every man of the people short of subsistence prostitutes his female children' (*Histories* 1. 196). Rather than pressing the amalgamated customs into a pattern in line with scattered references to other Eastern practices (or, for that matter, pressing what Herodotus has to say into a descriptive ethnography of 'historical' Babylon), we are more disposed than our nineteenth-century predecessors to see the two items as complementary components in Herodotus' project of thinking out the paradigmatic dynamics of 'Babylon'—this once independent hegemonic Eastern Other, but now long conquered and subject to the Persians. He must excogitate a distinctive niche for Babylon in his cabinet of ways to be un-Greek which explains how Cyrus' Persia conquered and supplanted it; and in so doing put his finger on the strengths and weaknesses, socio-political, customary-religious, solidary-hierarchical, of their culture as a system—in heyday, and in eclipse. And so we are less inclined to receive reports about extinct customs displaced by debased present ways as veridical documentary evidence; we may choose to bracket off the issue of referential adequacy, while reading the ethnography as a discursive project, engaged in the *construction* of an Other people.[33]

At this point in the argument, however, we must deal rather more explicitly with referential adequacy than we have up till now; asking directly what kind of testimony has been deployed to confirm the existence, at any time, or any place, of 'cultic prostitution'. There has never been any call to doubt that dedication of 'respectable' women, and men, to a lifetime or term of temple servitude was a common practice in societies of the East (and West), often with a frisson, suspicion, or imputation of sexual availability: these are the 'hierodules' of the ancient world.[34] But even as Western readers of Herodotus have always been sure that Herodotus' Babylon gives a hint of what went on in the Temples of Lust beyond their horizon (for which ample confirmation would surely be found in the primary documents of the Near East, if only they knew where exactly to look), so scholars of the Near East have matched this certainty with their own mirror-image of it. The fact is, as we shall soon see, that one side of modern scholarship has looked to the East to confirm Herodotus' account of Babylon, while the other has looked to Herodotus to provide a single clear example of an institution that their Eastern documents repeatedly fail to confirm. Each set of cultural historians has fed on the other's conviction that the lack, dubiety and paucity of corroborating evidence to set beside Herodotus' is a happenstance that can be effaced by a mixture of extrapolation with imagination.[35] For the rite of Mylitta to make sense, to have a matrix or context in Oriental culture, we have to envisage the full-blown 'sacred prostitution' in honour of Ishtar, Astarte, Ashtoreth, Inanna, Tanit, and the other 'Aphrodites'[36] of Canaan, of Phoenicia, of the Semitic peoples—those vast temple complexes, packed with divine love, for sale.

Few accounts of the ancient Near East pass Ishtar's sacred harlots by[37]— taking their cue from 'Western' analysts: 'Herodotus has certainly garbled the details', but his Babylonian rite is part and parcel of the world of Ishtar.[38] As we shall see, without Herodotus, the picture that even the most confid-ent scholar can produce is always revealed as embarrassingly tentative.[39] It can perhaps be made to seem somewhat less tentative under the rubric of 'Cultic prostitution as a case study in cultural diffusion'—encompassing western Africa in recent times and southern India, as well as many sections of the biblical world. In a review of precisely *how* diffused, E. M. Yamauchi offers this picture of Mesopotamia:

> W. G. Lambert summarizes our state of knowledge as follows: 'No one doubts its [cultic prostitution's] prevalence, especially with the cult of ISHTAR, but little is known of its functioning. The names of various categories of priestesses are known, all highly respectable ... but it is not known if all, or some, or even none of these were especially religious prostitutes. Money was presumably paid for favours received despite its being a glorification of a goddess.' [Of Syria and Phoenicia] it is generally assumed that the worship of the major Ugaritic goddesses—Asheras, Astarte, Anath, Qudshu ...—involved sacred prostitution though there are no explicit texts which can prove this. [Of Carthage and Sicily] the lack of evidence for sacred prostitution is surprising.

But in sum (again):

> the most explicit texts describing sacred prostitution in Mesopotamia are these late texts [viz. Herodotus' Mylitta, Strabo's version of the same story, plus an enigmatically intimidatory Abomination from the apocryphal Epistle of Jeremias, 6.43] which associate the institution with the ritual defloration of women by strangers in contrast to the association of the rite with temple personnel found in the earlier texts.[40]

It was cultural diffusion*ism* that produced the familiar picture of Ishtar's sacred whores, reading into the mêlée of names for different groups of temple servants, by more or less extravagant (and scarcely believable) acts of translation, the pre-postulated stereotype of the cult prostitute: '*istaritu* came to mean a sacred harlot. In my own editions ... I have consistently rendered this title by "virgin" ... The word really means "the undefiled" ... [it] came to be a euphemism ... "virgin-harlot".'[41] A recent authority on

Figure 2: Ivory plaque depicting the 'woman at the window'. Late ninth century BCE Height 83 mm. Courtesy of Metropolitan Museum of Art, New York (Near Eastern Department) (Fletcher Fund no. 57. 80. 11).

Mesopotamia, noting frankly that the various names for supposed religious prostitutes are mixed in with names for other acolytes, 'as if there were no real distinction between these groups', accepts that our information on the structure of the temple complexes does not allow us to know how labels correlated with functions, and goes on to conclude: 'It is probable that certain prostitutes, if not all of them, often went to sanctuaries, especially those of their protectress Ishtar.' This would account for Herodotus' *Histories* 1. 199, 'who seems to have seen so many of them exercising their profession there, that he mistakenly thought they included all the women of the country'.[42]

We should put alongside this radical re-writing of Herodotus' Babylon the case of the image of the 'woman at the window'. Every account of Ishtar that carries an illustration sports an example of this type of ivory furniture-panel (Figure 2). Not, perhaps, the most obvious promise of bodily availability in the flesh-pots of the Orient. The woman is at 'the typical Phoenician "upper window"', in 'a cult scene of Astarte worship, the woman being a prostitute votaress'. She 'is' in some (vital, graphically paradigmatic) sense, Astarte—because she must be (an/the) *istaritu*. Even (if) so, 'the subject is wholly Canaanite, but the woman wears an Egyptian wig and the window is supported by little columns with lotus capitals'.[43]

This minuscule decorative glimpse of Near Eastern worship through-and-as Lust, then, touts Astarte of Canaan *because* it shows an *Egyptian* sex-goddess—even though Yamauchi has trouble attesting any such practice as 'sacred prostitution' in Egypt itself:

> According to Albright sacred prostitution was 'apparently not known in native ... religion'. Attempts to prove its presence in Egypt rest on either dubious or late evidence ... It is once again the late classical texts that give us unambiguous references to cultic prostitution in Egypt. Herodotus I. 182 ... Strabo 17. 1. 46 ...[44]

In fact, both passages cited concern one priestess's sex with, or under the auspices of, *Zeus Ammon* (Amun). Not a hint of a goddess—or even a lotus position.

If we turn now to examine more carefully the case of the Babylonian marriage-auction, as it is recounted by Herodotus (with supporting evidence from a few other sources, including Strabo again), we shall find that this also slips all too easily out of our historical sights, undoing 'the rite of Mylitta' at the same time. 'Nothing is known of [the auction] from cuneiform sources ... The custom hardly seems probable. Both Strabo and Nicolaus Damascenus, however, say that the practice was still in use in their time.'[45] This kind of naivety is more than a century old, witness G. Rawlinson's note on Herodotus from the 1880s: 'Writers of the Augustan age (Strabo, Nicolaus Damascenus) mention this custom as still existing in their day. The latter testimony, coming from a native of Damascus, is particularly valuable.'[46] What the reader is bound to recall, unless determined to buttress the significance of the whole discursive edifice of 'sacred sexuality', is that Herodotus precisely underlined that the auction had lapsed before his day —and indeed had not survived the Persian conquest, which had delivered its quietus.

But what of Strabo and Nicolaus? On inspection, Strabo's account of this particular version of cultic sex does *not* 'mention' *anything* 'as existing in his day'. A present tense does not, we should remember, imply an eye-witness account—nor even proof that the institution described still existed at the time of writing; the ethnographer's present tense has quite different implications. Strabo here reports salient features of the culture of Babylonia in the present, summarizing Herodotus through (or more likely together with) an intermediary source: 'special to them is their setting up three sound men in charge of each tribe, who bring along the marriageable girls before the crowd, and offer the husbands-to-be the more prized ones first. That is how pairings are brought about' (16. 1. 20). The geographer is here excavating the historical strata sedimented in the area's culture, not reporting (let alone attesting or averring) life observed or observable way beyond the borders of the Roman Empire. He tells us how the Medes, the Armenians and the Babylonians took it in turn to rise and fall at each other's expense, and 'this was the situation that prevailed until the Parthian ascendancy. The Parthians rule the Medes and the Babylonians—but at no point the Armenians … We shall speak next about Mesopotamia and the tribes to the south, first proceeding for a little to tackle what is told about customs among the Assyrians. Now the rest of it is just like the Persians, but special to them etc.' (16. 1. 19). Strabo is explicitly retailing traditional ethnographical nuggets—not to say lore, legend, myth—and myth *not* vouched for, but presented to the reader *as myth* (*ta legomena*, 'the things said'). His project epitomizes each locality in terms of natural and cultural peculiarities—the ensemble of differences which vindicate an identity for a vicinity (its 'proprioceptors'). This is philosophy, not a holiday guide for globe-trotting or for armchair tourists, describing what you can still *see*.[47]

Nicolaus' 'Compilation of Customs' (*Ethon Sunagoge,* or *Peri Ethon*) survives only in fragmentary excerpts. The relevant item gives a précis of Herodotus' account, as a habit of 'the Assyrians'; this is a note, in the ethnographic present—but there is *no* modal inflection in its presentation, and we have no context. At least so far as we are concerned, the note belongs to the timeless world of factoids that it shares with our other excerpts, a collection of piquant 'data' anthologized by John Stobaeus for Byzantine bookworms.[48]

Essentially the same considerations apply to the 'corroborative' evidence supposed to document the survival of Herodotus' rite concerning Mylitta through the ages: Rawlinson's 'This unhallowed custom is mentioned [in Jeremias] … Strabo also speaks of it'[49] becomes, in a recent discussion:

> Four hundred years later the historian Strabo gives a similar account. He … adds a couple of minor details in his description which indicates that he did not simply copy Herodotus but took the information from an independent source or from an earlier one upon which Herodotus also drew. In either case it seems clear that we are not dealing with Herodotean invention.[50]

Following Herodotus' presentation, Strabo has the relevant item follow the auction, with a couple of other customs intervening:

> It is a custom for all Babylonian females according to some holy injunction to have sex with a stranger, turning up at a locale for love with a large retinue in a throng; each female is crowned with a bow-string. The male goes up and drops onto her lap as much money as is fine and couples with her, taking her away from the sanctuary. The money is considered sacred, the property of Aphrodite. (16. 1. 20)

Herodotus did not tell us that this 'most shameful' custom was in abeyance either in Cyrus' day or his own; on the other hand, Strabo is certainly not documenting its persistence to his day. Moreover, the copious temple-records from Hellenistic Babylonia in the cuneiform of conservative traditionalism will convince anyone that there is simply no room for a significant Ishtar cult, for a custom of ritual prostitution embracing the whole female population of Babylon, or, more generally, for any large-scale practice of cultic prostitution whatever. Even in the Hellenistic period—before, during and after the Seleucids—where a strikingly detailed picture is preserved of the calendar, timetable and agenda for the temple complexes, there is no trace of the organization, accountancy, housing, and so forth that would be required by any such institution.[51]

Fortified by this failure to find the sex-shop of Astarte's Holy Grail, we might briskly explore cracks in the rest of the assembled testimonia for cultic prostitution—Frazer's 'stores'.[52] We shall find again, for the most part, a mixture of emphatically *imperfect* tenses (the long-lost world of 'once upon a time') and the cultural constructions of the Other, the kind of present that exists forever outside the here and now of the eye-witness. Just as the huge swathe of cultural space annexed to cultic prostitution gave powerful impetus to the drive to locate some original humanity, so the impression of a huge arc of time has lent a spurious solidity to the postulated institution. But this impression, as inspection will show, derives from uncritical treatment of the evidence.

For Cyprus, referred to by Herodotus as having a similar custom to Babylon, there are long lists of references, almost all to mythological narratives, with just the Christian persiflage of Justin (citing, it is true, the much earlier Augustan writer Pompeius Trogus) telling that dowries were *formerly* earned by prostitution: *mos erat ...* ('the custom was, used to be ...').[53] At Heliopolis (Baalbec) the first Christian Emperor Constantine destroyed the temple of Aphrodite to abolish the prostitution of virgins to strangers— according to the claims of the historians of the Christian Church from Byzantium.[54] Herodotus (*Histories* 1. 93) has the Lydians prostituting their daughters without reference to cult or temple. Strabo (11. 14. 16), on the other hand, invokes the behaviour of Herodotus' Lydians as similar to the Armenians' cult of Anaitis at Acilisene, except that there 'the most high profile men of the nation consecrate their virgin daughters, the custom being for them to be prostituted for ages at the goddess' [temple], and after that to be given in marriage—and nobody objects to living with one of them'. '*Cult* prostitution' is therefore not securely attested for Lydia; but Armenia, significantly beyond the borders of the Empire, does seem to host a wondrous institution, in *a* present tense:

> Medes and Armenians have honoured all the Persian's rites, especially Anaitis', having put up shrines in various spots, above all in Acilisene. Here they dedicate ... consecrate ... The women deal with their lovers so charitably that they show them hospitality and give return gifts greater than the ones they get ... They *don't* take on any strangers who come along, but especially those of equal status.

If these women are more than just ethnographically present, Strabo is, nevertheless, taking away with one hand what he gives sacred prostitution with the other: this is at the same time just like common 'Lydian' prostitution *and* nothing like *any* form of prostitution—truly (as Strabo announces) a 'wonder'.

The one occasion where eye-witness status is asserted for the custom is an aside on the cult of Byblos in Lucian's parodic description of the rituals of divine Atargatis, *On the Syrian Goddess*—written in the second century CE in a humorously heavy imitation of Herodotus' characteristic style of Greek (*De Dea Syria* 6). Traditionally described as 'the same custom' as Herodotean Babylon's,[55] this is among 'the most explicit references to sacred prostitution in Syria and Phoenicia'.[56] It fits alongside (and trumps) Constantine's foundation of his church on the ruins at Baalbec. And it fits alongside Augustine's objection to the pagan practice of 'putting different gods in charge of different parts of the cosmos', for example by multiplying Venuses, and (at least from his totalizing, monotheistic, point of view) staying evasive whether 'the Venus who belongs to virgins (=Vesta)' is the same as 'the Venus who belongs to wives', and the same as 'the Venus of whores'. 'Which one', he asks, 'is she to whom the Phoenicians *used to* make a gift from the prostitution of their daughters before they hitched them to husbands?' (*City of God* 4. 10) Here Augustine builds the *City of God* out of sarcasm at the expense of the multiplicitousness of polytheism with avowedly dead material dredged from a lost past: another (crucially) imperfect tense. A further instance occurs when the Roman Valerius Maximus tells tales on the women of Carthage: 'There is a shrine of Venus at Sicca, where the matrons *used to* gather and process from there to hire themselves out, collecting dowries by mistreating their bodies, meaning to join together a fair marriage, to be sure, through so foul a knot'.[57]

Lucian's strikingly strong modality, by contrast, tells how 'I saw' the Adonis festival at Byblos, that requires women to crop their hair, or else, as a forfeit, go down to the sea-shore. There they 'become prostitutes for one day, and give themselves to foreign guests, thus probably representing the fruitful earth, which receives new seeds. Lucian, though a sceptic with a slight tendency towards cynicism, was nevertheless so impressed by the whole proceedings that he sought to get to the bottom of it.'[58] Now Lucian is clearly modelling his narrator on the Herodotean enquirer, holding *his* thinking up to put *ours* to the test, as he constructs one more entertainingly satirical tease at once of our credulity and of our rationalism. See how he continues, on Osiris: 'Every year a human head floats from Egypt to Byblos. It takes seven days to get there … It happened when I was in Byblos, and *I myself saw* the head in this city.' As we are told: 'He himself claims that the strange head was made of Egyptian "papyrus"'—for 'the head of Byblos' doubles in Greek as 'the head of paper' (*Bublinen/bublinen*).[59] This much is indeed true, true today as it was true in the second century CE: Lucian's rites *are* what Lucian writes—on *paper*, *Egyptian* paper. It is worth reading to the end to see how Lucian's self-satirizing narrator confects his identity with the shearing of locks, the shearing of his own locks, for his 'Syrian goddess', as the ultimate test of incorporation: do disbelievers, then, consign themselves to some stranger on the shore? Is the joke of the whole comic essay that sacred prostitution awaits readers who reject the gospel of the Syrian goddess—with their laughter?

Three more items which might confirm the institution of cult prostitution are outstanding, all from Strabo's *Geography*. The first has in Sicily 'a temple of Aphrodite that is honoured especially, full in Antiquity of female hierodules, dedicated in accordance with vows by both Sicilians and plenty of outsiders'. But this is how Eryx—'at least semi-Semitic', as Farnell punned—*used to be*: 'now like the town itself the temple is depopulated, and the horde of sacred bodies has given out' (6. 2. 6).[60] In (non-Semitic)[61] Pontic Comana, next, Strabo tells us there was a flourishing and populous centre, thronged at the festival of the goddess (Ma): 'there is a horde of women who work with the body, most of whom are sacred' (12. 3. 36). In the present tense, this time, but (at the least) vague about the religious implications: 'the custom of turning over the earnings from prostitution to the goddess was common among "secular" prostitutes'—whores with hearts of gold having a 'whip round'.[62] The one word 'sacred' (*hierai*) here does *not*, however, attest 'temple prostitution'.

And at this point, Strabo brings us back, finally, to the city that was the starting-point for this article: (non-Semitic)[63] Corinth. For he calls Comana 'a sort of little Corinth ... for there too because of the horde of whores who were sacred to Aphrodite, there used to be many a visitor attending the local festival. The traders and soldiers would spend to the limit, so there a proverb was coined to cover them, as follows: "Not for every man is the voyage to Corinth".' Here, then, is our final item, citing Strabo's earlier visit to Corinth in its own right.

There, too, we must now emphasize, Strabo does *not* present the Corinth of his day:

> The temple of Aphrodite was so rich that it had acquired more than a thous-
> and hierodule whores, dedicated by both men and women to the goddess.
> And because of them, the city used to be jam-packed and got wealthy. The
> ship-captains would spend up easily, and so the proverb says: 'Not for every
> man is the voyage to Corinth'.[64] Besides which, it is recorded that a whore
> said to the woman who insulted her ... (8. 6. 20)

Here is that characteristic imperfect tense, the evocative modality of a vanished past, nostalgically glamorizing the flesh-pots of run-down Corinth as the dregs of a once-proud cultic extravaganza unparalleled throughout Greece.[65]

Recall that 'the main source for temple prostitution in old Corinth is Strabo'.[66] He has little to say on the goddess who formed the focus of these rituals; but this has not prevented her conscription into a predictable

Oriental role. All the evidence we have shows that the goddess of Acro-Corinth, 'Armed Aphrodite', has always attracted sumptuous acclamation along the lines of 'congener of the Eastern Ishtar, goddess of love and war'.[67] Thus, according to H. R. H. Hall: 'It is evident now that she was not only a Canaanitish-Syrian goddess, but was common to all the peoples of the Levant. She is Aphrodite Paphia in Cyprus, Ashtaroth-Astarte in Canaan, Atargatis in Syria, Derketo in Philistia, Hathor in Egypt.'[68] Nor, to come back to earth, does Strabo pause to ponder the practicalities. Some modern writers have: 'The area around the temple slopes downward from the temple site and indicates no large area for one hundred or, in Strabo's time, a thousand girls. One might better think of the hierodouloi as having conducted their business within the heart of the city.'[69] But, if so, where (as we have asked before) does this leave *temple* prostitution?

We might better agree to discount the historical reality of the mythical *Tempelbrothel*—and to turn to the more important question of what was being said, and thought, with Corinth through the myth. Strabo's text, with its report that 'once upon a time' the city teemed with *Corinthiennes* for hire, presents Corinth as being like, but at the same time unlike, other Greek cities. He precisely does *not* call the women '*hierodoulous* ["sacred slaves"] **or** *hetairas* ["courtesans"]';[70] rather, he labels them the *paradox* of '*hierodoulous … hetairas*', 'sacred-slaves/courtesans'. In so doing, he proclaims that the courtesans of Corinth enjoyed a relationship with their goddess that was strikingly anomalous in Greek terms. Since Corinth was Aphrodite's city, we should expect that whores would enjoy a special status, along with the rest of the womenfolk, and the whole city, in line with the identity set in place by this collective self-dedication. Readers of Pindar and Simonides could, accordingly, love the tangle of thoughts and fantasies locked in their lyrics, reading the controversies in their commentaries disputing whether it was the hierodules whose prayers saved Corinth —was it the happy hookers? Or the merry wives?

We take it that, when Pindar invokes 'the lovely beds' of Corinth's 'common fund of wives', he is playing at confounding the marriage-beds of the women on whom the community depended (and whose nearness to the city's patron deity Aphrodite might rightly be called upon to exert influence on her in any crisis at the Isthmus), with 'the lust-filled sex' of the city's 'common prostitutes' available, at a suitably uncommon price, to everyone and equally close to the heart of *their* patron goddess Aphrodite. Pindar's chorus sings, then shies decorously away from, his expertly customized flattery—that the blessed city of Corinth can call on the powerful intercession of its womenfolk with their citadel's defender, Armed Aphrodite; or, to put it more bluntly than the poet will, Corinth provides the men of its community with wives who are as good in bed as the priciest call-girls in the up-town phonebook. The verbal play in the lyric is more than verbal dexterity or conceptual amphiboly. Rather, it parades an insider's cultural grasp of the unique difference on which Corinth founded its identity, and could pretend to rest its security: *all* its women were, truly, goddesses of love.[71]

If being 'a girl of Corinth' already placed you nearer to 'love' than other females,[72] in the same package comes an anomalous construal of Aphrodite —as the supreme local divinity. In her city, it was a basic political issue to ask which should be regarded as the normalizing line: to sacralize the brothel (town), or to seek heaven with high-priced sex-goddesses? For Corinth was set to play the space where desire fashioned the polis. The cultural myth of the city ran along lines of gender projected back through history, importing from the East all the transgressive cargo figured in the paradox of 'sacred prostitution'. For all that a visit to historical Corinth would not prove an expensive male ego-trip to a paradise of sex, Corinth retained its identity as the one town in Greece where, by hallowed tradition, all the glamour of the Orient was, truly, in place. History apart, those Herodotean women of Babylon have never ceased to colonize their myth of licensed lust. Auction of fantasy, 'sacred prostitution' underpins and blesses body shopping: 'Frauen als Ware'.[73]

Notes

We are grateful to anonymous readers for corrections, information and suggestions. The translations of Herodotus and Strabo are our own, unless otherwise indicated.

1. J. G. O'Neill, *Ancient Corinth, with a Topographical Sketch of the Corinthia*, Part 1: *From the Earliest Times to 404 BC*, Johns Hopkins University Studies in Archaeology 8 (Johns Hopkins University Press, Baltimore, MD, 1930), p. 50.

2. J. B. Salmon, *Wealthy Corinth: A History of the City to 338 BC* (Oxford University Press, Oxford, 1984), pp. 398–9 devotes less than two pages out of more than four hundred to this strange practice, before swiftly moving on to the 'secular prostitutes' of the city.

3. N. Spivey, *Understanding Greek Sculpture: Ancient Meanings, Modern Readings* (Thames & Hudson, London, 1996), p. 176.

4. B. MacLachlan, 'Sacred Prostitution and Aphrodite', *Studies in Religion*, 21/2 (1992), p. 146.

5. A. J. Bowen, *Plutarch: The Malice of Herodotus* (Aris & Phillips, Warminster, 1992), p. 142, on *De malignitate Herodoti* 39.

6. L. Kurke, 'Pindar and the Prostitutes, or Reading Ancient "Pornography"', *Arion*, 4.2 (1996), pp. 49–75 (esp. pp. 50–1).

7. Athenaeus, *Deipnosophistae* 13. 573c–4c, probably embroidering the (lost) *On Pindar* of the 4th/3rd centuries BCE peripatetic scholar-polemicist Chamaeleon of Heraclea (Kurke, 'Pindar and the prostitutes').

8. Esp. Kurke, 'Pindar and the Prostitutes', pp. 50–60 on *Olympians* 13 and fr. 122 (*skolion*).

9. Cf. Kurke, 'Pindar and the Prostitutes', pp. 64–5 and esp. n. 38, on Simonides *Epigram* 14 Page (cf. D. L. Page, *Further Greek Epigrams* [rev. edn; Cambridge University Press, Cambridge, 1981], pp. 207–11): the peripatetic philosopher Chamaeleon's no longer extant *Life of Simonides* may have been Athenaeus' source.

10. MacLachlan, 'Sacred Prostitution', p. 158.

11. MacLachlan, 'Sacred Prostitution', p. 158.

12. Kurke, 'Pindar and the Prostitutes', p. 66, 'map<ping> ... opposed value systems onto the civic space'.

13. The current fashion of opposing 'Greeks' and 'the Other' generally restricts alterity to cultures, peoples and customs that can be defined as non-Greek; but within Greek discourse, Othering begins at home and defines the relationships between the various Greek cities no less than external relationships. Modern scholarship tends to occlude the Otherness of Corinth by resorting to such technical terms as 'Orientalizing'.

14. MacLachlan, 'Sacred Prostitution', p. 145.

15. Salmon, *Wealthy Corinth*, p. 400.

16. E.g. J. G. Frazer, *The Golden Bough: A Study in Magic and Religion* (abridged edn; Macmillan, London, 1924), p. 331: 'If we survey the whole of the evidence on this subject ... we may conclude that a great Mother Goddess, the personification of all the reproductive energies of nature, was worshipped under different names but with a substantial similarity of myth and ritual by many peoples of Western Asia.'

17. S. Langdon, *Tammuz and Ishtar: A Monograph upon Babylonian Religion and Theology* (Oxford University Press, Oxford, 1914), p. 73.

18. Frazer, *Golden Bough*, pp. 330–1.

19. Cf. G. E. M. de Ste Croix, *The Class Struggle in the Ancient Greek World from the Archaic Age to the Arab Conquests* (Duckworth, London, 1981), pp. 153–4, on '"sacred" serfdom ... in the temple-estates' as 'survivals of forms of serfdom ... earlier widespread in Asia'.

20. Martin Bernal ('Burkert's Orientalizing Revolution', *Arion*, 4.2 [1996] pp. 137–47) still pursues his project of uncovering anti-Egyptian and anti-Semitic teleology in the Victorian research of both classicists and scholars of the Near East without reference to our topic—or to the pioneering works of theory involved in this aspect of the cultural interaction between 'West' and 'East'. (For pointed general critique of Bernal, cf. esp. G. MacLean Rogers, 'Multiculturalism and the foundations of Western civilization', in *Black Athena Revisited*, ed. M. R. Lefkowitz and G. MacLean Rogers [University of North Carolina Press, Chapel Hill, 1996], pp. 428–43, and esp. J. Ray's review of Lefkowitz and Rogers in the *Times Literary Supplement*, 14 February 1997, pp. 3–4, 'How Black Was Socrates?'). Burkert, too, looks elsewhere for his revision of our understanding of ancient Greek 'Orientalism'. We are suggesting that the legacy of 'sacred prostitution' deserves the closest of attention—and scrutiny.

21. Contemporary feminism re-founds the discourse by incorporating prostitution within labour, as 'sex-work', and thus distinguishing between 'sex as performance, capable of being detached from the body of the worker', and 'sex as an expression of an inner self, which when "sold" damages the woman involved' (W. Chapkis, *Live Sex Acts: Women Performing Erotic Labour* [Routledge, London, 1996]). This is predicated on modern refocusing of 'sex', i.e. heterosexual genital intercourse oriented to male ejaculation, and consequent realignment of the terms 'sexuality' and 'humanity'.

22. E. S. Hartland, 'Concerning the Rite at the Temple of Mylitta', in *Anthropological Essays Presented to Edward Burnett Tylor in Honour of his 75th Birthday Oct. 2 1907*, ed. W. H. R. Rivers, R. R. Marett and N. W. Thomas (Oxford University Press, Oxford, 1907), pp. 189–202; quote from p. 195.

23. The old entry, by F. R. Walton, was written for the first edition (Oxford University Press, Oxford, 1949), and included again in the second edition (1970). S. G. Pembroke wrote the new entry for the third edition (1997). The 'secular' article is by M. M. Henry.

24. A. Van Gennep, *The Rites of Passage* (Routledge & Kegan Paul, London, 1960), pp. 100–1: 'since little is known about the consecration rituals of the sacred prostitutes of antiquity, I shall cite several Hindu rites ...' Cf. L. R. Farnell, *Greece and Babylon: A Comparative Sketch of Mesopotamian, Anatolian and Hellenic Religions* (University of Edinburgh Press, Edinburgh, 1911), p. 279; Frazer, *Golden Bough*, pp. 330–1.

25. K. van der Toorn, 'Prostitution (Cultic)', in *The Anchor Bible Dictionary*, ed. D. N. Freedman (Doubleday, New York, 1992), vol. V, pp. 510–13, with pp. 511–12 on the 'payment of vow' hypothesis; full modern bibliography on p. 513.

26. Van der Toorn, 'Prostitution (Cultic)', p. 512.

27. A. T. Mann and J. Lyle, *Sacred Sexuality* (Element Books, Shaftesbury, 1996), pp. 42–3, 'The Whores of Babylon': enthusing over Herodotus 1.199, via N. Qualls-Corbett, *The Sacred Prostitute* (Inner City Books, Toronto, 1988), p. 34; J. Williamson-Magus, 'Temple Prostitutes. Reading', in *The Woman's Encyclopedia of Myths and Secrets*, ed. B. G. Walker (Harper & Row, San Francisco, 1983), pp. 819–21: "http://www.ucalgary.ca/~~hutton/Magus.html.

28. Hartland, 'Temple of Mylitta', p. 191; Farnell, *Greece and Babylon*, p. 279, n. 2.

29. Farnell, *Greece and Babylon*, pp. 268–9.

30. R. Jenkyns, *Dignity and Decadence: Victorian Art and the Classical Inheritance* (Harvard University Press, Cambridge, MA, 1992, pp. 119–25, quote from p. 119; for its economy—bazaar—of Orientalist/racist/sexist voyeurism, cf. S. Gilman, 'Black Bodies, White Bodies: Towards an Iconography of Female Sexuality in Late Nineteenth-Century Art, Medicine and Literature', *Critical Inquiry*, 12 (1985), pp. 204–42.

31. Farnell, *Greece and Babylon*, pp. 270 and 271; Hartland, 'Temple of Mylitta', pp. 192–3, brushing aside the problems of timing, imagines a peer-group cohort 'coming out' in their year. But was there a catch-clause in the engagement allowing for delay proportionate with desirability? Surely Herodotus must have pointed out that the auctioneer could take a rough guide for his pecking order from the time it had taken a deb to find her stranger?

32. Thus MacLachlan, 'Sacred Prostitution', p. 149, n. 14 still obediently reports that 'this Babylonian ritual took place just once, before marriage, with a stranger', before observing that the logic of Herodotus' terminology 'may exclude the possibility of defloration'. Cf. P. Friedrich, *The Meaning of Aphrodite* (University of Chicago Press, Chicago, 1978), p. 19: 'in some places a woman was expected to prostitute herself for one day, just before her marriage, in a temple to Astarte—but only to strangers, and with the proceeds to be spent on sacrifices' (an enthusiast's *tour de force* of inaccuracy).

33. See L. Kurke in her forthcoming book on Herodotus, chapters 5–6, esp. ch. 6 § II, 'Herodotean Alternatives: Reimagining the Public Sphere (*Histories* 1. 196, 1. 199)', on the intrication of prostitution within Herodotus' thinking on cultural economy. (We thank her for showing us this work in progress.) Hartland, 'Temple of Mylitta', p. 193 utterly suppresses the lien and dialectic between the homeostatic regulation of the marriage market and the depreciation of monetary face-value for the sacred sex: 'The payment seems to have been merely *pro forma*. It mattered not how small the coin was.' *Precisely* what mattered was that the value of the coin did *not* matter; cf. D. T. Steiner, *The Tyrant's Writ: Myths and Images of Writing in Ancient Greece* (Princeton University Press, Princeton, NJ, 1994), p. 165: 'the all-pervasive role of money, and its power to transform a man or woman into a commodity or sign, takes its place alongside other distinctions between Herodotus' worlds of East and West.'

34. Cf. *Oxford Classical Dictionary*, s.v. 'Hierodouloi' (F. R. Walton).

35. Cf. Kurke, forthcoming book, ch. 6, typescript pp. 10 and 11: 'There can be little doubt that these narratives are projections. Scholars of Babylonian history and culture find no native evidence for bride auctions, while temple prostitution was practiced only by a particular group of women (not, as Herodotus claims, universally) ... We must understand Herodotus' women as signifiers [within] figurations of different economies or systems of circulation.'

36. Mylitta is apparently 'Mulissu', Assyrian counterpart of Babylonian Ninlil, 'one of whose aspects is as a Mother', whereas 'the Babylonian goddess of sexual love is normally thought to be Ishtar ... who assumes the specifically sexual role as the Prostitute and Mistress of Love-making'. But no problem: 'in Assyria at any rate Ishtar and Ninlil were confused or merged in late times' (J. MacGinnis, 'Herodotus' Description of Babylon', *BICS*, 33 [1986], pp. 77–8).

37. A. Kuhrt, *The Ancient Near East: c. 3000–330 B.C.* (Routledge, London, 1995), pp. 1–2, is the exception; cf. D. Arnaud, 'La prostitution sacrée en Mésopotamie, un mythe historiographique?', *RHR*, 183 (1973) pp. 111–15; E. Fisher, 'Cultic Prostitution in the Ancient Near East? A Reassessment', *BTB*, 6 (1976), pp. 229–36; G. Lerner, 'The Origin of Prostitution in Mesopotamia', *Signs*, 11 (1986), pp. 236–54; further bibliography in E. A. Goodfriend, 'Prostitution: B. Cultic Prostitution in the OT', in Freedman, *Anchor Bible Dictionary*, vol. V, pp. 509–10.

38. H. W. F. Saggs, *The Greatness That Was Babylon: A Survey of the Ancient Civilization of the Tigris-Euphrates Valley* (Sidgwick & Jackson, London, 1988), pp. 302–3.

39. Cf. J. N. Postgate, *Early Mesopotamia: Society and Economy at the Dawn of History* (Routledge, London, 1992), p. 106: 'it is possible that the practice of sacred prostitution, reported more than a thousand years later by Herodotus in rather lurid terms, was already current in Old Babylonian times.'

40. E. M. Yamauchi, 'Cultic Prostitution: A Case Study in Cultural Diffusion', in *Orient and Occident: Essays Presented to Cyrus H. Gordon on the Occasion of his Sixty-fifth Birthday*, ed. H. A. Hoffner, Jr (*AOAT* 22, Neukirchen-Vluyn, 1973), pp. 215, 219 and 221. For Strabo, see below. The third century BCE Septuagint *Epistle of Jeremias* (=Baruch VI 42–3) says: 'the women also with cords about them, sitting in the ways, burn bran for perfume; but if any of them, drawn by some that passeth by, lie with him she reproacheth her fellow, that she was not thought as worthy as herself, nor her cord broken.' Pembroke, *OCD* s.v. 'Prostitution, sacred' generously concedes: 'some distinctive features repeated [here as in Herodotus]'. What will-to-power is required to conclude: 'This *accords* exactly with Herodotus (only the bran being added), and as it is not possible that we are dealing with a borrowing from Herodotus, it seems that a genuine tradition is re*corded*' (MacGinnis, 'Herodotus' Babylon', p. 78: our italics)? Cf. Farnell, *Greece and Babylon*, p. 270: 'the wish is father to the thought', though *he* was speaking in judgement over the anxiety of 'devoted Assyriologists' to impugn Herodotus' veracity in order to discount that 'an ancient civilisation of otherwise advanced morality could have sanctioned such a practice'.

41. Langdon, *Tammuz and Ishtar*, pp. 81–2; cf. Farnell, *Greece and Babylon*, p. 282, '"kadistu", that is, "pure" or clean in the ritualistic sense, or as Zimmern interprets the ideogram, "not unclean"'. Cf. Goodfriend, 'Prostitution, OT', pp. 507–9, on the *qadistu*.

42. J. Bottéro, *Mesopotamia: Writing, Reasoning, and the Gods* (1987; University of Chicago Press, Chicago, 1992), p. 189. On names for temple servants, MacLachlan, 'Sacred Prostitution', p. 146: 'in no case is the title of each category linked specifically to ritual prostitution'.

43. D. Harden, *The Phoenicians* (Penguin, Harmondsworth, 1971), pp. 122, 175–6, 284 n. on fig. 62.

44. Yamauchi, 'Cultic Prostitution', pp. 216–18. Cf. D. Montserrat, *Sex and Society in Graeco-Roman Egypt* (Kegan Paul International Press, London, 1996), p. 125: 'cultic prostitution or *hierodouleia* was not an Egyptian tradition, though it might have gone on at such places as the precinct of the foreign deity Astarte at Saqqara.'

45. MacGinnis, 'Herodotus' Babylon', pp. 76–7. For recent re-examination, cf. R. A. McNeal, 'The Brides of Babylon: Herodotus 1. 196', *Historia*, 37 (1988), pp. 54–71, who wonders: 'where Herodotus picked up his information. Did he copy it from Hecataeus? ... At some point in the misty beginnings of Greek historical writing, this Babylonian story was invented by someone and then had a long life as a kind of literary topos. It appears, with slight variations, in Nicolaus Damascenus and again in Strabo' (p. 69); R. Rollinger, *Herodots babylonischer logos. Eine kritische Untersuchung der Glaubwürdigkeitsdiskussion* (Innsbrucker Beiträge zur Kulturwissenschaft 84, Innsbruck, 1993), p. 180 and n. 655.

46. G. Rawlinson, *The Histories of Herodotus* (Murray, London, 1880³), vol. I, p. 321, n. 8.

47. For Strabo's project, see L. A. Thompson, 'Strabo on Civilization', *Platon*, 31 (1979), pp. 213–29; F. Lasserre, 'Strabon devant l'Empire romain', *ANRW*, II.30.1 (1983), 867–96.

48. Nikolaos von Damaskos, F. Jakoby, *Fragmente der griechischen Historiker* (Brill, Leiden, 1923–58), F103 w (131). Aelian *Varia Historia* 4.1 gives a very similar lemma after Herodotus (as he does, in the same batch of miscellaneous excerpts, for the Lydians' prostitution of their daughters).

49. Rawlinson, *Herodotus*, vol. I, p. 325, n. 1.

50. MacLachlan, 'Sacred Prostitution', pp. 149–50.

51. Cf. G. J. P. McEwan, *Priest and Temple in Hellenistic Babylonia*, Freiburger altorientalische Studien 4 (Freiburg University Press, Freiburg, 1981).

52. Conveniently updated, sorted, and analysed by W. Fauth and M.-B. von Stritzky in *Reallexikon für Antike und Christentum*, s.v. 'Hierodulie'.

53. Yamauchi, 'Cultic Prostitution', p. 220 for the uncritical list; cf. MacLachlan, 'Cultic Prostitution', pp. 152–4, notably missing the temporality of Justin's imperfect tenses.

54. Hartland, 'Temple of Mylitta', pp. 189–90: Socrates and Sozomen. Christian writers were always concerned to find 'immorality' (in their terms) in 'pagan' ritual, on whatever scanty 'evidence'.

55. W. W. How and J. Wells, *A Commentary on Herodotus* (Oxford University Press, Oxford, 1912), vol. I, p. 151 on 1. 199. 1, 'from personal inquiry'. Cf. R. A. Oden, 'Studies in Lucian's *De Dea Syria*', *Harvard Semitic Monographs* 15 (Scholars Press, Missoula, MT, 1977), pp. 77–8, on Byblos, Aphrodite and Astarte.

56. Yamauchi, 'Cultic Prostitution', p. 219.

57. Valerius Maximus 2. 6. 15.

58. G. Herm, *The Phoenicians: The Purple Empire of the Ancient World* (Gollancz, London, 1975), pp. 113–14. Cf. Hartland, 'Temple of Mylitta', p. 192: 'The rite as there practised was therefore, at all events in the second century A.D., an alternative to the dedication of hair ... Thus the woman would repeat the expiation once a year, whether married or single, so long as she was unwilling to shear her locks, *or preferred the alternative sacrifice of her chastity*.' Hear satire cackle at *this* Victorian glimpse of libertinage!

59. Hartland, 'Temple of Mylitta', p. 192.

60. Cf. Pembroke, *OCD,* s.v. 'Prostitution, sacred': 'the cult of Aphrodite at Eryx ... once again a thing of the past by [Strabo's] time ...'. He adds, decisively: 'in all these cases, the adjective [sacred] denotes no more than manumission by fictive dedication.'

61. Farnell, *Greece and Babylon,* p. 272.

62. MacLachlan, 'Sacred Prostitution', p. 154, n. 25.

63. Farnell, *Greece and Babylon,* p. 272.

64. Apostolius, *Proverbs* 13.60 offers three explanations for this saying: either because the *hetairai* prayed to Aphrodite for Corinth in the great war; or because landing in port there is hard; or because only the rich can afford the *hetairai*.

65. So H. Conzelmann, *Korinth und die Mädchen der Aphrodite. Zur Religionsgeschichte der Stadt Korinth, Nachrichten der Akademie der Wissenschaften im Göttingen aus dem Jahre 1967. Philologisch-Historische Klasse,* 8 (1967), pp. 245–61, esp. p. 250: 'He is speaking in relation to a rupture in the history of Corinth from the city's Golden Age'; Pembroke, *OCD,* s.v. 'Prostitution, sacred': 'admittedly writing long after the city's destruction in 146 B.C.'; *pace* D. M. Halperin, *One Hundred Years of Homosexuality and Other Essays on Greek Love* (Routledge, London, 1990), p. 106: 'temple-prostitution on a grand scale reminiscent of the ancient Near East appears to have occurred only on the periphery of the Greek world—with the possible exception of Corinth, where in Roman times (according to Strabo ...) the famous and wealthy shrine of Aphrodite owned more than a thousand temple-slaves who worked as prostitutes, making Corinth the Amsterdam of the ancient world.' Cf. C. K. Williams, II, 'Corinth and the Cult of Aphrodite', in *Corinthiaca: Studies in Honor of Darrell A. Amyx,* ed. M. A. Del Chiaro (University of Missouri Press, Columbia, MO, 1986), p. 20, n. 35: 'in the time of Strabo at least a thousand girls served the goddess.' Feel the longing, the desire, in this collective delusion—presently being turned, for real, to mind-colonization, or to delivering faith, on the Alpha course at London's Church of the Holy Trinity at Brompton, by a group of new Christians: 'the congregation believe they are saving England's capital for Jesus. Mr Millar tells them: "The enemy is devouring and destroying London." Simon Downham, a younger priest, illustrating a letter of Paul to the Corinthians, informs worshippers that ancient Corinth had many places of worship, including a temple with 1,000 prostitutes. The city was a cross between New York, Los Angeles and Las Vegas. "Strangely like contemporary London," he told us' (D. Kennedy, 'Smart Route to the Lord', *The Times,* 'Weekend', 14 December 1996, p. 1: the photograph is captioned, 'they are young, professional, good-looking—and they have found God in droves', but is dominated by attractive, well-to-do, young *women.*

66. Kurke, 'Pindar and Prostitutes', n. 3. Strabo lived through the Caesarian and Augustan refoundation of Colonia Laus Iulia Corinthiensis (cf. J. Wiseman, 'Corinth and Rome I: 228 BC–AD 267', *ANRW,* 2.7.1 [1979], pp. 438–548, esp. pp. 491–7; p. 468, Wiseman accepts that 'The famous temple of Aphrodite, which stood on the highest point (575 m) of Acrocorinth and in whose sacred service prostitutes offered themselves to citizens and visitors in the city below, has left little trace').

67. Kurke, 'Pindar and Prostitutes', p. 17.

68. H. R. H. Hall cited by O'Neill, *Ancient Corinth,* pp. 100–1.

69. Williams, 'Corinth and Aphrodite', p. 21, thinking of Xenophon's 100 votaries. Pembroke, *OCD,* s.v. 'Prostitution, sacred', amusingly points out that 'the number given [by Pindar] is strictly a total of limbs rather than of persons'.

70. Yamauchi, 'Cultic Prostitution', p. 220 (our emphasis). Cf. Conzelmann, *Korinth,* p. 251: 'Strabo explicity marks that he means prostitutes by "Hierodules" by writing hetairas.'

71. Commentators treat this Pindaric flourish with prosaic stolidity. Pembroke in *OCD*, s.v. 'Prostitution, sacred', must stand for all: 'a *skolion* which explicitly anticipates a degree of moral opprobrium and seeks to forestall this with a coy invocation to "necessity".'

72. **Kor**inthia **kor**e ('a girl of Corinth') was proverbial for a man-pleaser (Plato, *Republic* 3. 404d)—as if the town was *named* for its girls. The verb *Korinthiazomai* ('to go Corinthian') meant to 'whore' or 'pimp'.

73. Rollinger, *Herodots babylonischer logos*, p. 181 (with n. 657).

Men Without Clothes:
Heroic Nakedness and Greek Art

ROBIN OSBORNE

Clothes are the cause of nudity. (Minutes of the Vienna Psychoanalytic Society)[1]

Classical Greece has become the cultural reference point by which the public display of the naked male body is justified: the German magazine editor who in 1994 published photographs of Prince Charles only partially concealed behind a bath towel, attempted to claim the purloined private image as suitable for the public stage with reference to his appearing 'like a Greek statue'. For us, appeal to the Greeks can indeed be the bath towel which alone preserves our academic respectability, but if we wish to understand the role of the exposed male body in Greek art, no such defence is possible. The issue is pointedly highlighted by Denis Diderot in his imaginary dialogue with a sculptor on the topic of female beauty:

> 'Well, to answer without torturing my mind too much, when I want to make a statue of a beautiful woman, I have a great number of them undress; all offer both beautiful parts and badly shaped parts; I take from each what is beautiful.' 'And how do you recognize what is beautiful?' 'Obviously, from its conformity with the antique, which I have thoroughly studied.' 'And if the antique did not exist, how would you go about it? You are not answering my question ...'[2]

For Kenneth Clark the ideal early Greek male nude was 'calm, pitiless and supremely confident in the power of physical beauty'.[3] Modern discussion of male nudes focuses on their structure and their musculature, while discussion of female nudes focuses on their sexuality (hence the dismay at the boundary crossing of Robert Mapplethorpe's *Lady: Lisa Lyon*).[4] But what were the connotations of nudity in antiquity, and just how asexual was the naked male body? This paper reviews what scholars in the past have made of the nakedness of men in Greek art and then surveys chronologically the naked male body in archaic and classical Greek art, probing the protocols of fleshly display and the changing boundaries of what was acceptable.

Scholarship on classical Greek art is divided in its interpretation of the exposed male body. For one tradition the exposure of male flesh is an act of heroization.[5] Among contemporary scholars, this tradition can be seen behind Brunhilde Ridgway's comment that in the scenes of fighting on the sculpted frieze of the late fifth-century temple of Athene Nike at Athens 'the unrealistic attire of the fighters may have been meant to support a generic identification, *whereas complete nudity might have entirely removed the action from the human sphere*'.[6] Most recently Nigel Spivey has written: 'Greek men did not normally walk around with no clothes on, so if figures are glimpsed naked (or nude) in the context of what appears to be a "realistic" scene, then the chances are that the scene has been elevated from the realistic to the supernatural.'[7] Those who deny heroization may nevertheless stress idealization: so Andrew Stewart, who writes that 'so-called heroic nudity is nothing of the sort', explains the dominance of the male nude in Greek sculpture by exclaiming that 'if the artist's wish was to portray man in an "ideal" or rather archetypal and generalizing way, then what better device was there to reveal both beauty and arete [excellence, virtue], while affirming the superiority of men over women, and soon, of Greeks over barbarians?'[8]

But a second tradition regards the element of idealization in the exposed male body as minimal. Although Sir John Boardman admits that 'The idealizing tendency in Classical sculpture ... is abetted by the male nude', he claims:

> In Classical Greece the nude (men only) *was* acceptable in life. Athletes at exercise or competition went naked and it was possible to fight near-naked. Youths and even the more mature took no pains to conceal their private parts on any festive, and no doubt many more ordinary, public occasions ... In Greek art, therefore, the nude could carry no special 'artistic' connotation, nor could it exclusively designate a special class, such as hero or god.[9]

Christoph Clairmont wants to go even further, and has asserted that the naked male of Greek sculpture 'is not likened to a hero. The fact that the heroes of Greek mythology are mostly, but not exclusively, depicted naked is sheer coincidence.'[10]

At issue here is the role of undress in Greek life. Insistence that Greek sculpture looks as it does because Greeks themselves looked like that goes back to the founding father of classical art history, the eighteenth-century German scholar J. J. Winckelmann, in whom, at least, there is an element of wishful thinking:

> The forms of the Greeks, prepared to beauty, by the influence of the mildest and purest sky, became perfectly elegant by their early exercises ... By these exercises the bodies of the Greeks got the great and manly contour observed in their statues, without any bloated corpulency. The young Spartans were bound to appear every tenth day naked before the ephors, who, when they perceived any inclinable to fatness, ordered them a scantier diet ... The

gymnasia, where, sheltered by public modesty, the youths exercised themselves naked, were the schools of art ... Here beautiful nakedness appeared
with such a liveliness of expression, such truth and variety of situations, such
a noble air of the body, as it would be ridiculous to look for in any hired
model of our academies ... The fairest youths danced undressed in the
theatre; and Sophocles, the great Sophocles, when young, was the first who
dared entertain his fellow-citizens in this manner ... Then every solemnity,
every festival, afforded the artist opportunity to familiarize himself with all
the beauties of Nature ... The probability still increases, that the bodies of the
Greeks, as well as the works of their artists, were framed with more unity of
system, a nobler harmony of parts, and a completeness of the whole, above
our lean tensions and hollow wrinkles.[11]

Against such a view, those who stress idealization deny that Greek men
can normally have worked or fought unclothed. So Martin Robertson says
of the sixth-century dedicatory figure of a man carrying a sacrificial calf
that 'A Greek of this time would not have gone about in a single little
garment exposing the whole front of his body', and supports his claim that
the Parthenon frieze does not represent the Panathenaic procession as it
ever took place by observing that 'young men for instance did not ride
naked in classical Athens'.[12] Andrew Stewart points out that statues of unclothed men were produced before it became conventional for men to
compete unclothed in athletics, and he sees the latter as the adoption of
'a kind of absolute and archetypal state' which served to 'certify athletes as
a class apart'.[13]

Little external evidence is available to settle the arguments about the
relationship between exposed bodies in Greek art and exposed bodies in
Greek life. The main body of evidence for life comes from art itself, both
Greek sculpture and the scenes on Greek pots, but the relationship between either sculpture or the scenes on pots and life is itself open to discussion.[14] Texts support the view that at least some gymnastic and athletic
activities were practised with bodies unclothed,[15] but textual evidence
for bodily exposure in other circumstances is limited and not always easy
to interpret. Nevertheless it is important to stress that the textual evidence
clearly indicates that at Athens, at least, opportunities to observe male
genitalia were limited and that viewing young men's penises was sexually
provocative. In Aristophanes' play *Clouds* insouciant youthful nakedness is
a feature of the golden Marathonian past,[16] vanished from the present, and
when in his *Wasps* the character Bdelykleon asks his father Philokleon
'Give me an example of what good ruling Greece does you?', Aristophanes
has Philokleon reply: 'When boys are inspected [to see that they are
eighteen] we get a good view of their genitals.'[17] This latter exchange draws
attention to the way the unclothed male body went on display in controlled
contexts: the Athenian Council which inspected these young men was
made up of men aged over thirty; at the Olympic games too, women were
prohibited from being spectators. It is common to note that Winckelmann's

claims about the Greeks were not unrelated to changes in attitudes to sexuality and the body that he desired to promote in his own day, and a similar motivation can be found behind parallel recent claims that what you see on pots is what you got in life,[18] but the ancient texts give us good reason to believe that male nudity in life was sexually charged in classical antiquity as well for modern scholars.

To understand why any particular sculpted or drawn body is clothed or unclothed, we need to be able to establish what the options were. No artistic image is produced in a vacuum, and in the case of any particular image we can and must establish the alternative traditions against which, at any given moment in time, the choice of an artist or of his client to have a particular image is to be understood.

Male figures in the various regional styles of Greek art in the eighth century, known as 'Geometric' art because of the dominance of geometric ornament in pottery decoration, are not clothed. Breasts are indicated or separate legs are replaced by a solid or decorated panel from which two feet project to gender a figure as female. Maleness is positively indicated not by clothing but by arms and armour and by such occupations as driving a chariot. In statuettes maleness may be positively indicated by making male genitalia manifest. Some males are prominently belted but this apparently does not imply clothing.

In geometric drawing and sculpture, therefore, to be a man is to be un-clothed. Several arguments suggest that this was not also true of geometric life. Practicality suggests that those who donned more or less elaborate armour would not neglect more elementary protection for parts vulnerable in war or to accidents liable to occur when animals are handled or metal worked. The Homeric poems, which draw on an oral tradition certainly alive and well in the eighth century, clothe their male characters and associate stripping of the body and exposure of genitals with dishonour and shame. More generally, clothing plays an important part in exchange and in the making of symbolic statements in epic poetry, and in the one instance where a hero displays his body along with his heroic prowess, when Odysseus casts off his clothes to tackle the suitors at the very beginning of *Odyssey* 22, that it is rags that he casts off may be as important symbolically as the nakedness he reveals.[19] Already in the *Odyssey*, however, the encounter between the newly cast up Odysseus and Nausikaa does suggest the latent possibility, and sexuality, of the naked male body beautiful.[20]

Given that the clothed man is unknown to eighth-century artists, and that they had the option of showing a woman instead of a man but not of showing a man clothed, it is inappropriate to ascribe any particular value to the unclothing of any particular male in geometric art. Historians some-times worry about the lack of correspondence between art and what they believe to have been the case in life, and so talk of the 'ceremonial nudity' of a youth with a ram and deduce from this 'ceremonial nudity' that the activity in question is sacrificial rather than workaday, or suggest that the

contrast between the largely negative associations of the removal of clothing for the Homeric warrior and the uniformly unclothed bronze warrior
figures demonstrates 'the early existence of different kinds of nudity in Greek
culture. The nudity of a heroic warrior is apotropaic and must symbolize
his valor and perhaps even divine favor'.[21] The contrast between the generally negative value of being without clothes in the Homeric poems and
the absence of clothes from all men in drawing and sculpture does indeed
demand explanation, but the very consistency with which men are unclothed argues for the exposed body as being essential to being a man, not
as a feature of a particular sort of man.[22] The unclothed body marks gender
difference, and suggests that marking gender difference was important, but
there seems no reason to read anything more into it.[23]

The 'conventional' exposure of the male body in geometric art suggests
that it is clothing, as much as the unclothed body, which needs to be explained in early Greek art. In geometric art clothing marks out a character
as 'not a man'. Later, in seventh-century Greek art, men are not infre-
quently clothed, but it is arguable that clothing marks out figures who are
in some way deserving of special attention. Where getting a story over is
what is important men frequently remain unclothed—so Odysseus and his
men are unclothed as they blind the Cyclops.[24] But elsewhere, when an
artist wishes to confront viewers with the recognition of everyday experience, men are often clothed and their clothing treated in considerable
detail. This can be illustrated nicely from the mid-seventh-century pot of
Corinthian manufacture known as the Chigi Vase (Figure 1): here the top
frieze, which shows, perhaps for the first time in art, heavily armed troops
about to clash in battle, clothes both the warriors and the boy playing the
flute; the middle frieze seems to have clothed all participants in the tableau
of the judgement of Paris and clothes most of those involved in the chariot
procession and lion hunt, but leaves at least one huntsman naked but for a
belt; the lowest frieze showing boys ambushing small animals leaves most
of the human participants naked. Armour is clearly itself part of the subject
of the top frieze (two men are shown behind the main lines still arming
themselves); the conjunction of the familiar and the exotic (whether mythical beauty-contests or foreign lion hunts) seems essential to the central
frieze; only the bottom frieze is essentially an adventure story. The naked
huntsman in the centre frieze embodies the tension there between on the
one hand emphasizing the similarity between exotic hunts or Paris' judgement of goddesses and the everyday activities of hunting and girl-spotting,
and on the other hand the uncluttered telling of a story.

It is, I suggest, clothing that is the marked signifier in seventh-century art,
not the unclothed body, and there is no reason to think that the significance
of the unclothed male in art changed immediately there was a possibility
of men being clothed. To leave a man without clothes in seventh-century
painting or sculpture is to offer the viewer no context in which to place
him other than the context of the figure's own actions. This is particularly

Figure 1: Protocorinthian *olpe* known as the Chigi Vase; mid-seventh-century BCE. Rome, Villa Giulia. Photo: Hirmer Fotoarchiv, Munich.

important for understanding the development and popularity of the *kouros* type in sculpture (Figure 2).

Although small bronzes of naked standing figures are known from the end of the eighth century onwards, the large stone type of naked male figure with feet slightly apart and arms by sides, known as the *kouros*, appears only in the late seventh century. Although analysis of proportions leaves no doubt that sculptors were inspired by large Egyptian sculptures, the Egyptian parallels have been rid of their loin-cloths, their determined expressions, and their associations with particular (ruling) figures, before they appear in Greek sanctuaries and as markers on Greek graves. The *kouros* type dominated free-standing sculptural representation of individual men from the end of the seventh to the beginning of the fifth century. That long popularity seems closely linked to the difficulties involved in pinpointing exactly what the *kouros* represents: it is clear that it cannot in every case represent the god to whom it is dedicated, since some are dedicated to the goddesses Athena and Hera, or the dedicant (since men dedicate *korai*, the clothed female equivalent). Some have argued that the nakedness of the figure *does* makes it specifically an athlete, but the absence of the *aryballos* (a flask to hold perfumed oil) that identifies the athlete in archaic grave reliefs, or the strigil that serves the same purpose in classical sculpture counts against this.[25] Rather this figure would seem to offer a template in which any man can fit himself, whether to feel sympathy for the dead in whose place he might have been or to place himself as a model of humanity before the gods. Either specific action or a specific age for the figure require clothing: once a figure is shown carrying a calf (as with the Moskhophoros from the Athenian Acropolis mentioned by Martin Robertson in the quotation above), or is shown distinctly immature (as with the figure of Dionysermos from Ionia), at least minimal clothing is provided.[26]

But if the *kouros* carries on the tradition of unmarked nakedness, other sculptures and painted pottery of the sixth century reveal that the unclothed male was becoming an increasingly complex figure. Athenian tombstones, for example, regularly carry reliefs of individuals seen in profile.[27] Some are clothed, notably with armour, but the great majority are naked. Of these some carry a staff or other object which does little to specify their role in life, but a large proportion identify themselves, by discus, bound hand, or oil flask, as men who engage in athletics. These unclothed bodies have become contextualized, and the viewer is encouraged to see in the absence of clothing the realities—or at least the idealization—of the gymnasium. Real-life contexts of nakedness have for the first time been invoked in sculpture. More or less contemporaneously, as sculpture begins to invoke the one public context in which males might be viewed unclothed, pots begin in the middle of the sixth century to invoke both private and public contexts in which men might be unclothed, first with lewd dancers and sexual activity—where the erect phallus might best be seen as an accoutrement which sexualizes as it contextualizes—and then with athletes.[28]

Figure 2: Sixth-century *kouros* probably from Boiotia. British Museum B474. Photo: courtesy of the Trustees of the British Museum.

Neither in sculpture nor in the painting of pottery is there a clean break between the unmarked unclothed male and the marked naked man, but in the course of the sixth century the male body lost its semiotic innocence. We can understand what is happening equally in social and in artistic terms. An elite which expresses its superiority over the run of men by the ability to make lasting memorials of its dead will also create a demand for ways by which some of its members can demonstrate their superiority over others. One area of possible competition is size of monument, but another is its specificity, the invoking of the dead person as a particular type of individual by making reference to their achievements in life. To make such reference demands the display of the range of public achievements of which members of the elite were proud, demands that features of the sculpted monument be seen to invoke particular features of the life lived and not just its bare male humanity. Similarly, the demand for figurative pottery seems to have moved from semi-public pots such as amphorae which may have stood about storing wine or oil, or the mixing-bowls for wine which seem to have been popular as wedding gifts around 600 BCE, to smaller private vessels seen only when in use at the, perhaps increasingly fashionable, formalized male drinking parties known as symposia. Such vessels could display the owner's wit and culture in many ways, but that they should do so by offering reflections of acceptable, and in due course unacceptable, behaviour on the very occasions on which they were used, was surely inevitable.[29]

In artistic terms, the challenge to both sculptors and painters in the sixth century can be seen as the challenge to allude to the known world in an ever richer way, to absorb the viewer's interest and attention by encouraging a continuous and varied flow of associations—something some artists sought to achieve by combining texts with their painting or carving. There is an inevitable tension, however, between this aim and the aim, most apparent in the *kouros*, of offering an image with which any man can associate himself, for the richer the skein of allusions the greater the specificity which must result (Figure 3). The final destruction of the *kouros* type by this specificity is to be seen in such early fifth-century figures as the Anaphe *kouros*, illustrated here, or the Kritian boy; in these figures the traditional static *kouros* pose is transformed into a specific movement, and the traditional agelessness of the *kouros* transformed into a specific adolescence; the power of the *kouros* to stand in for men in general is utterly lost. The unclothed male can no longer stand to the viewer in a relationship of identity: a new relationship is formed. This new relationship, which is the basis of what E. Gombrich famously called 'the Greek revolution', is one in which voyeurism becomes for the first time one of the options for the viewer.[30] The varied sexual attraction exercised by the remarkable Riace Bronzes, which perhaps date to around 460 BCE, on different modern viewers shows very clearly that their unclothed mature male bodies can no longer make a pretence at sexual innocence: the viewer stands to the statue in a relationship of desire.[31]

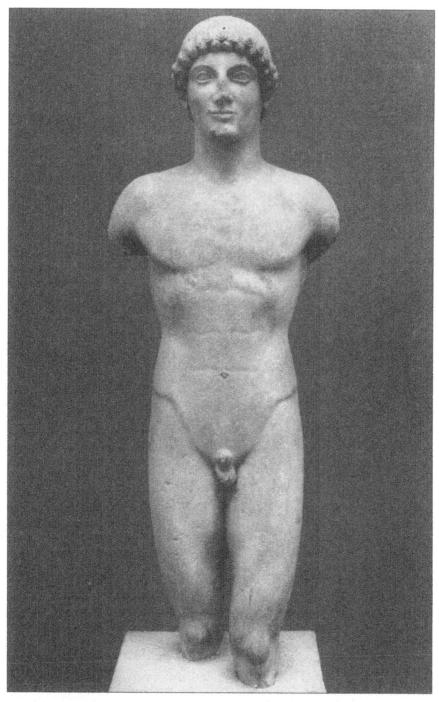

Figure 3: Early fifth-century *kouros* from Anaphe. British Museum B475. Photo: courtesy of the Trustees of the British Museum.

The most remarkable monument to the sexualizing of the unclothed body may well be one now lost. The Athenians had erected, perhaps in the last decade of the sixth century, what Pliny (*Natural History* 34.70) believed to be the first official portrait statues to commemorate the killing of the tyrant Hipparkhos by Harmodios and Aristogeiton. This original 'tyrannicide' group was taken away by Xerxes in the sack of Athens in 480 BCE, and the Athenians had Kritios and Nesiotes produce a new group. That group, although now lost, inspired both direct copies and imitation in other contexts, including on painted pottery, and we have a good idea of the appearance of the balanced pair in striding active poses. It is likely that the tyrannicide pair were markedly distinguished as to their maturity by means other than merely the beard of the older man. By the time that Thucydides wrote, Harmodios and Aristogeiton were held to have been lovers, and the murder of Hipparkhos the indirect result of Hipparkhos' lack of success in seducing Harmodios.[32] Antenor's original group seems unlikely to have conveyed much of that relationship, but in the later group the aggressive display of the unclothed male bodies may well have acquired a sexual edge.

The same sexualizing process can be traced on pots too. Black-figure pottery shows an increasing interest in scenes which are not identifiably mythological and which make more or less direct reference to real life. Such reference is in part pioneered by the scenes of athletics which were painted on the oil amphorae awarded as prizes at the games associated with the great festival of the Panathenaia from the 560s onwards. It is in athletic scenes that sensitivity to male nakedness is first apparent, when on vases destined for an Etruscan market painters of the so-called Perizoma group add loin-cloths to running figures.[33] The development of the red-figure technique at the end of the sixth century enabled bodies to occupy space and not simply be flat silhouettes, as they had been in the earlier black-figure technique, and the shadow-play which kept painted scenes at a distance from the viewer's experience gave way to possibilities of intimacy which necessarily made real-life experiences part of the painter's agenda. The painter's desire to emulate real-life experiences is inseparable from the painting of desire.

From around 500 BCE onwards, therefore, the decision to show an unclothed male was a decision in which a number of different factors played a part. Artists who chose to show men unclothed might do so because they wished to signal that they belonged to a long artistic tradition, because they were imitating life, or because the display of male sexuality was relevant to their artistic aims. The way in which the sexuality of the unclothed male was newly subject to negotiation on painted pottery from the end of the sixth century onwards is well illustrated by one particular iconographic development: the representation of the ligaturing of the penis, often known as 'male infibulation', and by the way in which some habitually clothed male figures are treated.

Ligaturing, the restraint of the penis usually by tying it up in some fashion, is represented on vases and, very occasionally, in sculpture.[34] In early red-figure vases, between about 510 and about 460 BCE, youths are represented in athletic contexts tying up their penises, or with penises tied up, and mature men are represented with ligatured penises in the context of the post-sympotic revel known as the *komos*. During the same period some satyrs are also shown with ligatured penises.[35] What unites all these activities? Although the activities of the *komos* could indeed be athletic, and are particularly so portrayed when satyrs are involved, the factor common to all these scenes would seem to be not violent physical activity but discourse about sex. Athletes were both peculiarly in the public eye and in danger of immodest display, and were held to perform better if they refrained from sexual activity;[36] the symposium was the place where control over bodily appetites was displayed in the face of opportunities to lose control; satyrs' bodies were used to parade humanly improper degrees of indulgence and transgression. By taking the ligaturing of the penis out of the athletic context in which it may have been at least occasionally employed, and out of the context of use by sexually immature youths, and by redeploying it in mature human or fantasy situations in which it had no role in genital protection but was rather a signifier of discourse about sexual control, early red-figure artists make it abundantly clear that the display of the naked male body is no longer insouciant: men's bodies are actively sexual.

The place of ligaturing in discourse about sex is well illustrated by comparing its use by the painter Douris on a wine-cooling vase (*psykter*) in the British Museum and on a cup in Berlin.[37] The *psykter* (Figure 4a and b) shows a group of satyrs performing various more or less athletic feats in order to drink wine out of a range of vessels. Of the eleven satyrs shown, eight have their penises ligatured. One satyr has a penis which is unligatured but not erect, and it is he alone who is not entirely naked, but wears, as if in theatrical costume, a highly decorated cloak round his shoulders, Thracian boots and a travelling hat, and carries a herald's staff: he is dressed up as the god Hermes, his boots and cloak deliberately made to be mortal equivalents of Hermes' own accustomed dress, rather than identical with that dress. Two other satyrs have erect penises: one is performing the feat of balancing on the tip of an erect penis a vase which is being filled from a jug by one of his companions; the other overlooks and approaches with a great stride from the rear a satyr who is attempting to drink from a cup while doing a hand-stand. The presence of these sexually excited satyrs in the two most extraordinary stunt performances makes it clear that sex, as well as drink, is a focus of attention here. These satyrs are shown both as the most 'cool' and urbane of men, and as the most transgressive: to represent satyrs is always to raise the question of sexual activity.

The exterior of the Berlin cup by Douris shows mortal men in a post-sympotic revel (Figure 5). Like the satyrs on the *psykter*, these men put on display a range of drinking vessels. Two play the double pipes of the *aulos*,

Figure 4a and 4b: Attic red-figure *psykter* by Douris of *c.* 490 BCE. British Museum E768. Photos: courtesy of the Trustees of the British Museum.

Figure 5: Attic red-figure cup by Douris of early fifth-century date. Staatliche Museen Berlin Antikensammlung 2289.

two dance, another throws his head back as singers regularly are shown to do. In this *komos*, all the participants whose genitals are visible have their penises ligatured. All these mature, bearded men, who exhibit the acceptable degree of wine-induced excitement, are thus visibly shown to retain their urbanity, even in the heat of the wine. The ligaturing draws attention to what is absent, draws attention to the gap between the behaviour exhibited in this civilized revelry and the behaviour familiar among satyrs.

The importance of the ligatured penis for our understanding of the display of the unclothed male body lies precisely in the way in which it comes to be used to draw attention to an absence. To show scenes of men engaged in sexual activity, such as appear on certain shapes of pot particularly during this period from about 510 to about 460 BCE, carries no necessary implications for the unclothed male body as sexual. To show the penis ligatured, however, is to display the penis as an essentially sexual organ, and not merely a marker of the male gender. By taking over a practice which may have been employed by athletes for purposes of comfort or modesty and applying it in fantasy contexts, where it can have no practical place, artists turn the ligaturing of the penis into a way of denying that the naked male body can ever fail to be sexually engaged.

While men and other gods regularly appear naked, whether in myth or real-life contexts, in sixth- and early fifth-century art, one divine figure stands out: the god Dionysos is always clothed.[38] Young or old, beardless or bearded, gods regularly appear naked or in a sufficiently unclothed state to reveal their genitals during this period. Not Dionysos, who is rarely even bare-chested. Though regularly surrounded by satyrs who are not only not clothed but who display their sexual excitement, Dionysos remains clothed, just as, in the midst of drunken display, he remains sober.[39] Although Dionysos' dress can be paralleled by that worn by other male figures, there is no doubt that his robes, usually including a long garment, became inseparable from his image. This is particularly nicely seen when Dionysos is shown taking part in battles against the Giants: not only is his spear often also a *thyrsos* (a giant fennel stalk crowned with ivy), but when he is shown arming his costume is incongruous, and while his opponents may be shown as naked hoplites, the god himself never is (Figure 6).[40]

Dionysos' clothing is closely related to the peculiar character of the god. Not only is his dress an object of attention in literary texts, particularly but not at all exclusively, in Euripides' *Bacchae*, but the cult image of Dionysos, which was a head on a draped pole, points to the peculiar unimportance of the body for this god. That stands out particularly clearly when the mask-idols of Dionysos are compared with the other divine image which lacks an anthropomorphic body: the Herm. Herms have square pillars for bodies, with short stubs for arms, but they also have an erect phallus. Dionysos' bodilessness emerges, by contrast with the Herm, as in particular a denial of sexuality.

Making sense of Dionysos' clothing is revealing both about how Dionysos differs from other gods and about the changing meaning of the unclothed

Figure 6: Attic red-figure cup by Oltos of *c.* 500 BCE. British Museum E8. Photo: courtesy of the Trustees of the British Museum.

male body. Dionysos is exceptional among gods in the extent to which he attracts images which cannot be related to myths. The Dionysiac entourage of satyrs and/or maenads attracts the attention of sixth-century vase painters in its own right, and from the early fifth century there are also scenes of activity around a mask-idol of Dionysos on a series of vases which scholars have associated with the festival of the Lenaea.[41] Whatever the relationship of these scenes to ritual activities familiar to Athenians, there is little doubt that maenads in some sense reflect the activities of Dionysiac devotees. Sexual relationships between gods and mortals in myth were one thing, sexual relationships between gods and mortals as part of the normal encounter with the god of any (female) worshipper were another. By the end of the sixth century at least, when there has been a change in iconography such that maenads have become an object of interest in their own right and the *thyrsos* has appeared as their regular attribute, the bodilessness of Dionysos has to be read as a strong denial of the god's sexuality and an affirmation that, for all that phalloi were paraded as part of Dionysiac cult activity, enjoying sex was not itself part of what it was to worship this god.[42] The emphasis on the clothing of Dionysos, which in the earliest representation of the god may simply mark him out from ordinary men, has to be seen by 500 BCE as a powerful symbol of his undoubted sexual power being kept under check, the visual equivalent of the marked lack of any mythological tradition of Dionysos as rapist. The universal concern to keep the unclothed body of Dionysos off the scene argues very strongly for the strong sexual overtones of the naked body of at least the mature bearded male.

Until the middle of the fifth century, therefore, the story of the unclothed male body is arguably the story of a conventional way of showing men becoming increasingly problematized because of the changing priorities of representational art. The unclothed male body, which in geometric art could find a place in scenes of all sorts, comes to carry with it a sexual charge which makes it good, sometimes scandalous, to think with in certain contexts, but which makes it impossible to employ in others. The long tradition of representative practice in which the unclothed male body dominated sculptural and graphic imagery can be seen to be threatened by the additional burden which the richness of reference to the particular achieved in early fifth-century art. This richness of reference forced a confrontation between artistic traditions and real-life practice. As we have seen in examining the representation of ligaturing, early fifth-century vase painters, painting largely for consenting adult males in private, exploited this confrontation to encourage critical thought about behavioural conventions. In public sculpture, however, that confrontation was arguably distinctly more problematic, for outside the contrived and controlled circumstances of the symposion it was harder to maintain the playful fantasy that displayed the unclothed body in carefully captured real-life contexts to which it was alien. What the fifth-century sculptor needed was a way of escaping from real life and its associations, a way of preventing the very richness of his allusions to the world from giving his creations an all too specific fantasy life.[43]

Around the middle of the fifth century there is a subtle but dramatic change in sculptural style which has been much discussed. The Riace Bronzes inhabit a different world from the classic male nude, Polykleitos' Doryphoros; the particularism and sensual bodily presence of the former is replaced in the latter by a focus on the shared and the typical. The sculptural convention of showing men without clothes has been rescued, and its sexual charge dissipated.

What is at issue in mid-fifth-century art is very well shown by continuing the story of the representation of Dionysos. From the third quarter of the fifth century, perhaps from the time of the Parthenon pediments (Figure 7), Dionysos is regularly shown without clothes in Athenian art in particular and in Greek art in general. But the removal of the clothes is not an isolated event, it goes together with the removal of the beard. The mature Dionysos, whose body is kept under wraps, is joined by a youthful Dionysos whose body is displayed (Figure 8).[44] Exhibiting the body of Dionysos, and exhibiting it in public sculpture, has become acceptable provided that that body is sexually immature.

What is true of Dionysos is also more generally true of males in sculpture. In the Parthenon sculptures all the bodies which are on display, whether on the pediments, in the metopes, or on the frieze, are the bodies

Figure 7: Figure of Dionysos from the East Pediment of the Parthenon, *c.* 435 BCE. British Museum 303. Photo: courtesy of the Trustees of the British Museum.

of the beardless. Bearded men appear on the frieze, both as occasional features of the cavalcade and among the officials and other personages at the east end, but they are all clothed or otherwise have their genitals obscured. The famous free-standing sculptures of male nudes of this period, such as Polykleitos' Doryphoros and Diadoumenos, are similarly always beardless. The men who appear in Attic grave reliefs obey the same rule: beardless men may be naked, the bearded are clothed.[45] So, when Lykeas and Khairedemos are shown as two hoplites on a grave stele of *c.* 400 BCE, the latter is beardless and naked, the former bearded and clothed (Figure 9).[46] This convention that bearded men are not shown naked in normal circumstances endures throughout the fourth century, and has its effect even on the imagery of so quintessentially mature a figure as Herakles. Although Herakles is still shown bearded and without clothes, a youthful Herakles type is developed, perhaps stimulated by a sculpture by Polykleitos, in which the hero is shown beardless. It is this type that prevails, for example, in Athenian decree reliefs where, once more, all naked male figures are beardless.[47] Though the convention of not showing bearded men naked was perhaps stronger at Athens than elsewhere, exceptions are rather thin on the ground.[48]

In vases the picture is more complicated, but something of the same pattern can be discerned. Bearded males without clothes continue to appear, but few such figures are of ordinary mortals. Satyrs remain bearded and naked, as do other 'monstrous' figures,[49] but gods (other than Dionysos)

Figure 8: Squat lekythos by the Makaria Painter, *c.* 400 BCE. British Museum E 703. Photo: courtesy of the Trustees of the British Museum.

Figure 9: Grave relief of Lykeas and Khairedemos, *c.* 400 BCE. Peiraieus Museum 385. Photo: Hirmer Fotoarchiv, Munich.

may also be shown bearded and without clothes, as in the scene of their combat against Giants on a cup by the painter Aristophanes.[50] There is certainly no hard and fast rule that bearded men are not represented naked on vases, but such representation is infrequent, and when it occurs it seems to be specially motivated—as, for example, in the bell krater by the Nikias painter showing the end of a torch race, where it seems to be important to indicate that the leader of the running team was not a youth.[51]

What has happened to the unclothed male body seems best explained by returning to early fifth-century *kouroi* and the Riace Bronzes. The same richness of sculptural reference which gives the Riace bronzes their unavoidable sexual charge also renders the Anaphe *kouros* (Figure 2) or Kritian Boy definitely boys, and it is in the genitals, above all, that that boyishness is signalled. Beardlessness is now not a denial of age, as it was in archaic *kouroi*, but an affirmation of youth, a sign of not having entered into the man's world and in particular of not having become sexually active. The distinction visible in the way vase-painters employ the ligaturing of the penis, where the athletes who use it are all beardless and tend to have a ligature which realistically shows the ends of the string, while the revellers (and satyrs) who use it are all bearded and no string is actually shown, foreshadows this differentiation between the sexuality of the beardless and of the bearded.

The emasculation of the beardless figure, which even allows a naked Dionysos to enjoy the company of women, should be seen as heavily conventional, not unrelated perhaps to literary claims that boys take no pleasure in being the passive partners in a homosexual relationship (as in Xenophon, *Symposion* 8.21). Although beardless figures include some who are in all respects shown as youthful, the beardless body is very often a sculptural construct, an idealization, distanced from the male body of life by its combination of beardless immaturity with distinctly mature musculature. The naked beardless men in fourth-century Athenian grave reliefs include men who in other respects are clearly physically in their prime. But the development of the convention helps to indicate the significance of the naked male body. Only in circumstances where there was a strong desire to maintain the central position of the naked male body in the representation of the human figure is the development of this artificial convention comprehensible. The convention enables the naked male body to be enjoyed in sculpture as it was enjoyed in life, on such occasions as the competition for manly beauty (*euandria*) at the Panathenaia.[52] The convention recovers the archaic artistic tradition that men need no clothes and makes it possible to continue it in a new world in which art's enriched reference to the situations of ordinary life had put it under threat.

Tracing the history of the unclothed male body in Greek art has shown how changing artistic practices meant that the representation of the naked male was no unchanging sign. An unclothed body in geometric and archaic art was a body gendered as male; once sexually explicit scenes, and figures and scenes with rich reference to the circumstances of daily life, developed, nakedness could no longer be a symbol simply of gender. After what may, in retrospect, be seen as something of a crisis of representation during the early years of the fifth century, when traditions of representing men naked were exploited as ways of exploring male sexuality, classical art developed a new convention which rescued the unclothed male body as an artistic standard by limiting its representation to youthful and 'sexually immature' males (or figures which belong outside the purely human world).

This history shows that there is justification neither for claims that in respect to nakedness art merely imitated life nor for claims that nakedness heroizes. To show a male figure without clothes was certainly to invoke the beautiful body of the young athlete and to claim the athletic body as the model of all it was to be a man. The artificiality of the claim that the beard-less body could be asexual was soon exposed by vase painters who from time to time put young men's sexual activity defiantly on display.[53] And sculptors who adhered to the convention came themselves to make clear that the conventional asexuality of the unclothed beardless youth offered the male body for display only at the price of questioning his masculinity.[54] That such awareness of the fragility of the convention did not destroy that convention is evidence of the fundamental role which it played in estab-lishing and maintaining a distance between art and life such as to ensure that the discourse about life which art maintained was kept distant from the sordid particulars of specific lives.

Any means of establishing a distance from the grubby reality of daily life will have its political uses. The transformation of Athenian imagery and iconography in the middle of the fifth century was a political as well as an artistic act; the Roman emperor Augustus and later autocratic rulers have known what they were doing when they have encouraged the re-adoption of classical imagery and its conventions. The activities of snooping photo-graphers attract little praise from the royals whose images they capture, but the distancing from the sordid particulars of daily life which the image of the naked beardless male still has the power to effect is one that royalty should surely welcome.

Notes

1. Quoted by Adam Phillips, *London Review of Books* (4 January 1996), p. 6. I am grateful to Simon Goldhill for drawing my attention to this passage and to him, John Boardman, Jas Elsner, Bert Smith, Nigel Spivey and Maria Wyke for comments on an earlier draft.

2. Denis Diderot, *Sur l'art et les artistes* (Paris, 1967), p. 37; tr. by Francette Pacteau, *The Symptom of Beauty* (Reaktion, London, 1994), p. 21.

3. Kenneth Clark, *The Nude: A Study of Ideal Art* (John Murray, London, 1956), p. 37.

4. Robert Mapplethorpe, *Lady: Lisa Lyon by Robert Mapplethorpe*, text by Bruce Chatwin (Viking, New York, 1983); see Susan Butler, 'Revising Femininity', in *Looking*

on: *Images of Femininity in the Visual Arts and Media*, ed. Rosemary Betterton (Pandora, London, 1987), pp. 120–6, and Lynda Nead, *The Female Nude: Art, Obscenity and Sexuality* (Routledge, London, 1992), pp. 8–9.

5. The most subtle and sophisticated exposition of this position is N. Himmelmann, *Ideale Nacktheit in der griechischen Kunst* (De Gruyter, Berlin and New York, 1990). This work contains many pertinent observations but nevertheless seems to me to beg the question on the fundamental issue. See the review by T. Hölscher in *Gnomon*, 65 (1993), pp. 519–28. In particular Himmelmann's omission of the sexualized body, which Hölscher (p. 528) notes, is what I here try to make good.

6. B. S. Ridgway, *Fifth-century Styles in Greek Sculpture* (Princeton University Press, Princeton, NJ, 1981), pp. 90–1 (my emphasis).

7. N. Spivey, *Understanding Greek Sculpture* (Thames & Hudson, London, 1996), pp. 112–13.

8. Andrew Stewart, *Greek Sculpture: An Exploration* (Yale University Press, New Haven, CT, 1990), pp. 79, 106.

9. John Boardman, *Greek Sculpture, the Classical Period* (Thames & Hudson, London, 1985), pp. 239, 238 (original emphasis).

10. Christoph Clairmont, *Classical Attic Tombstones* (Akanthus, Kilchberg, 1993), vol. 1, pp. 145–6.

11. J. J. Winckelmann, 'On the Imitation of the Painting and Sculpture of the Greeks' (1755), tr. H. Fuseli, quoted from David Irwin, *Winckelmann: Writings on Art* (Phaidon, London, 1967), pp. 61–8. See Himmelmann, *Ideale Nacktheit*, pp. 1–28 for a full history of the development of views on male nakedness in Greek art.

12. Martin Robertson, *A History of Greek Art* (Cambridge University Press, Cambridge, 1975), pp. 94, 311.

13. Stewart, *Greek Sculpture*, p. 106.

14. See Mary Beard, 'Adopting an Approach II', in *Looking at Greek Vases*, ed. Tom Rasmussen and Nigel Spivey (Cambridge University Press, Cambridge, 1991), pp. 12–35 and Robin Osborne, 'Whose Image and Superscription Is This?', *Arion*, n.s. 1 (1991), pp. 255–75.

15. Thucydides 1.6.5 is the classic text, and M. McDonnell, 'The Introduction of Athletic Nudity: Thucydides, Plato, and the Vases', *Journal of Hellenic Studies*, 111 (1991), pp. 182–92 the most recent discussion.

16. *Clouds* 961–89; cf. also *Birds* 137–42.

17. *Wasps* 577–8.

18. On Winckelmann see Alex Potts, *Flesh and the Ideal: Winckelmann and the Origins of Art History* (Yale University Press, New Haven, CT, 1994). Recently note e.g. Catherine Johns's paean on Greek sexual liberation in *Sex or Symbol? Erotic Images of Greece and Rome* (University of Texas Press, Austin, 1982), or K. J. Dover's unshockable Greeks in *Greek Homosexuality* (Duckworth, London, 1978).

19. This is a traditional crux since by *Odyssey* 22.488 Odysseus has his rags on again.

20. *Odyssey* 6.127–246.

21. Tamsey Andrews talks of 'ceremonial nudity' when discussing the youth with a ram in the Sackler Museum, Harvard (Catalogue no. 1970.26), and Susan Langdon talks of 'different kinds of nudity' and of the 'apotropaic' nudity of the heroic warrior when discussing a helmeted warrior figure in the Menil Collection, both in *From Pasture to Polis: Art in the Age of Homer*, ed. S. Langdon (University of Missouri Press, Columbia, MO, 1993), at pp. 149 and 196.

22. I am not persuaded by Himmelmann (*Ideale Nacktheit*, p. 32) that male nudity carries aristocratic connotations in geometric art.

23. Compare L. Bonfante, 'Nudity as Costume in Classical Art', *American Journal of Archaeology*, 93 (1989), pp. 543–70 (at p. 549).

24. This is so both on the Protoattic amphora from Eleusis (Eleusis Museum) and on the Aristonothos krater from Cervetri (Museo dei Conservatori, Rome), which was perhaps made in the Greek west.

25. C. Sourvinou-Inwood, *'Reading' Greek Death* (Oxford University Press, Oxford, 1995), pp. 227–70.

26. Moskhophoros: Athens Akropolis Museum 624; Dionysermos: Louvre MA3600.

27. G. M. A. Richter, *The Archaic Gravestones of Attica* (Phaidon, London, 1962).

28. Both the pots and the grave reliefs show how untrue for the sixth century is the claim made by Spivey, *Understanding Greek Sculpture*, p. 113 that nudity is heroized by association, for in both media many who are demonstrably not heroes are naked, just as in both pots and architectural sculpture many who are heroes are clothed.

29. On the self-reflexive world of the art of the symposion see F. Lissarrague, *The Aesthetics of the Greek Banquet* (Princeton University Press, Princeton, NJ, 1990).

30. E. Gombrich, *Art and Illusion: A Study in the Psychology of Pictorial Representation* (Phaidon, London, 1960), ch. 4.

31. See O. Taplin, *Greek Fire* (Cape, London, 1989), pp. 87–9. I discuss this further in 'Sculpted Men of Athens: Masculinity and Power in the Field of Vision', in *Thinking Men: Masculinity and its Self-representation in the Classical Tradition*, ed. Lin Foxhall and John Salmon (Routledge, London, 1998).

32. Thucydides 6.54.

33. J. Boardman, *Athenian Black Figure Vases* (Thames & Hudson, London, 1974), pp. 112, 211.

34. W. Sweet, 'Protection of the Genitals in Greek Athletics', *Ancient World*, 11 (1985), pp. 43–52; E. J. Dingwall, *Male Infibulation* (John Bale, Sons and Davidson Ltd, London,1925). Dingwall's fascinating book insists, mistakenly in my view, on refusing to identify the ligature with the *kunodesme* referred to in some ancient sources, and on distinguishing between those representations in which some form of tie is clearly shown and those in which the penis is curled up without a tie. He achieves this by not sufficiently acknowledging the overlap between the types of males shown in his two classes, and as a result denies a connection with male modesty for either of his classes, preferring views about ligaturing preventing powers leaking, which are based on a Japanese parallel, and the curled penis being a sign of pederasty, sexual excess and moral degradation. I hope to discuss Dingwall and ligaturing at greater length elsewhere.

35. See F. Lissarrague, 'The Sexual Life of Satyrs', in *Before Sexuality*, ed. D. Halperin, J. Winkler and F. Zeitlin (Princeton University Press, Princeton, NJ, 1990), pp. 53–82, at pp. 58–60, to which I am much indebted for what follows.

36. M. Foucault, *The History of Sexuality* vol. 2: *The Use of Pleasure* (Penguin Books, Harmondsworth, 1985), pp. 119–20, citing Plato, *Laws* 840a.

37. BM E768 (J. D. Beazley, *Attic Red-Figure Vases*, 2nd edn (Oxford University Press, Oxford, 1963; [hereafter *ARV²*]), p. 446, no. 262); Berlin 2289 (*ARV²*, p. 435, no. 95).

38. The relevance of Dionysos to discussions of male nudity is brought out by Himmelmann, *Ideale Nacktheit*, pp. 27, 46–7. I know of only one image of Dionysos dating from before the middle of the fifth century BCE in which the god appears naked: the Dionysos on the silver coinage of Serdaioi in southern Italy. My discussion of

Dionysos is heavily indebted to the article by C. Gasparri, in *Lexicon Iconographicum Mythologiae Classicae* (Artemis Verlag, Zurich and Munich, 1981–), vol. 3.1, pp. 414–514. The Serdaioi coin is no. 76 in Gasparri's catalogue. On Dionysos in sixth-century art see T. H. Carpenter, *Dionysian Imagery in Archaic Greek Art: Its Development in Black-Figure Vase Painting* (Oxford University Press, Oxford, 1986).

39. See Michael Jameson, 'The Asexuality of Dionysus', in *Masks of Dionysus*, ed. Thomas Carpenter and Christopher Faraone (Cornell University Press, Ithaca, NY, 1993), pp. 44–64, esp. pp. 47–53.

40. See Gasparri catalogue no. 620 (for thyrsos-spear and naked opponent) and no. 609. Dionysos himself appears naked in such combats only from the end of the fifth century (see Gasparri no. 630 by the Jena Painter).

41. I discuss these further in 'The Ecstasy and the Tragedy: Varieties of Religious Experience in Art, Drama and Society', in *Tragedy and the Historian*, ed. Christopher Pelling (Oxford University Press, Oxford, 1997), pp. 187–211. On the 'Lenaean' vases see also F. Frontisi-Ducroux, *Le dieu-masque: une figure du Dionysos d'Athènes*, (Flammarion, Paris, 1991).

42. Arguably an exactly parallel phenomenon with regard to wine is visible in the 'Lenaean' vases. There maenads ladle wine from large pots and carry it round in various forms of cup, but they are never seen to drink, and, given the taboos on women drinking wine, can reasonably be assumed not to drink. Just as only making Dionysos bodiless could remove assumptions of sexual activity from rituals involving manipulations of male genitalia, so only putting the vessels into the hands of women could remove assumptions of inebriation from rituals involving manipulations of wine.

43. The voyeurism of the kinds of sexual narratives which these naturalistic statues elicit is also, of course, on display in the art of those who from Michelangelo to Mapplethorpe have turned to the Greek model to justify a more or less explicitly homoerotic art.

44. For a very rare example, from this same period, of a bearded Dionysos whose genitals are not concealed see ARV^2, p. 632, no. 3, printed as Figure 4 in Jameson, 'The Asexuality of Dionysus'.

45. Of three exceptions to this rule that I know, one (Clairmont, *Classical Attic Tombstones*, vol. 1, no. 100 [Athens National Museum 2004]) involves one Agakles, a bearded man shown as an athlete—a pankratiast—who has occupational reasons for being unclothed; the second (Clairmont, vol. 2, no. 192 [New York Metropolitan Museum 40.11.23]) involves the naked victim of a warrior, where the nakedness seems to be a mark of the man's weakness and helplessness; and only the third (Clairmont, vol. 2, no. 957 [Budapest Museum of Fine Arts 6259]) seems clearly problematic. In this last relief a bearded naked man, with cloak over his shoulder, stands beside a clothed woman. It is possible that this man too was intended as an athlete, since signs that he wore a crown have been detected (Clairmont, vol. 2 p. 829). But it should also be noted that the piece may not be Attic: Clairmont regards the suggestion, on quite different grounds, that it is Boiotian as being 'not without its merits' (p. 828). Naked bearded men certainly appear on Boiotian monuments: cf. the stele of Rhynkhon, W. Schild-Xenidou, *Boötische Grab- und Weihreliefs archaischer und klassischer Zeit* (Schön, Munich, 1972), no. 44.

46. Peiraieus 385, Clairmont, *Classical Attic Tombstones*, vol. 2, no. 156. Clairmont (vol. 2, p. 106) remarks: 'Hölscher has rightly pointed out that in the case of Chairedemos one should not speak in terms of heroic nakedness, Lykeas having as much reason as his companion to be depicted naked but he actually wears clothing.' In fact what

T. Hölscher says ('Ein Kelchkrater mit Perserkampf', *Antike Kunst*, 17 [1974], pp. 78–85 at p. 81, n. 32) is 'Take the grave relief of Khairedemos and Lykeas from Salamis, which has been explicitly cited as evidence of the heroizing meaning of nakedness ... both stand by one another with shield and spear, one is clothed and the other is naked. Obviously they are also of the same status: the naked man is not because of his nakedness raised to some fundamentally different world from the clothed man' (my translation). That Hölscher is correct does not entail that there is *no* reason why Lykeas is clothed.

47. For Herakles in Athenian decree reliefs see Carol Lawton, *Attic Document Reliefs* (Oxford University Press, Oxford, 1995), nos. 72, 82, 85, 133, 157 and 158. The young Theseus appears naked in no. 187 (a rather later example) and some other hero in no. 148. See also O. Palagia in *Lexicon Iconographicum Mythologiae Classicae*, vol. 4.1, pp. 747–8, nos. 326–30 on the beardless Herakles of these reliefs, and p. 758 for the possible role of a Herakles by Polykleitos in popularizing the beardless type.

48. It is a peculiarity of the frieze from the Mausoleion that there bearded hoplites *are* shown naked.

49. So Theseus' opponents are all bearded on the cups by the Kodros painter and by Aison *ARV²*, p. 1269, no. 4, p. 1174, no. 1.

50. *ARV²*, p. 1318, no. 1.

51. *ARV²*, p. 1333, no. 1.

52. See N. Crowther, 'Male Beauty Contests in Greece: the *euandria* and the *euexia*', *Antiquité Classique*, 54 (1985), pp. 285–91. N. Spivey, *Understanding Greek Sculpture*, pp. 36–7 suggests that there was a pederastic element to the appreciation of the male body in the *euandria* competition, but it is clear that more was at stake in the competition than sexual attraction.

53. As on a wine jug by the Shuvalov Painter, Berlin 2412 (*ARV²*, p. 1208, no. 41).

54. As in Praxiteles' Apollo Sauroktonos or Lysippos' 'Farnese' Herakles. I explore this theme at greater length in 'Sculpted Men of Athens'.

Women's Costume and Feminine Civic Morality in Augustan Rome

JUDITH LYNN SEBESTA

> Augustus was eager to revive the traditional dress of the Romans. One day in the Forum he saw a group of citizens dressed in dark garments and exclaimed indignantly, 'Behold the masters of the world, the toga-clad race!' He thereupon instructed the aediles that no Roman citizen was to enter the Forum, or even be in its vicinity, unless he were properly clad in a toga.[1]

In the terms of Augustan ideology, the avoidance of Roman dress by Romans was another sign of their abandoning the traditional Roman way of life, character and values in preference for the high culture, pomp, and moral and philosophical relativism of the Hellenistic East. This acculturation of foreign ways was frequently claimed to have brought Republican Rome to the edge of destruction in both the public and private spheres.[2] Roman authors of the late first century BCE depict women in particular as devoted to their own selfish pleasure, marrying and divorcing at will, and preferring childlessness and abortion to raising a family. Such women were regarded as having abandoned their traditional role of *custos domi* ('preserver of the house/hold'), a role that correlated a wife's body and her husband's household. A Roman wife was expected to maintain her body's inviolability and to preserve her husband's possessions, while increasing his family by bearing children and enriching his wealth through her labors.[3]

The mindful care of the ideal wife was epitomized in the legendary story of the chaste Lucretia, who became an important symbol of wifehood in Augustan literature. In recounting the events that led to the fall of the last king of Rome, the Augustan historian Livy relates how Lucretia's husband and his friends amused themselves during a tedious siege of a nearby city by boasting about the virtues of their wives. To settle the contention, they made an unexpected journey home and discovered that all the wives, save Lucretia, were attending dinner parties. Only Lucretia was found at home, weaving cloth for her husband.[4] Though by the late Republic upper-class women may have mostly abandoned this traditional occupation of Roman wives, according to the biographer Suetonius Augustus none the less regarded it as a still potent symbol of a wife's virtue and devotion to her husband's

Figure 1: Altar of Augustan Peace, Rome. Relief of Tellus. Photo: J. Sebesta.

household, and required his wife, Livia, to weave his garments in order to set an example for other Roman wives.[5]

Two important aspects of Augustus' program to reform public and private morality involved legislation and public 'propaganda'. Augustus instituted legislation concerning the proper exercise of female sexuality. These laws prevented unmarried persons from receiving inheritances and legacies and rewarded freeborn women who had three or more children by removing them from statutory guardianship. An essential part of his program of cultural and moral renewal was the creation of a 'new pictorial language' that gave the Romans a new image of themselves as heirs of the traditional Roman morality that had gained them an empire.[6]

Within this pictorial language, depictions of female subjects were used as 'moral signs' of civic morality and health.[7] Such female subjects included deities or personifications of fertility and regeneration.[8] On the quintessential Augustan monument, the Altar of Augustan Peace, the healthy state (*Tellus*) that Augustus presented himself as restoring is depicted as a full-breasted woman who caresses twin babies and holds on her lap various fruits and cereals, symbols not only of the regeneration that accompanies peace, but of the additional children she will yet bear[9] (Figure 1). In the panel accompanying this scene is another female figure (Roma) who represents civic morality. Depicted as an Amazon, armed with helmet, shield, sword and spear, Roma sits enthroned, with one breast exposed, on a pile of weapons captured from the enemy. As Eve D'Ambra notes, 'No doubt, she serves as an appropriate defender of the honor of the city and empire because she is chaste and pure. The body of Roma, replete with bronze armor, repels advances, both sexual and military ...'[10] An image of a mortal woman serving as dual sign of civic health and morality adorned the frieze of another Augustan monument, the Basilica Aemilia. Here, in the Forum, the civic heart of Rome, the image of the legendary Tarpeia connects the destruction of Rome with the wrong use of female sexuality. According to Livy, in his account of the reign of the first king of Rome, Romulus, the Sabines were nearly successful in their siege of Rome due to the treason of Tarpeia, daughter of the commander of Rome's citadel. Whether she was seduced by love of the Sabine commander or by greed for Sabine gold with which to adorn her body and make herself more desirable—Roman authors differ as to her motivation—she let the Sabines into the citadel. The relief depicts her fate: as each Sabine soldier passed by, he threw his shield upon her. Tarpeia is shown half-covered by the shields, arms spread wide in a fruitless gesture for mercy.[11] All three of these reliefs (Tellus, Roma and Tarpeia) show how the female body was troped as the body politic in Augustan pictorial language: a woman who is a *custos* (preserver/defender) of her chastity is configured as a defender of the state's health and survival and a provider of future citizens, while a woman who yields her body to lust (whether of sex or luxury) betrays the state to its destruction.

Another important part of the Augustan pictorial language was the establishment of distinctive 'Roman' costume. Since Augustan ideology viewed public peace and social stability as particularly 'dependent on the proper conduct of women in domestic life and the encouragement of productive sexuality',[12] Augustus not only made the toga once again the national costume of Roman men, but also re-established the distinctive costume for their wives: the white *stola,* which they wore over their tunic, and the woollen bands (*vittae*), with which they bound their hair. Thus in the friezes of the Altar of the Augustan Peace, members of Augustus' family, proudly wearing toga and *stola,* pose as models of the traditional Roman family that Augustus wanted to reinstate in place of the sexual immorality that was thought to have conduced to the collapse of the Roman Republic[13] (Figure 2). Just as the toga signified the Roman male in his civic role as 'master of the world', so the woman's costume signified her in her private role as protector (*custos*) of her body, its sexuality and her husband's house/hold.

In re-establishing what he thought was traditional Roman costume, Augustus was undoubtedly influenced by the research of such antiquarian scholars as Varro (116–27 BCE) and Verrius Flaccus (deceased BCE 4), tutor to Augustus' own grandsons.[14] They shared their contemporaries' view that Romans were abandoning the traditional Roman way of life, and this sense of a lost or disappearing past spurred their interest in collecting and investigating what information they could find on 'antique' Rome. These antiquarian authors treat the subject of costume neither comprehensively nor

Figure 2: Altar of Augustan Peace, Rome. Members of the family of Augustus. The girl (third figure from the right) wears a *toga praetexta*, as do the two younger boys. Photo: J. Sebesta.

systematically. Rather, their attention is caught by interesting etymologies or explanations of costume items.

As the antiquarian accounts of early Republican costume suggest, the protection of a woman's sexuality began in childhood. Children of both sexes wore the *toga praetexta*. This toga had a border of purple (*praetexta*) that indicated its wearer was in an 'inviolable' state. The *praetexta*, for example, adorned the togas of magistrates who presided over sacrifices as one of the duties of their offices and the toga worn by the mourning son who conducted his parent's funeral, and it bordered the veils of the Vestal Virgins. The *praetexta* on a garment, therefore, signified prohibition and precaution; the wearer was inviolable (*sacer*), and those nearby were not to pollute his/her inviolability by word or deed, particularly not by sexual language, acts, or gestures.

That the purple border on the child's toga also signified inviolability to the Romans is indicated by the words of the orator Quintilian: 'I swear to you upon that sacred *praetexta*—by which we make sacred and venerable the weakness of childhood.'[15] Verrius Flaccus, moreover, defines 'praetextate speech' as speech devoid of ill-boding words that would harm a child if uttered in its presence.[16] The *toga praetexta*, therefore, indicated that the child was to be treated with respect, especially in reference to actions or speech that concerned sexuality. Cicero plays on this reverence owed the child in its sexual immaturity when he cites, in the climax of his denunciation of the debauchery of Apronius, the fact that at a banquet Apronius danced naked before a boy clothed in a *toga praetexta*.[17]

On the processional panel of the Altar of Augustan Peace, the artists depicted the grandchildren of Augustus prominently in the foreground. These grandchildren correspond to the theme of 'the blessings of children' represented elsewhere on the altar by the twin babies whom Tellus fondles on her lap. Clad in their *togae praetextae* on this important public monument, Augustus' grandchildren also serve as exempla of the respect that individuals and society owe to children (Figure 2).

Though the child's costume represented sexual inviolability for both sexes, the costumes worn by youth and maiden in the rite of transition to adult status were partly the same and partly different, reflecting their ambiguous state of transition to their divergent adult roles. Both youth and maiden wore the *tunica recta*. It was called *recta* ('upright') because ritual required that it be woven on the upright loom, the earliest loom used by the Romans.[18] This tunic may have had purple bands that, like the child's *praetexta*, indicated sexual inviolability.[19]

The divergence in costume concerned the treatment of the head and its hair. Puberty is a significant watershed in the course of life because it is the 'time when gender meanings become inscribed in bodily practices'.[20] Molly Myerowitz Levine comments:

> As a signifier, hair operates both metonymically and metaphorically. In its metonymic mode hair stands for the 'whole person'. As such, hair is useful for rituals implying movement and exchange, passage and negotiation, changes in status … Hair serves as both metonym and metaphor particularly in the case of adolescent rites of passage. These transformations, which are enacted as ritual death by the metonymic cutting of hair, enable the adolescent's rebirth into a higher cultural order.[21]

Through mapping mature sexuality on to the head and its hair, the Romans transformed these into a metonym for the sexual maturation of the genitals, which is marked in both sexes by the growth of pubic hair and, in the case of the male, also by the appearance of facial hair. As Carol Delaney explains, 'The genitals are clearly the site of gender; but since they must be hidden, their meanings are displaced to the head, where they can be publicly displayed … As different meanings are attributed to the genitals of each gender, so too are the heads of men and women treated differently.'[22] Thus, argues Levine, hair should be seen not solely as a *locus eroticus*, but as a 'locus for the statement of social attitudes regarding the proper or desired relationship between nature and culture'.[23] The Roman puberty rituals involving the youth's beard and the maiden's hair were complementary actions which youth and maiden performed upon themselves to signify their readiness to assume the adult roles in society that sexual maturation brought.

When the youth shaved his beard and dedicated it to the household gods, he performed an act of separation that connected his sexual maturation with his role as mature male, the role of citizen-soldier: he signified his willingness to separate himself from the social body through death in battle.[24] Significantly, after this transition from childhood to adulthood, the youth began his military service. As a symbol of his willingness and capability to defend the state as its warrior, the youth assumed the plain white toga of manhood (*toga virilis*) and was enrolled in the census list.[25] From this time on, if he so chose, a man could indulge himself sexually outside the bounds of marriage (provided he did not do so with the children and wives of his fellow citizens).

While the ritual of assuming the *toga virilis* continued to be an important ritual in the late Republic, Augustus took steps to link the donning of this garment more closely to the young man's responsibility to the state. According to his biographer, Suetonius, he encouraged sons of senators to gain early familiarity with public affairs immediately after they assumed the *toga virilis* and required them to gain experience as officers both in infantry and cavalry units. [26]

Once a young man gained the right to wear the *toga virilis*, he would doff it only when assuming special, temporary civic or social duties, such as when a magistrate, an officer of a military unit, or a mourner at the funeral of a family member. Even in such situations he simply wore a different kind of toga.[27] The costume of the adult male citizen, therefore, varied not according to his age or marital status, but according to his civil status, that is, as a 'private' citizen (one holding no elective or religious office), an elected official, or chief mourner. On the Altar of Augustan Peace, the adult males of Augustus' family are depicted wearing either military cloaks to signify that they were currently serving as officers or the *toga virilis* to signify their participation in state affairs[28] (Figure 2).

The transition of the maiden (*virgo*) to her adult status was through marriage. Verrius Flaccus seems to have done much research on the symbolism of bridal costume, which indicates that this was a topic of great interest to Augustan ideology. His research ties the symbolism of the bridal costume to the important concepts of Augustan ideology that concern women and their fertility within marriage.

On the evening before her marriage, the maiden confined her hair with the yellow hairnet she had woven. The confinement of her hair was an act of association that signified the binding and confining of her mature sexuality first to pre-marital chastity, and then, after marriage, to her husband.[29] As she was required to weave both the *tunica recta* and her hairnet (*reticulum*), her production of these garments indicated that she had mastered the skill most emblematic of her adult role as *custos domi*.[30]

These two garments, moreover, covered her head and her body, which therefore became loci of her sexuality. Before she even took on the role, through marriage, of *custos domi*, she proved herself as the *custos* of her chastity which she 'protected' through the garments she had woven. Her future costume changes, as bride, *matrona* ('married woman') and *materfamilias* ('mother of the extended family'), also involved distinctive garments for her head and body, mapping chastity on to each of these two loci.

Through the rite of marriage, the young woman transferred her sexuality to her husband and his family line. On her wedding day she tied her *tunica recta* with the bridal belt. This belt (*cingulum*) was made from the wool of a ewe (symbolizing fertility) and 'tied' to her not only her fertility, but also her role of wool worker. The belt was knotted with the *nodus Herculaneus* ('knot of Hercules'), which Romans considered difficult to untie. Verrius Flaccus states that this knot was used because it too signified fertility, for Hercules had fathered seventy children.[31] Moreover, Verrius Flaccus adds, the belt itself was to be untied only by the bride's husband in their wedding bed. Verrius Flaccus explains that just as the wool was carded into long strands and spun together, so her husband should be bound and tied with her. Given that the knot was so difficult to untie, the bridal belt signified not only that the bride's chastity was tied to her husband, but that it was indissolubly tied—no other man should, through adultery, 'untie' the belt.

The second locus of the bride's sexuality, her head, was dressed in a special hairstyle and covered by the bridal veil. The bridal hairstyle (*seni crines*, 'six tresses') was, according to Verrius Flaccus, 'the most ancient hairstyle … which commits brides' chastity to their husbands'.[32] Over her hair the bride wore the special bridal mantle (*flammeum*).[33] The importance of veiling the bride is indicated by the etymology of the Latin verb *nubere* ('to veil herself' = 'to be married') that was used only of women. In preparation for the wedding ceremony, the bride completely veiled her hair. At the conclusion of the marriage ceremony, she was uncovered by her husband, an act that symbolized the surrender of her virginity to him.[34]

The clothing of the married woman (*matrona*) visually represented her chastity and marked her as a woman to whom respect ought to be shown.[35] Both loci of sexuality—head and body—had to be covered completely by her garments. The *matrona* bound her hair with fillets (*vittae*) made of long rolls of carded wool that were tied at intervals to form 'beads'.[36] Such fillets also adorned anything that was religiously pure to warn of its inviolability: sacrificial animals, sacred trees, altars, columns and so on. Like the hairnet of the maiden, these fillets expressed the binding (reservation) of the *matrona*'s sexuality to her husband and indicated her inviolability. When out in public, the *matrona* wore the *palla*, a large rectangular mantle that she draped over her head and wrapped around her body. That this veiling of her head and body out of doors was an important act is shown by an anecdote concerning Sulpicius Gallus, consul in 166 BCE, which is related by Valerius Maximus, a historian who dedicated his work to Augustus' adopted son and successor, Tiberius. When his wife left his house one day unveiled, Gallus divorced her, stating: 'By law, only my eyes should see you … That you should be seen by other eyes … links you to suspicion and guilt.' By unveiling her head and body, his wife had in essence removed herself from the category of married women, and his divorce recognized and legally ratified her self-exclusion.[37]

The *matrona* covered her body—her second locus of sexuality—with the *stola*, a long, strapped dress resembling a modern full-length slip, which covered her feet.[38] The garment is clearly depicted on the official statues of Augustus' wife, Livia (Figure 3). The *stola* was often called simply 'the long

Figure 3: Livia, wife of Augustus. She wears a *stola* and fillets in her hair and has her *palla* pulled up over her head. National Museum, Naples, Inv. 6041. Inst. Neg. Rom. 76.1157

dress', and its length protected the lower legs and feet of its wearer from the gaze of others.[39] There was a similar taboo that forbade the priestess called the *flaminica Dialis*, the 'archetypal *matrona*', to allow others to view her lower legs and feet. This priestess was specifically forbidden to climb higher than three steps of any staircase or ladder that had no risers to block the view of her limbs.[40] To see a woman's ankles and feet uncovered was essentially equivalent to seeing her 'naked', a right reserved only to her husband. Thus, as Paul Zanker points out, 'In the context of the (Augustan) social legislation the *stola* became a symbol of female virtue and modesty'.[41]

These costume items (*stola, palla, vittae*) are prominently worn by the women of Augustus' family on the Altar of Augustan Peace (Figure 2). The folds of the long *stola* flow over their feet, and the *palla* is pulled over their heads. Although one figure, identified as Antonia minor, has let her *palla* slip from her head, none the less she has wrapped it tightly around her body in the way that art historians call the *pudicitia* ('modesty') pose and displays the *vittae* binding her hair. Her dedication to chastity is further indicated by her pose: she turns her head towards her husband Drusus and gazes deep into his eyes.[42]

A woman became a *materfamilias* when her husband became a *paterfamilias*, that is, when upon the death of his own father, he assumed the 'power of a father' (*patria potestas*) over his own descendants. Though a *paterfamilias* assumed no special costume, a *materfamilias* adopted a new hairstyle, the *tutulus*. The *tutulus* was formed by twisting locks of hair around the top of the head to form a high chignon and then fastening them in place with fillets.[43] In his discussion of this traditional hairstyle, the Augustan antiquarian Varro offers an etymology for *tutulus* that connects the woman's head and hair, a locus for feminine fertility, with the citadel, the locus for the protection of the state. He suggests that *tutulus* derives either from *tueri* ('to protect') or *tutissimum* ('most protected') for, he argues, either the head must be protected for the sake of its hair or because the highest part of the city, the citadel, was the most protected.[44] In linking the hair of the *materfamilias* to the citadel, Varro reiterates the trope (discussed above with regard to Augustan pictorial language) of the female body as a moral sign of civic morality and health: the *tutulus* is etymologized as the protector (*custos*) of the woman's hair, itself a trope for feminine sexuality, just as the citadel is the protector of Rome.

In the preface to his comprehensive *History of Rome*, written just after Augustus became sole ruler, Livy expressed the hope that his contemporaries would profit from the instructive instances of courage, patriotism and morality that they were about to read in his account of the regal and Republican periods of Rome. Drawing upon the past idealized both in the pages of Livy and in the researches of antiquarians such as Verrius Flaccus and Varro, Augustan ideology used visual imagery of both art and costume and revived Republican symbolism in its cultural program to restore a sense of the morality and honor of the Roman people.

Integral to this Augustan program was the restoration and honoring of the traditional role and qualities of the Roman woman and her family and household. Augustan ideology expected a proper Roman wife to prove herself a good *custos domi*. Devoting the fertility of her body to her husband and her labors to his household, she was to waste neither the 'wealth' of her fertility nor her energies. The ideal *matrona* or *materfamilias* was expected to find fulfillment in her children, deriving from them, as the roots of *matrona* and *materfamilias* show, honor during her lifetime and praise on her tombstone after her death. Her assiduous devotion to her husband's home was configured as the task of weaving, which also served as a metaphor for her preoccupation with the material prosperity of her husband's household. Lastly, her role of *custos domi* also encompassed the ideal of inviolable matronal chastity. She was to be as fertile as Tellus, industrious as Lucretia, impregnable as Roma. If, in Augustus' words, the 'toga-clad race' were the 'masters of the world', their wives, dressed in the *stola*, were the guardians of Rome itself.

Notes

1. Suetonius, *Life of Augustus* 40.5 (my translation). See also P. Zanker, *The Power of Images in the Age of Augustus*, tr. A. Shapiro (University of Michigan Press, Ann Arbor, 1988), p. 163. The Roman toga was a white garment.

2. See Zanker, *The Power of Images*, pp. 1–2.

3. See T. Pearce, 'The Role of the Wife as *Custos* in Ancient Rome', *Eranos*, 12 (1974), pp. 16–23.

4. Livy, *History of Rome* 1.57.

5. Suetonius, *Augustus* 73. Women's epitaphs of the late Republican period often contain the eulogy 'She kept the house. She worked her wool.'

6. Zanker, *The Power of Images*, pp. 162–6.

7. N. Kampen, 'Reliefs of the Basilica Aemilia', *Klio*, 73 (1991), p. 454.

8. Eve D'Ambra, *Private Lives, Imperial Virtues: The Frieze of the Forum Transitorium in Rome* (Princeton University Press, Princeton, NJ, 1993), p. 88.

9. This matronly figure incorporates the iconography of other Augustan symbols, viz. Peace (Pax), Venus, the goddess who dispenses fertility, and Ceres, the goddess of grain and fruits. Thus, this matronly figure 'deliberately combines various tokens of blessing and happiness', according to Zanker, *The Power of Images*, p. 175.

10. D'Ambra, *Private Lives*, p. 89. The iconography of Roma also owes something to that of the goddess Athena, the virginal defender of Athens, who was frequently depicted with helmet, spear and armor.

11. Kampen, 'Reliefs of the Basilica Aemilia', pp. 451–2. On the trope of the female-body-as-state, see Patricia K. Joplin, 'Ritual Work on Human Flesh: Livy's Lucretia and the Rape of the Body Politic', *Helios*, 17.1 (1990), pp. 51–70.

12. D'Ambra, *Private Lives*, pp. 89–90.

13. Zanker, *The Power of Images*, pp. 156–9.

14. Verrius Flaccus' work survives in an epitome made by Festus, grammarian of the second century CE.

15. Quintilian, *Education of an Orator* 340.

16. Festus 282, 283L. Persius, in *Satires* 5.30–1, calls the *praetexta* of his child's toga the guardian (*custos*) of his childhood.

17. Cicero, *Verrine* 3.23, cited by Julia Heskel in 'Cicero as Evidence for Attitudes to Dress in the Late Republic', in *The World of Roman Costume*, ed. Judith Sebesta and Larissa Bonfante (University of Wisconsin Press, Madison, 1994), p. 139.

18. Festus 342L, 343L: 'Manly garments are called "*recta*" that fathers take care to have made for their sons for the sake of good omen. They are called "*recta*" because they are woven by women who stand and weave at the top of the loom.' The warp hung from the upper beam of the loom and was kept taut by weights attached to the bottom of each warp thread. The weaver stood before the loom weaving down from the top beam. Romans began to use the vertical two-beamed loom in the first century CE, and by the end of the second century CE the traditional warp-weighted loom had largely disappeared from use in Italy. See J. P. Wild, *Textile Manufacture in the Northern Roman Provinces* (Cambridge University Press, Cambridge, 1970), p. 63.

19. Festus quoted in Nonius Marcellus 864L, states that the *tunica recta* was also *regilla*. T. Tucker, *An Etymological Dictionary* (Ares Publishers, Chicago, 1976), states that *regilla* means 'striped, worked in bars'. N. Boëls-Janssen, *La Vie Religieuse des Matrones dans la Rome Archaïque, Coll. de l'École française de Rome*, no. 70 (Ecole française de Rome, Palasi Farnese, Rome, 1993), pp. 71–3 argues that this term indicates that these stripes were purple, like the *praetexta*.

20. C. Delaney, 'Untangling the Meaning of Hair in Turkish Society', in *Off with Her Head! The Denial of Women's Identity in Myth, Religion, and Culture*, ed. H. Eilberg-Schwartz and W. Doniger (University of California Press, Berkeley, 1995), p. 60.

21. Molly Myerowitz Levine, 'The Gendered Grammar of Ancient Mediterranean Hair', in *Off with Her Head!*, ed. Eilberg-Schwartz and Doniger, p. 85. She further notes that *capillus* ('hair') means 'little head'.

22. Delaney, 'Untangling the Meaning of Hair', p. 60.

23. Levine, 'Gendered Grammar of Hair', p. 88.

24. Upon certain occasions, this death was accomplished through a rite of self-dedication and sacrifice (*devotio*). In this rite the soldier ritually dedicated himself as a sacrificial victim through whose death the army would receive victory and life; see, for example, Livy, *History* 8.9.5.

25. *Vir*, from the root *vir-* ('strong, vigorous'), denotes the male in his status as warrior; see Tucker, *An Etymological Dictionary*, p. 259.

26. Suetonius, *Life of Augustus* 38.

27. Festus 272, 273L states that the male relative conducting the last rites for the deceased wore a *toga praetexta pulla*, a dark-colored toga with a purple border. The *praetexta* here indicated his religiously pure state while he was conducting a religious rite. A praetextate *toga virilis* was worn by magistrates who also conducted religious rites as one of the functions of their office.

28. As it was forbidden by law to wear armor and weapons within the city, military costume consisted of the military cloak (*sagum*) worn over the tunic.

29. *Virgo* is derived from the same base as *virere* ('to be ripened for child-bearing'). See Tucker, *An Etymological Dictionary*, p. 259 and Boëls-Janssen, *La Vie Religieuse*, p. 64.

30. Festus 364L: 'The white *regilla* tunics and the yellow hairnets are made by each young woman standing at her loom and weaving at the top of her loom; the young

women go to bed clad in these garments the evening before their marriage for the sake of good omen, a custom also observed when young men are given their manly togas.'

31. Festus 55L. This square knot (*nodus Herculaneus*) was frequently used for good omen on rings, torques, pins and earrings, as well as on the diadem of the Macedonian royal house. On its apotropaic power, see Boëls-Janssen, *La Vie Religieuse*, pp. 75–6; Pliny, *Natural History* 28.6.17, 18.6; J. Heckenbach, 'De nuditate sacra sacrisque vinculis', *Religionsgeschichtliche Versuche und Vorarbeiten*, 9.3 (1911), p. 106. On the costume of the bride, see L. La Follette, 'The Costume of the Roman Bride', in *World of Roman Costume*, pp. 54–64.

32. Festus 454L. The passage is somewhat fragmentary; I have inserted the word 'commits'. See also La Follette, 'The Costume of the Roman Bride', p. 56.

33. As its name indicates, the bridal veil (*flammeum*) was 'flame-colored', an intense orange-yellow. This dye was made from the stamens of the crocus, a flower part that had been used since the Bronze Age (and continues to be used in some Mediterranean countries) to promote women's menstrual and reproductive cycles. On dye from the crocus, see Ovid, *Heroides* 20 (21).162, 168. On the crocus and women's hygiene, see Ellen Reeder, 'Representing Women: The Wedding', in *Pandora: Women in Classical Greece*, ed. Ellen Reeder (Princeton University Press, Princeton, 1995), p. 127. See also E. J. W. Barber, *Women's Work: The First 10,000 Years. Women, Cloth, and Society in Early Times* (W. W. Norton, New York, 1994), pp. 114–16 and 162. On the use in European cultures of the *Crocus sativus* for promoting menstruation, see W. H. Lewis and M. Elvin-Lewis, *Medical Botany: Plants Affecting Man's Health* (Wiley & Sons, New York, 1977), p. 325.

34. Levine, 'The Gendered Grammar', p. 96.

35. J. F. Gardner, *Women in Roman Law and Society* (Indiana University Press, Bloomington, 1986), p. 117. This respect included using only pure speech. Thus Ovid (*Art of Love* 1.31–2, 3.483) warns that a *matrona* should not read his racy love poetry.

36. See J. Pley, 'De lanae in antiquorum ritibus usu', *Religionsgeschichtliche Versuche und Vorarbeiten*, 11.2 (1911), pp. 3–39.

37. Valerius Maximus, *Memorable Deeds and Sayings* 6.3.10 (my translation). Valerius' interest in this anecdote reflects the continuing Augustan interest in the moral traditions of the Republic. For a similar attitude in Turkey, see Delaney, 'Untangling the Meanings of Hair', p. 64. See also L. Bonfante, 'Nudity as Costume in Classical Art', *American Journal of Archaeology* 93 (1989), pp. 545, 567–9. To see a married woman naked is to place oneself in the position of her husband. Thus, when Gyges sees the queen of Lydia naked and she realizes he has done so, she demands that Gyges either kill her husband and make himself king, or kill himself (Herodotus, *Histories* 1.10).

38. On the *stola* see B. I. Scholz, *Untersuchungen zur Tracht der römischen matrona* (Bohlau, Köln, 1992).

39. (*vestis longa*): Ovid, *Art of Love* 1.31; *Poems of Sadness* 2.248; *Letter from Pontus* 3.3.52; *The Roman Calendar* 6.654. On protecting the body from others' gaze: Aulus Gellius, *Attic Nights* 6.12. See also Scholz, *Untersuchungen zur Tracht*, p. 141, n. 13.

40. Servius, on *Aeneid* 4.646; J. H. Vanggard, *The Flamen: A Study in the History and Sociology of Roman Religion* (Copenhagen Museum Tusculum Press, Copenhagen, 1988), pp. 92–3. On the *flaminica* as the archetypal *matrona*, see N. Boëls-Janssen, 'La Prêtesse aux Trois Voiles', *Revue des Études Latines*, 67 (1989), p. 133. The *flaminica Dialis* was the wife of the chief priest of Jupiter and her costume included elements of the costume of the bride, the *matrona* and the *materfamilias*.

41. Zanker, *The Power of Images*, p. 165.

42. There could be no question in the minds of her contemporaries of Antonia's devotion to her husband, Drusus. After his death in 9 BCE, within a few months of the dedication of the Altar, she refused steadfastly to marry again, thus becoming an exemplum of the concept of *univira* ('wife of one man'), a traditional Republican feminine epithet of honor that was also esteemed in Augustan ideology.

43. L. Bonfante, *Etruscan Dress* (Johns Hopkins University Press, Baltimore, MD, 1975), pp. 8, 62, 70, 75–6. See also L. Sensi, 'Ornatus e status sociale delle donne romane', *Annali della Facoltà di Lettere e Filosofia Perugia*, n.s. 4 (1980–1), p. 73.

44. Varro, *Latin Language* 7.44. The etymology of *tutulus* is unknown.

The Ideology of the Eunuch Priest

LYNN E. ROLLER

Eunuchs were a regular part of the gendered world of Mediterranean antiquity. Most eunuchs were castrated involuntarily, many as slaves and prisoners of war. This paper examines a different class of eunuch, the eunuch priest. This was a free man who, as a mature male, castrated himself voluntarily by removing his testicles with a sharp object, an act undertaken as a token of his dedication to the deity he served.[1]

All of the eunuch priests known from ancient Mediterranean society were attendants on so-called Oriental divinities, deities whose cults originated in western Asia. Of these, the most prominent one is the Great Mother Goddess, known in Greece and Rome as Cybele, whose priests will form the principal subject of this paper. The Great Mother was originally a deity of Phrygia, a region of central Asia Minor (modern Turkey). Evidence for her worship first appears in the early first millennium BCE, and she remained a conspicuous figure in the religious life of Mediterranean antiquity until the dominance of Christianity in the fourth and fifth centuries CE. Despite her Phrygian origins and her continuing identification as a Phrygian deity, the Great Mother is best known through her cult centers in the Greek world and in the city of Rome. In the Greek world she was addressed as Meter, the Mother, and her civic shrines could be found in several Greek cities. In the city of Rome the Great Mother, the Roman Magna Mater, gained even more public visibility, as she acquired the role of a patriotic, protective divinity, worshipped at an important temple in the very heart of the city. The ubiquity and public presence of the Mother Goddess are marks of a deity who enjoyed a great deal of dignity and respect in Mediterranean antiquity. Yet this circumstance forms a sharp contrast to the position of her eunuch priests, whose asexual condition caused them to be viewed with disgust and loathing outside the goddess's Phrygian homeland. In some cases the eunuch priest was described as a man who had deliberately made himself into a woman, taking on all of the negative implications that were attached to a woman's body in antiquity. In other cases the eunuch was addressed as a being who was a grade below a woman, as one 'neither man nor woman', whose appearance and manners incorporated the most disagreeable aspects of both male and female.

It is the ancient reaction to the priests' intermediate gender identity and the implications of such reaction for ancient attitudes towards gender and the status and appearance of both men and women that I wish to explore here. It is important to understand that we are not examining the actual circumstances of the lives of these eunuch priests, but rather the ancient perception of them. In no case does the voice of a eunuch survive to inform us about the individual's attitude towards his castrated state and his reasons for choosing this asexual path. Moreover, we are poorly informed about the identity, ethnic background, social class and economic status of these eunuchs. We do, however, have abundant ancient literary and historical sources which present a vivid picture of how Greek and, more especially, Roman society viewed a man who had voluntarily relinquished his masculine identity and the masculine place in society by voluntarily relinquishing his testicles.

There appear to be two unspoken assumptions which underlie negative reactions to the gender status of a self-castrating eunuch priest. The first is the automatic assumption of male superiority, in particular of the superiority of masculine appearance. The second is the firm conception that it was necessary to have gender and to play the biological and social role assigned to one's gender to be fully human. There is already a considerable literature on the identity of the eunuch priest, but many modern studies have uncritically echoed the pejorative and judgemental language of Mediterranean antiquity, a circumstance which has obscured efforts to understand the source and motivations of ancient reactions to the institution of sacred eunuchism.[2]

Since the institution of sacred eunuchism was connected with deities whose origins lay in the ancient Near East, it would seem logical to look there for information on the priests' origins and status. Yet evidence for the practice in western Asia is extremely limited. Eunuch priests played a role in the religious cults of Mesopotamian divinities in the second millennium BCE, but their influence did not extend beyond this area.[3] Therefore it seems unlikely that there is a direct connection between the sacred eunuchs of early Mesopotamia and the eunuch priests of the Mother Goddess in Greece and Rome. In contrast, the cult of the Phrygian Mother Goddess, prominent in central Asia Minor during the first millennium BCE, does offer a direct thread between Phrygia, Greece and Rome, for the name, physical appearance and iconography of the deity worshipped in Greece and Rome form close parallels with the Phrygian goddess.[4] In the Phrygian homeland of the Mother Goddess, however, evidence for the existence of eunuch priests is very limited, particularly before the third century BCE when Phrygia came under Greek political control and cultural influence. No text in the Phrygian language provides any explicit reference to the existence of eunuch attendants on the Mother. Moreover the eunuch deity Attis, whose status in Greek and Roman myth as the Mother's consort supposedly provided the model for the eunuch priest, does not exist in Phrygian iconography and cult practice.[5] There are a few statuettes of beardless males found in conjunction with representations of the goddess which may represent eunuchs, since males were normally depicted with beards in the art of western Asia.[6] Beardlessness could, however, simply indicate youth, and so even this feature is not a sure indicator of a eunuch.

Given the scarcity of comprehensible texts from early Phrygia, the limited evidence for eunuch priests in the Mother's homeland should not be taken as proof of their absence. In fact, a few texts in Greek and Latin from the first two centuries BCE do furnish clear information on the activities of eunuch priests in their communities in Asia Minor. Two episodes recorded by the historians Polybios and Livy indicate that these priests were influential figures in political as well as religious matters. During the Roman siege of Sestos, in western Asia Minor, in 190 BCE, the Mother's priests, the Galli (the term is discussed below), approached the Roman army and persuaded it to spare the city (Polybios 31.6; Livy 37.9.9). In 189 BCE. when the Roman army was maneuvering against the Celts in central Asia Minor near Pessinous, an important Phrygian cult center, the Mother's priests met the army and predicted victory, thus encouraging the Romans' military efforts (Livy 38.18.9). While we learn nothing of their sexual status from these references, the historians record that the priests wore their sacred costumes and insignia. An idea of what that costume was is furnished by an inscribed votive relief from Kyzikos, in north-western Asia Minor, dedicated in 46 BCE by a priest, a Gallus named Soterides.[7] The relief depicts him in woman's clothing, a long gown and a veil, implying that within Asia Minor the eunuch priest identified himself as a woman in his physical appearance (Figure 1).

In general, the evidence from Asia Minor suggests that the priest was a figure of dignity who enjoyed the respect accorded to one chosen to be the representative of his community. There is nothing in the evidence from Asia Minor to suggest that sacred eunuchism was widespread and required of the Phrygian Mother's priests. Indeed, the opposite, as a Greek inscription from the first century CE makes clear; the text records that the office of chief priest of the Mother at Pessinous was hereditary, passing from father to son.[8] This circumstance clearly indicates that not all Phrygian priests of the Mother were eunuchs dedicated to life service of the goddess. Thus the custom of sacred eunuchism did not receive any particular comment in the goddess's Asiatic homeland. Certainly the eunuch priest did not attract the kind of sensational notice there that he did in Greece and Rome. This will be an important point to remember when evaluating the Greek and Roman attitudes towards eunuch priests.

Evidence for the worship of the Phrygian Mother Goddess in the Greek world appears during the sixth century BCE,[9] yet secure references to priests of this divinity first appear only in the fourth century BCE, when we begin to hear of an individual known in Greek as a metragyrt, meaning a priest who collects alms for Meter, the Mother. This individual is regularly

Figure 1: Votive relief from Kyzikos dated to 46 BCE, depicting a Gallus worshipping the Phrygian Mother Goddess. Photo courtesy of the Musée du Louvre.

described in very negative terms. He was someone dishonorable (Aristotle, *Rhetoric* 32), a beggar (Athenaios 12.541e), the lowest form of life (Athenaios 6.226d; Plutarch, *Cleomenes* 36). In his capacity as a priest, the metragyrt was accused of using his religious office to prey on the rich and on individuals weakened by disease or personal distress. For example, by representing Meter as one of the deities responsible for epilepsy, her priest could present himself as the means of curing this disease (Hippocrates, *On the Sacred Disease* 4), although the author of the Hippocratic text was most scornful of his ability to do so. The metragyrt could claim to be a suitable nurse for children (Athenaios 6.226d, quoting Antiphanes), thus insinuating himself into a household (Clement, *Protreptikos* 2.20, quoting Menander). Plato was particularly contemptuous of such beggar priests and prophets "who stand at the doors of rich men and persuade them by means of spells and charms that they have special powers from the gods" (Plato, *Republic* 2.364b). Clearly Greek intellectuals viewed the metragyrt as a charlatan of the worst kind who routinely used the position of his religious office for his own selfish ends. There is, however, no reference to the metragyrt's gender or his sexual identity as a basis for the negative reaction to his activities. He is always described as masculine (since Greek is a highly gendered language, this is quite clear in the original Greek texts), and there is no indication that the priest's sexual status affected his appearance or behavior.

The negative impression we receive of the metragyrt stands in direct contrast to the generally favorable picture given of the goddess Meter herself. Meter was honored with a temple in the center of Athens and a cult statue by a major artist.[10] She received a temple at the important sanctuary of Olympia, and she was the object of cult in other Greek cities.[11] Why should the goddess receive such respect and admiration, while her priests were viewed with such contempt? The answer may lie in the way in which Meter's ethnicity was perceived. In the cities and sanctuaries where she was revered as an important divinity, she was given a good Greek pedigree. She was addressed as the Mother of the gods and equated with the Greek divinity Rhea, mother of the Olympian deities.[12] Yet where the priest of Meter was castigated for his improper behavior, he is frequently mentioned in the same context as rites and activities viewed as non-Greek, often as Oriental. He uses charms and spells (Plato, *Republic* 2.364b), he thumps his drums and clashes cymbals (Athenaios 12.541e; Plutarch, *Cleomenes* 36; Clement, *Protreptikos* 7.65, quoting Menander), and generally behaves in an undignified fashion. Such actions were regularly associated with other non-Greek divinities such as Adonis, of Syrian origin, and Sabazios, a Phrygian like the Mother Goddess.[13] These rites were described with contempt because of the negative attitudes expressed by many Greeks towards those who worshipped the divinities of the Near East.[14] Thus what upset many Greeks about the metragyrts was not their position as attendants on Meter, but their use of foreign ways. According to their accusers, the metragyrts took advantage of the charm of the exotic to achieve nefarious ends.

The suspicious reaction to the Mother Goddess's foreign priests first becomes coupled with accusations of cross-gendered behavior in the second century BCE, when the eunuch priest enters the literary language to become the standard image of the attendant to the Phrygian Mother. In a series of six epigrams from the Greek Anthology (*Anthologia Palatina* 6.217–20, 234, 237) we meet a priest of the Mother Goddess whose appearance and gender status mark him as someone deviant from normal masculine behavior. The epigrams all record the same anecdote: the priest, wandering across the countryside in Asia Minor (some epigrams place the episode in Pessinous, others near Sardis), takes shelter in a cave; here he meets a lion who tries to devour him but the priest uses his ritual insignia, his raucous music and his wild dance to drive the lion away or render him harmless.[15] This priest is usually called a Gallus (*Anthologia Palatina* 6.217.1, 220.8, 234.1, 237.1), the term which in later Greek and Roman literature was regularly used to describe the emasculated priest of the Magna Mater.[16] One epigram gives this priest's name as Atys, or Attis (*Anthologia Palatina* 6.220.3), the name of the Mother's eunuch lover in Greek and Roman myth,[17] and in another epigram, *Anthologia Palatina* 6.218, the priest is called a metragyrt, the term for the alms-collecting priest of the Greek Meter introduced above, indicating that these epigrams refer to the same goddess and attendant.

Yet the priest whom we meet in these epigrams differs markedly from the metragyrt of fourth-century BCE Greek comedy and philosophy. He is explicitly described as a eunuch (*Anthologia Palatina* 6.219.5), a half-woman (*Anthologia Palatina* 6.217.9), recently castrated (*Anthologia Palatina* 6.234.1). His appearance and manners are, in Greek terms, distinctively feminine: he has long dainty tresses, which can be neatly plaited under a hairnet or worn long and loose to toss in the wind; he wears women's clothes and women's perfume (*Anthologia Palatina* 6.234.5); he has a high-pitched piercing voice; and he engages in frenzied and agitated movement and dance of the type usually associated with hysterical, i.e. feminine behavior. Yet his feminine qualities do not make him a woman: the eunuch is quite clearly conceptualized as male, as the Greek masculine pronoun and adjectives describing him make clear. Instead, he is a figure of caricature whose appearance and mannerisms exaggerate feminine attributes for humorous effect. The story of the epigrams further reinforces the allusion to feminine traits, for the priest does not face the lion boldly and attack him, as a real hero should, but instead defends himself with the marks of his effeminate status. He shakes his long hair, thumps his drum, or dances his dance, and the divine spirit of the goddess moves through him to drive the lion away. *Anthologia Palatina* 6.218 carries the caricature even further, as the lion itself tosses its mane and joins in the dance.

The introduction of the emasculate priest of Meter into Greek literature, interestingly, parallels the spread of the cult of the emasculate god Attis in the Greek world. A divine Attis, absent in Phrygia and a latecomer to the Mother's Greek cult, first becomes a visible presence during the second century BCE.[18] The junction of Attis' worship with Meter's is surely a reinforcing factor in the increasing prominence of eunuch priests. Such prominence evidently for the first time made these priests an element to be reckoned with in Greek society, and the epigrams offer a vivid look at the reaction, both amused and hostile, to individuals who flouted the norms of conventional gender roles. The epigrams seem designed not to belittle feminine appearance and behavior, but to express amazement that a man would willingly adopt such feminine qualities. The eunuch priest's castrated state has reduced him to an undesirable condition in ways evident through his dress, hairstyle, voice and mannerisms, but unrelated to his sexual activities.

The epigrams do much to inform us about contemporary Greek opinions and assumptions about the superior nature of masculinity. Their portrait of the Gallus lays the background for similar assumptions that underlie the portrayal of the eunuch priest in Roman literature.

First, some comments are in order about the Roman goddess whom the eunuch priests served and her place in Roman religion and society. The Magna Mater, or Great Mother, came to Rome in 204 BCE from Asia Minor, where the Romans had gone to fetch her at the command of the Sibylline books.[19] The goddess came as an Asiatic divinity, an outsider introduced into the Roman pantheon, but she also had a very Roman persona through her identification as a divinity of the Trojans, the mythological ancestors of the Romans. Her arrival, heralded by omens and portents, was celebrated with great fanfare, and her divinity was made manifest by miracles from her first appearance in Rome.[20] The Magna Mater received an important shrine on the Palatine near some of Rome's most venerable religious sanctuaries, and she was honored with a public festival, the Megalesia, celebrated in April. The rites for the Magna Mater included many features which were common to the rituals celebrated for other divinities of good Roman pedigree: a public procession in which the image of the deity was carried through the streets, sacrifices and communal banquets, and games consisting of musical and theatrical performances.[21] Along with the Mother came Attis, the god who functioned as the Mother's eunuch consort. Attis's presence in Roman cult is evident from the large number of figurines depicting him which were dedicated in the Great Mother's Palatine temple. Several of these figurines illustrate Attis with his clothes pulled back to draw attention to his genitalia, while other figurines found in the same votive deposit depict the male phallus.[22] This circumstance suggests that elements of sexuality, particularly male sexuality, were prominent in the Mother's worship from the early years of her presence in Rome.

The impact of the Mother's eunuch priests on her Roman cult is less clear. The goddess's eunuch attendants presumably accompanied her on her journey from Asia to Italy, although initially there is no evidence of their presence in Rome. The first unequivocal evidence for a eunuch priest of the Magna Mater active in Rome appears roughly a hundred years after the goddess's arrival; we learn of a slave who castrated himself in the service of the Great Mother in 101 BCE and as a result was exiled from Rome and forbidden ever to return.[23] An even more marked indication of the Romans' attitudes to eunuch priests occurred in 77 BCE, when a slave named Genucius received a legacy from his master. As a eunuch priest of the Magna Mater, Genucius was ultimately denied his inheritance on the grounds that he was neither man nor woman. Genucius was not even allowed to plead his own case, on the grounds that his "obscene presence and corrupt voice" might pollute the court.[24] The Romans carried the Greek distaste for the eunuch's effeminacy one step further, by declaring that his lack of male sexual organs made him not a woman but a non-person in the eyes of the law.[25]

This forms a sharp contrast to the portrayal by the historians Polybios and Livy of these same eunuchs, the Galli, in Asia. As we saw earlier, the historians describe these priests as figures of influence and dignity in their home communities, whose functions included intervention in diplomatic and military situations. There, when the Galli were engaged in affairs of state, especially when acting in a manner favorable to the Romans (predicting Roman victory), they are not described as having feminine voice and manners; on the contrary, the historians stress the traditionally masculine quality of boldness needed for an unarmed priest to confront an army in the field. We see the same circumstance in the reception given to one of the Mother's Asian priests who came from Phrygia to Rome in 102 BCE, in this case also to declare the Phrygian Mother's support for Rome's military undertaking. This individual was received with great acclaim in Rome, and while much attention was directed to his exotic costume, his gender and sexuality received no comment.[26]

These episodes encapsulate the Romans' two-sided response to the eunuch priest. When he was identified primarily with his Asian homeland, he was viewed as an exotic, non-threatening figure, particularly when he reinforced the Romans' positive view of themselves. But when he was active in Rome, in the Magna Mater's civic cult, he became an outsider, a foreigner, whose unconventional gender and sexual status were viewed with alarm and disgust. Permitting such conduct in Rome would appear to imply support for clearly unmasculine behavior.

This paradox becomes prominent in the literature of the first century BCE and continues so until late antiquity. I have chosen to focus my discussion of this paradox through a review of the portrait of the Roman eunuch priest presented in the literature of the first centuries BCE and CE. There is an especially rich corpus of evidence from these two centuries to illustrate Roman attitudes towards the gender and body of the eunuch.[27]

We perceive one reaction to the priests, that of grudging tolerance, in descriptions of the conduct of their official duties. The Roman poet Lucretius, writing *c.* 60 BCE, offers a vivid picture of the Galli's role in the principal Roman festival, the Megalesia, held to honor the Great Mother.

The chief feature of this festival was a public procession in which the Mother's eunuchs paraded in full armor and flashing weapons, as her image was carried through the streets (Lucretius 6.621–43). Lucretius' language effectively communicates a note of almost menacing tension.[28] As the Galli approach, drums thunder, cymbals clash and horns threaten with their raucous sound. Armed men jump around the sacred image of the goddess, shaking the fearsome crests of their helmets and exulting in blood. The eunuch priests' asexual condition seems inconsistent with such a militaristic atmosphere, and the poet has to resort to the rather contrived expedient of explaining their castrated state as an inducement for normal people to be fruitful, multiply, and obey their parents; in other words, to follow traditional Roman values and not to be like the Galli.[29] Half a century later, Ovid's description of this same festival projects a similarly arousing ambience, as the poet stresses the howling, the thundering drums and the jingling cymbals, the instruments which accompany the soft "half-men" who carry the image of the goddess through the streets of the city; the poet confesses himself frightened by the scene (Ovid, *Fasti* 4.181–90).

The paradox of the priests' situation, distasteful even if a necessary part of an important public religious rite, is most clearly articulated by Dionysios of Halikarnassos, describing this same festival and procession. Dionysios comments on the many unattractive episodes of Greek myth, including the castration of Uranus, and compliments the Romans on avoiding them, even in cults which have come to Rome from abroad and in which many foreigners participate. His principal example is the festival of the Magna Mater and the un-Roman quality of the priests, both men and women, their brightly colored costumes, their habit of begging and their loud raucous music (Dionysios, *Roman Antiquities* 2.19). He calls these qualities degenerate, typical of foreigners; no Roman, he says, would be so lacking in decorum. Such careful separation of ritual practices into the Roman and the foreign is a mark of how strongly the Romans felt that these priests and their rites were alien to the cultural values of the city, even as the eunuchs were engaged in their most basic religious obligations to the Magna Mater, an important Roman deity.

The language used to describe the Galli's private activities in Rome was not so tolerant. Most references to the Galli make it clear that many Romans viewed them with utter contempt, calling them "pretty things", "little doves", "half-women" (*Anthologia Palatina* 7.222). Galli were clearly perceived as disgusting creatures, whose depraved character was evident both through their distinctive appearance, marked by brightly colored costumes, unusual headdresses, frizzy hairstyles and perfume, and also through a propensity for licentious indulgence in alcohol and sexual activities. Moreover, the Galli's degraded conduct was directly linked to their lack of masculinity. In *Anthologia Palatina* 7.233 we meet for the first time a Gallus described in feminine grammatical construct; this was Aristion (a masculine name), "she who used to toss her hair among the pines in honor of

Cybele", as the poet tells us, "and she could drink three tumblers of wine neat". And there was Trygonion, the Little Dove, who "was the flower of the eunuch band in their clubhouse; she alone among the half-women [eunuchs] loved the rites of Aphrodite" (*Anthologia Palatina* 7.222.2–4).[30]

The eunuch's sexual activities were all-inclusive, as the poet Martial describes in the first century CE; to him, the Gallus was an equal opportunity lover, skilled at oral sex with both men and women (Martial 3.81).[31] It was not the indulgence in such behavior that the Roman authors objected to; indulgence in offbeat sexual activities with one's social inferiors was an unspoken prerogative of the Roman male citizen.[32] Their objections arose from the fact that the Mother's priests, foreigners and non-citizens, could use their status as sacred eunuchs to gain impunity from charges of sexual misconduct. They were even accused of using their sacred status to suborn gullible women, with the unspoken implication that women were particularly susceptible to womanish men.[33] The complaints of Plato are re-echoed, but with explicit sexual overtones.

Even more telling than direct descriptions of the Galli and their activities are texts in which the eunuch priest forms a metaphor for the author's reflections on the social role of masculinity and asexuality. I have chosen two examples of such indirect musings to illustrate different images evoked by the eunuch priests: the haunting lament on the loss of masculinity found in Catullus' poem 63, and the politically charged images of Virgil's *Aeneid* equating the eunuch with the effeminate Oriental enemy of Rome.

Poem 63 of Catullus uses the figure of the eunuch priest to explore its narrator's ambiguity about the social constraints, including gender constraints, which define his world. The narrative recounts the actions and reactions of Attis, a young devotee of the Magna Mater, who consciously adopts the eunuch priest's identity and thereby acquires the eunuch's alien status. The poem starts with an air of eagerness, as Attis travels swiftly from his home to Phrygia. There he castrates himself abruptly while in a frenzy induced by the wild music and orgiastic excitement of the goddess's rituals. Attis's initial reaction to his new asexual persona is one of exultation.[34] He leads the goddess's band of followers on into a kind of delirious wandering, ended only by the cleansing quiet of sleep. The coming of the light, however, wakens him from this trance and forces him to confront the reality of his new state: he is no longer a man, but neither is he a woman, only a counterfeit woman, a *notha mulier* (63.27). He laments his action bitterly: his loss of gender means that he has cut himself off from everything of value, from homeland, property, friends and family (63.59), all the structures that define his world. The goddess's reaction is to draw Attis into her world, loosing her constant companion, her lion, from her chariot and sending him to drive Attis into the dark forests where the eunuch will spend the rest of his life as her slave (63.90).

Among the many complex issues raised by this poem,[35] I wish to address the implications of the poet's choice of the eunuch priest as a metaphor for an individual totally estranged from his social milieu. He is physically separated from his (unnamed) home by his journey to Phrygia; culturally separated from his normal life by abandoning the cultivated world of the city for the dark forest and wild beasts, the world of the goddess; and bodily separated from his former life as a whole person by the act of emasculation (he calls himself *pars mei*, 'part of myself', 63.69). The eunuch priest becomes a vehicle by which the poet expresses his own sense of alienation, for the Attis within the poem is surely the poet himself, as his frequent repetition of *ego* ('I') and *mihi* ('me') indicates.[36] By identifying himself with the self-castrating god who was worshipped along with Cybele in Rome, the poet can distance himself from his own masculine identity. He can play the feminine role, for once Attis has amputated his genitals, the poet abruptly shifts grammatical gender to have the narrator speak in the feminine voice. As a woman, he is cut off from the Roman benefits of masculinity: he has permanently lost the social contacts of the forum, palestra, stadium and gymnasium which define the masculine place in society (63.60). No longer is he sought after, nor is his presence courted (63.65–6). Not only his gender but also his civic identity (63.55) and his freedom (63.90) are gone. Yet he is not a woman, but a pseudo-woman, and as such has no place in the gendered world of normal Roman society. Writing as a eunuch, the poet can identify with the powerless state of a woman, but still remain acutely conscious of his own masculinity. Attis has sunk below the status of both man and woman to become a non-person, a complete outcast.[37]

The poet's choice of a Gallus as a symbol of alienation is one of the most telling comments on Roman reactions to the eunuch priest. The picture here of the eunuch priest is unremittingly negative, that of an individual who is outside the bounds of any social organization or contact. There is no comment on the eunuch's personal appearance and sexual behavior, nor is there any of the humorous or scatological language found in the epigrams. The message seems rather that to be a real person, a whole being, one must be a gendered being who plays the appropriate gender role in one's social as well as one's sexual life. The narrator seems eager at first to move beyond the constraints of gender and create a new identity for himself, and the early part of the poem reflects that eagerness: the voyage to a new place, the emotionally arousing features of the Galli's rites, the wild music, the trance-like state of the goddess's followers, appear to offer the capacity to transform him into a new and potentially better person. But in the end the only transformation achieved is to a state of slavery and alienation.

The second metaphorical use of the ambiguously gendered and asexual status of the Gallus, in Virgil's *Aeneid*, adds powerful political overtones to these personal musings on gender, sexuality and identity. The Great Mother Cybele aids the poem's hero Aeneas at many critical points throughout the *Aeneid*: her guiding star and her sacred mountain rescue Aeneas and his family from burning Troy (*Aeneid* 2.693–7, 788), ships built from the timber of her sacred groves protect Aeneas from Rutulian attack (*Aeneid* 9.110–13), her insignia embellish Aeneas' ship (*Aeneid* 10.156–7), and her chariot and her sacred image symbolize the great and glorious future of Rome (*Aeneid* 6.784–7). Yet her priests, the Galli, exemplify weakness and effeminacy, values which stand in stark contrast to the stalwart nature and noble virtue of the Italians whom Aeneas will soon lead to form the new Roman state.[38]

Indirect references to the Galli are found in all parts of the poem. When Aeneas and his companions arrive at Carthage and attract the attention of the Carthaginian queen Dido, they are disparagingly compared by the Carthaginian Iarbas to the castrated priests of the Mother: Aeneas is "that Paris [the archetype of an effeminate coward] with his half-male band" (*Aeneid* 4.215). After Aeneas' arrival in Italy, on the eve of a great battle, the Italian warrior Turnus prays: "Grant that I may … tear open with my strong hand the breastplate of this Phrygian eunuch, and befoul his hair, curled with a hot iron and wetted with myrrh, in the dust" (*Aeneid* 12.97–100). Similarly, in another battle scene, Numanus taunts the Trojan warriors as de-sexed foreigners, using the feminine form of address to emphasize their lack of manly virtues: "Your garments are dyed with yellow and shining purple; you delight in idleness and dancing; you wear sleeved tunics and ribboned caps; you who are really Phrygian women, not Phrygian men— go to the heights of Dindyma, where the flute gives a two-pronged song to your accustomed ears. The drums … call you: leave fighting to the men" (*Aeneid* 9.614–20). All of the negative aspects of the eunuch priest's appearance, his frizzy hair, his perfume, his brightly colored clothes and distinctive headdress, his Phrygian background, his susceptibility to emotional ritual, and most of all his castrated state (the Trojans are repeatedly called *semiviri*, 'half-men'), are used to castigate the Trojans as weaklings who cannot stand up to the deeds of real (Latin) men. Like the epigrams on the Gallus and the lion, and the epitaphs of the Galli Trygonion and Aristion, the language emphasizes the weakness and lack of manly virtues associated with feminine appearance and lack of male sexual potency.

In creating this image of contempt, Virgil drew on contemporary opinion that viewed the Gallus as a despised effeminate. At first reading, it seems an odd choice of metaphor with which to characterize the poem's hero Aeneas and his followers, and seems doubly inconsistent with the powerful portrait of the Magna Mater which permeates the whole *Aeneid*. Yet it is another example of the paradox noted above, the positive image of the deity coupled with the negative stereotypes of her priests. Virgil resolves this inconsistency in a speech given by Juno at the end of the poem. Yielding to Jupiter's plan that gives success to the Trojans, Juno imposes one last condition, that the conquered Italians not change their voices or their clothing (*Aeneid* 12.825); even though the Trojans have conquered, good sturdy Italian speech and manners will prevail. Once again it is the womanish speech and dress of the Galli which is offensive; in becoming the new rulers of

Italy, the Trojans will rise above the implied effeminacy of their Asiatic background to adopt the masculine appearance and habits of the Italians.

To Virgil, and indeed to most contemporary Romans, the degrading aspects of the eunuch priest's appearance—his hair, his voice, his clothing—and his anomalous sexual state were reinforced by the taint of his Asian background. Yet emphasizing the eunuch's foreign qualities is another way of placing him outside the mainstream of Roman society, of distancing him from approved Roman masculine behavior. To be of Asian origin was not automatically a mark of inferiority; as has been noted earlier, the Romans regarded the eunuch priest as a figure of dignity and respect within his Asian homeland. Yet to bring these "Asian", i.e. unmanly, ways to Rome was, to Virgil, clearly unacceptable. His portrait reinforces the perception of Catullus, that the eunuch priest in Rome was a social outcast. As such, he became a convenient peg on which to hang the most disagreeable stereotypes of conduct unbecoming to a man.

Taken as a whole, the Roman comments on the eunuch priest offer insights into the status not only of eunuchs but also of men and women. The eunuch was despised for several reasons—because he adopted feminine dress and appearance, because he was sterile, because he was thought to be sexually promiscuous—but most of all because he turned his back on the values and duties of a Roman man. On one level this portrait of a eunuch priest reinforces the unspoken assumption that masculine appearance and habits are superior: it may be all right for a woman to dress in brightly colored clothes, dye and curl her hair, and speak in a high-pitched voice, but real men don't do these things. If they do, they cut themselves off from the opportunity of participating in the social privileges of masculinity. On another level, this emphasizes a more basic belief, that gendered behavior along socially conventional lines is necessary for full humanity. The individual who deliberately made himself sterile has stepped outside the boundaries of behavior appropriate for either sex. He has completely estranged himself from the bonds of family and state.

In sum, the eunuch priest in his Asian homeland was an unsurprising figure, well accepted as part of the cult of the Mother Goddess and only one of several classes of priests serving the goddess. In the Greek world the priests of the Greek goddess Meter evoked a considerable amount of scorn for their raucous rites and begging habits, but little comment on their gender and sexual orientation. Only in the second century BCE do we begin to find the eunuch priest attracting attention for his castrated state and womanish ways. The increasingly negative reaction of Greek and Roman society to the eunuch priest, moving from amused interest to criticism to disgust, reflects in part the increasing prominence of the Mother Goddess in the Greek and Roman worlds and the concurrently increasing prominence of the eunuchs who attended her. It also shows how firmly the boundary between the sexes was perceived and how critical people were of individuals who crossed that boundary. To an extent, this was because the eunuch priest challenged the unspoken implication of masculine superiority. Even more than direct comments on a woman's body, masculine reactions to eunuch priests (and all of our sources on these priests are male) underscore the high worth credited to masculine appearance and masculine genitalia. The man who voluntarily gave up these advantages was a low creature, despised as an individual who had deliberately forgone the rights and privileges associated with the possession of a male body. Moreover, the eunuch priest's asexual condition kept him from filling the gender role of either a man or a woman, a circumstance which separated him from the legal and social privileges deriving from citizenship and from membership of a family. Nowhere in the literature of Mediterranean antiquity is there any intimation that the eunuch priest represented a third gender, a holy state to be respected, as is true of eunuchs in some other cultures.[39] Ultimately the eunuch priest was a being "neither man nor woman", lacking in the most elemental quality of human identity, the possession of gender.

Notes

1. Self-castration by eunuch priests is described in several ancient sources: Lucretius 2.621; Lucian, *Dea Syria* 51; Pliny, *Natural History* 35.165; Juvenal 6.514. Such descriptions emphasize the sensational aspect of self-castration, and some modern commentators have doubted whether castration could have been performed in this way, although our ancient sources are internally consistent on this point. Many commentators have assumed that men who acted thus were mentally deranged (e.g. Walter Burkert, *Structure and History in Greek Mythology and Ritual* [University of California Press, Berkeley and Los Angeles, 1979], p. 105), although ancient sources which describe self-castration give no support for this assumption. Valuable insight into the questions of how and why a man might choose to become a eunuch priest is provided by Serena Nanda and her studies of the eunuch priests of the Mother Goddess in contemporary India; see *Neither Man nor Woman: The Hijras of India* (Wadsworth, Belmont, CA, 1990), and "Hijras: An Alternative Sex and Gender Role in India", in *Third Sex, Third Gender: Beyond Sexual Dimorphism in Culture and History*, ed. Gilbert Herdt (Zone Books, New York, 1994), pp. 373–417; the Indian initiate to the Mother Goddess cult is castrated by a member of the community of emasculates, the hijras, with the initiate's full knowledge and consent; Nanda, *Neither Man nor Woman*, pp. 26–9.

2. Modern scholarship on eunuch priests is conveniently summarized by G. M. Sanders, *Reallexikon für Antike und Christentum*, 8 (Hiersemann, Stuttgart, 1972), pp. 984–1034, s.v. "Gallus"; see also Burkert, *Structure and History*, pp. 102–5, 108–11, both good examples of negative, judgemental attitudes towards the practice of sacred eunuchism. M. Beard, "The Roman and the Foreign: The Cult of the "Great Mother" in Imperial Rome", in *Shamanism, History, and the State*, ed. N. Thomas and C. Humphrey (University of Michigan Press, Ann Arbor, 1994) pp. 164–90, is an interesting, if atypical, effort to explore the paradox of simultaneous acceptance and repulsion that characterized the cult of the Mother Goddess and her eunuch priests.

3. Sanders, "Gallus", p. 988; Burkert, *Structure and History*, pp. 110–11; Will Roscoe, "Priests of the Goddess: Gender Transgression in Ancient Religion", *History of Religions*, 35 (1996), pp. 213–17.

4. For a summary of the evidence for the Mother's cult in Phrygia, see Lynn E. Roller, "Phrygian Myth and Cult", *Source,* 7 (1988), pp. 43–50. On the name of the Phrygian Mother Goddess and its transmission to Greece and Rome, see Claude Brixhe, "Le nom de Cybèle", *Die Sprache,* 25 (1979), pp. 40–5. The Phrygian cult images of the deity and their transmission to Greek images have been thoroughly explored by Friederike Naumann, *Die Ikonographie der Kybele in der phrygischen und der griechischen Kunst. Istanbuler Mitteilungen,* Beiheft 28 (E. Wasmuth, Tübingen, 1983). The most recent survey of the cult of the Mother Goddess, Maarten Vermaseren, *Cybele and Attis* (Thames & Hudson, London, 1977), gives a general introduction to the identity and cult practices of the goddess and her eunuch priests, but contains many errors and should be used with caution. An older work, Henri Graillot, *Le culte de Cybèle, mère des dieux, à Rome et dans l'empire romaine* (Fontemoing, Paris, 1912), is still of value.

5. Lynn E. Roller, "Attis on Greek Votive Monuments: Greek God or Phrygian?", *Hesperia,* 63 (1994), pp. 245–62.

6. Such statuettes include two small figurines of beardless males holding a bowl or a bird of prey, the standard symbols of the Phrygian Mother, from the Phrygian site of Gordion; Machteld J. Mellink, "Comments on a Cult Relief of Kybele from Gordion", in *Beiträge zur Altertumskunde Kleinasiens,* ed. R. M. Boehmer and H. Hauptmann (Philipp von Zabern, Mainz, 1983), p. 352, pl. 72; for two youthful beardless male musicians, a flutist and a lyre player, who flank a statue of the goddess from Boğazköy, see Roller, "Phrygian Myth and Cult", p. 44, fig. 2; and for a silver statuette of a mature beardless male from Bayandir, near Elmali, a piece found together with a fine ivory statuette of the goddess, see Engin and Ilknur Özgen, *Antalya Museum* (Ana Basim A. S., Istanbul, 1988), p. 38, no. 41.

7. See Folkert von Straten, "Images of Gods and Men in a Changing Society: Self-identity in Hellenistic Religion", in *Images and Ideologies: Self-definition in the Hellenistic World,* ed. A. Bulloch, E. S. Gruen, A. A. Long and A. Stewart (University of California Press, Berkeley, Los Angeles and London, 1993), pp. 255–6, fig. 17.

8. Two inscriptions record the career of Tiberios Claudios Heras, active in the religious life of the community; he was chief priest of the goddess Meter nine times, along with six terms of service as priest of the Imperial cult and one as high priest of the *koinon* ('the community'). As chief priest of Meter he held the title of 'Attis', an honor which he shared with his son, Tiberios Claudios Deiotarus. For the inscriptions, see John Devreker and Marc Waelkens, *Les fouilles de la Rijksuniversiteit te Gent a Pessinonte 1967–1973,* I, Dissertationes Archaeologicae Gandenses 22 (De Tempel, Brugge, 1984), pp. 19–20 and p. 221, nos. 17, 18.

9. A summary of the evidence for the earliest cult of the Greek goddess Meter is given by Martin P. Nilsson, *Geschichte der griechischen Religion,* II, 2nd edn (C. H. Beck, Munich, 1961), pp. 725–7; see also Lynn E. Roller, "The Great Mother at Gordion: the Hellenization of an Anatolian Cult", *Journal of Hellenic Studies,* 111 (1991), pp. 135–6.

10. On Meter's temple in Athens, see S. G. Miller, "Old Metroon and Old Bouleterion in the Classical Agora of Athens", in *Studies in the Ancient Greek Polis,* ed. Mogens Herman Hansen and Kurt Raaflaub (Franz Steiner Verlag, Stuttgart, 1995) pp. 133–56 with earlier bibliography; the cult statue is discussed by G. I. Despines, Συμβολὴ στὴ μελετὴ τοῦ ἐργοῦ τοῦ Ἀγορακρίτου (Hermes, Athens, 1971), pp. 111–23.

11. On Meter in Olympia, see K. Hitzl, *Die Kaiserzeitliche Statuen, Ausstattung des Metroons,* Olympische Forschungen 19 (De Gruyter, Berlin and New York, 1991), pp. 8–14. The worship of Meter in Thebes is described by the Greek poet Pindar, *Pythian Odes* 3.77–9. For the worship of Meter in Magnesia, see Plutarch, *Themistokles* 30.

12. The earliest testimonium to Meter as mother of the Greek gods is the sixth-century BCE Homeric Hymn 14.

13. H. S. Versnel, *Ter Unus: Isis, Dionysos, Hermes: Three Studies in Henotheism* (E. J. Brill, Leiden, 1990), pp. 103–5 (Adonis) and pp. 114–18 (Sabazios), discusses the testimonia for ancient Greek attitudes to these Asiatic deities.

14. See Demosthenes, *On the Crown,* 18.259–60, for a scornful assessment of those who participate in such ecstatic rites. For opposition specifically to deities of Asiatic origin, Demosthenes, *On False Legislation* 19.281; Josephus, *Apionem* 2.37.

15. The epigrams have been discussed as a group by A. S. F. Gow, "The Gallus and the Lion", *Journal of Hellenic Studies,* 80 (1960), pp. 88–93.

16. On the origin of the word "Gallos", see E. N. Lane, "The Name of Cybele's Priests the "Galloi", in *Cybele, Attis and Related Cults: Essays in Memory of M. J. Vermaseren,* ed. E. N. Lane (Brill, Leiden, 1996), pp. 117–33. Lane argues convincingly that the term Gallos first appears in the Greek language in the mid-third century BCE and that it derives from 'Galatian', referring to the Celtic tribes who invaded Anatolia in the third century BCE; these people eventually settled in Phrygia, becoming prominent in many of the older Phrygian centers of the Mother's worship, including Pessinous.

17. Attis is also the title used by the Phrygian Mother's priests in her shrine at Pessinous, Polybios 21.37.4–7; B. Virgilio, *Il 'Tempio Stato' di Pessinunte fra Pergamo e Roma nel II–I Secolo A.C.* (Giardini, Pisa, 1981).

18. A god Attis first appears in Greek cult during the fourth century BCE (see Roller, "Attis on Greek Votive Monuments"), and his worship is widely attested during the Hellenistic period. The first certain indication of a religious festival honoring Attis, the Attideia, occurs in the Piraeus (the port city of Athens) in the second century BCE, see Robert Garland, *The Piraeus from the Fifth to the First Century B.C.* (Gerald Duckworth, London, 1987), pp. 129–31.

19. The events surrounding the arrival of the Magna Mater in Rome are complex and have been the subject of much controversy. An excellent discussion of the problem is given by Erich Gruen, "The Advent of the Magna Mater", in *Studies in Greek Culture and Roman Policy* (E. J. Brill, Leiden, 1990), pp. 5–33.

20. For a full review of the ancient evidence for the event, see E. Schmidt, *Kultüber-tragungen* (A. Topelmann, Giessen, 1909), p. 1, n. 1. For a thorough discussion of the historical circumstances surrounding this event, see Gruen, "Advent of the Magna Mater".

21. Patrizio Pensabene, "Scavi nell'area del Tempio della Vittoria e del Santuario della Magna Mater sul Palatino", *Archeologia Laziale,* 9 (1988), pp. 54–67, summarizes the architectural history of the Magna Mater's Palatine temple. The goddess's principal Roman festival, the Megalesia, is vividly described by the Roman poets Lucretius, 6.621–43, and Ovid, *Fasti* 4.179–372. The nature of the Magna Mater's rites is discussed by K. Summers, "Lucretius' Roman Cybele", in *Cybele, Attis and Related Cults: Essays in Memory of M. J. Vermaseren,* ed. E. N. Lane (Brill, Leiden, 1996), pp. 337–65. On the Magna Mater's place in the Roman festival calendar, see H. H. Scullard, *Festivals and Ceremonies of the Roman Republic* (Thames & Hudson, London, 1981), pp. 97–100.

22. Maarten Vermaseren, *Corpus Cultus Cybelae Attidisque,* vol. III (E. J. Brill, Leiden, 1977), illustrates a number of Attis figurines, nos. 12–14, 17–18, 32–8, 58–67, 78–85, 119–32, 151–61. The phallic figurines are nos. 13, 69–72.

23. Obsequens 44a.

24. Valerius Maximus 7.7.6. On this passage, see T. P. Wiseman, *Catullus and his World: a Reappraisal* (Cambridge University Press, Cambridge, 1985), p. 204, and Beard, "The Roman and the Foreign", p. 177.

25. Note also the Roman treatment of a hermaphrodite, who could not be legally recognized as a third gender, but had to be classified as either male or female; see Yan Thomas, "The Division of the Sexes in Roman Law", in *A History of Women: From Ancient Goddesses to Christian Saints*, ed. Pauline Schmidt Pantel (Harvard University Press, Cambridge, MA and London, 1992), pp. 84–7.

26. In 102 BCE one of the Mother's priests at her shrine in Pessinous, entitled Battakes, came to Rome and petitioned to address the Senate in order to predict the Romans' victory and power in war. This petition met with a rather mixed reception, but when the plebeian tribune who opposed allowing the Phrygian priest to speak died of a fever shortly thereafter, the circumstance was seen as an omen of the goddess's power and created great public acclamation for the priest. We receive a vivid picture of the priest's colorful attire and his headdress, like a crown, considered particularly unsuitable for a Roman, but learn nothing of his gender and sexual status. Diodoros 36.13; Plutarch, *Marius* 17.5–6.

27. There is much additional material from later centuries on the eunuch priest, particularly in the literature of late antiquity. In late antique sources, however, the eunuch's gender and sexual status are couched as an element in the debate between pagan and Christian, a topic which deserves more discussion than I can give here.

28. This is well analyzed by Summers, "Lucretius' Roman Cybele".

29. Lucretius 2.614–17: "they assign Galli to her [the Great Mother] because those who violate the divinity of the Mother and are ungrateful to their parents are thought unworthy to bring living progeny into the light"; and 640–4: "they accompany the Great Mother with arms ... so that they may wish to defend the fatherland and be a source of protection and pride to their parents."

30. On the clubhouse of the Galli on the Palatine in Rome, see T. P. Wiseman, "Philodemus 26.3 G-P", *Classical Quarterly,* 32 (1982), pp. 475–6, and Wiseman, *Catullus and his World*, p. 204.

31. Note also the comments of Horace, *Satires* 1.2.119–22 (quoting Philodemus), on the Gallus as a suitable lover for a coy woman; see also Wiseman, *Catullus and his World*, p. 203.

32. Moses I. Finley, *Ancient Slavery and Modern Ideology* (Penguin, Harmondsworth and New York, 1980), pp. 95–6; Wiseman, *Catullus and his World*, pp. 10–14, quoting Seneca, *Controversies* 4, *Praef.* 10: the role of receptive partner in sodomy was the mark of a slave or freedman.

33. Juvenal, *Satires* 6.511–26.

34. After Attis' castration (lines 4–7) the poet frequently uses the feminine forms of pronouns and adjectives to describe Attis. I have chosen to retain the masculine pronoun in this discussion, however, since it seems to me that Catullus is not exploring the character of a woman, but rather that of a man who is uncertain of his own gender identity.

35. This poem has been much discussed, which is hardly surprising given its powerful language and volatile subject matter, and numerous readings, political, religious and didactic, have been applied to it. My discussion does not pretend to place this poem in the context of Catullus' whole oeuvre, an effort which would be out of place in an essay devoted to the eunuch as cross-gendered body; rather, I am most interested in its use of the eunuch as a vehicle for personal reflections on gender roles. The best introductions to this poem for the general reader are the works of Michael Putnam, "The Art of Catullus 64", *Harvard Studies in Classical Philology,* 65 (1961), pp. 165–205, and "Catullus 11: Ironies of Integrity", *Ramus,* 3 (1974), pp. 70–86, and also Wiseman,

Catullus and his World; an interesting reading is offered by S. A. Takács, "Magna Deum Mater Idaea, Cybele and Catullus' *Attis*", in *Cybele, Attis and Related Cults: Essays in Memory of M. J. Vermaseren*, ed. E. N. Lane (Brill, Leiden, 1996), pp. 367–86.

36. On this point, see Paul W. Harkins, "Catullus 63 and 64", *Transactions of the American Philological Association,* 90 (1959), pp. 102–11; Eve Adler, *Catullan Self-Revelation* (Arno Press, New York, 1981), pp. 130–3; Micaela Janan, *When the Lamp Is Shattered: Desire and Narrative in Catullus* (Southern Illinois University Press, Carbondale and Edwardsville, 1994), pp. 104–7.

37. The narrator's status as outcast mimics the status of a real slave in Rome, as Cybele becomes the *domina*, the mistress, both of Catullus' mind and of his body; cf. Wiseman, *Catullus and his World*, p. 181.

38. On the role of the Magna Mater and the Galli in the *Aeneid*, see the excellent discussion by T. P. Wiseman, "Cybele, Virgil and Augustus", in *Poetry and Politics in the Age of Augustus*, ed. T. Woodman and D. West (Cambridge University Press, Cambridge, 1984), pp. 117–28.

39. Some aspects of sacred eunuchism are discussed in *Third Sex, Third Gender: Beyond Sexual Dimorphism in Culture and History*, ed. Gilbert Herdt (Zone Books, New York, 1994), especially the chapter by Nanda, 'Hijras', discussing eunuch attendants on the Mother Goddess in contemporary India, and one by Kathryn M. Ringrose, "Living in the Shadows: Eunuchs and Gender in Byzantium", also in *Third Sex, Third Gender*, pp. 85–109, on eunuchs in the Byzantine court, who claimed a special status of chastity because of their asexual condition.

Why Aren't Jewish Women Circumcised?

SHAYE J. D. COHEN

Classical rabbinic Judaism has always been, and in many circles still is, a male-dominated culture, whose virtuosi and authorities are males, whose paragon of normality in all legal discussions is the adult Jewish male, whose legal rulings in many areas of life (notably marriage and ritual observance) accord men greater privilege than women, and whose values define public communal space as male space. Within this culture women are unable to initiate a marriage or a divorce, are obligated to dress modestly in public and to segregate themselves behind a partition in synagogue, and are excluded from the regimen of prayer and Torah study that characterizes, and in the rabbinic perspective sanctifies, the life of Jewish men. In this culture women are socially and legally inferior to men.

Of all the rituals from which women are excluded by rabbinic culture, the exclusion from circumcision is at once the most obvious and the most problematic. What sets circumcision apart from all the numerous other ritual practices that are observed by men but not by women is its status as a boundary marker. From Hellenistic to modern times, in the eyes of Jews and non-Jews alike, circumcision has functioned as a sign marking the boundary between Jews and non-Jews (gentiles). As a New Testament writer explains, gentiles are 'called the uncircumcision by what is called the circumcision' (Ephesians 2:11).[1] Unlike many other Jewish observances, circumcision is often understood as defining who is 'in' and who is 'out'. Circumcision is a sign of the covenant between God and Israel (Genesis 17). A gentile man's conversion to Judaism is signaled through circumcision. In the Middle Ages, and perhaps even before, both Christians and Jews attributed to circumcision a sacramental power akin to that which Christians attributed to baptism. Circumcision thus marks a Jew as a Jew and even has the power to make a gentile into a Jew.[2] However, there is something paradoxical about this identification of circumcision with Jewishness, because approximately half of all Jews living at any given moment are uncircumcised. If circumcision serves to define Jews as Jews, what of Jewish women? Why do Jewish men bear a covenantal mark on their flesh but not Jewish women? Are women Jews the same way that men are Jews?

If 'we' wished to answer these questions, clearly our answers would be determined by our methods and perspectives, which in turn would be determined by who 'we' are. If 'we' are contemporary Jews, especially those sensitive to gender issues, we might wish to argue that male circumcision needs to be abolished or de-emphasized as a ritual marker precisely because it has functioned within history to discriminate invidiously against women; or we might wish to argue that the Jewish community needs to invent a ritual as powerful as circumcision to mark the birth of baby girls. If 'we' are anthropologists, especially those informed by gender issues, we of course would argue that the Jewishness of women is very different from the Jewishness of men—we might even argue that only men are really Jews. We would observe that the same rabbinic culture that celebrates maleness, patriarchy and circumcision, is also the same rabbinic culture that ascribes Jewishness by descent to the offspring of a Jewish mother and a non-Jewish father but not to the offspring of a Jewish father and a non-Jewish mother. Perhaps a Jewish woman's Jewishness is less than that of a Jewish man, as indicated by the absence of any covenantal mark on her body, but rabbinic culture compensates her for this deficiency by declaring her, not him, the essential vehicle for imprinting Jewishness by birth. If 'we' are sociologists, especially qualitative sociologists informed by gender issues, we would want to interview contemporary Jewish women to understand how (or whether) their Jewish identity has been affected by the absence of an embodied representation. Do they feel 'less Jewish' because of the absence of a covenantal mark? We should like to know the thoughts and feelings of a Jewish mother whose son is about to be circumcised; beyond her obvious concern for the well-being of her child, what does she think of the fact that her eight-day-old son is about to be welcomed as a Jew by the community in a ceremony which the boy's father also experienced but which she did not? If 'we' are Freudians, or psychoanalytically inclined, we would argue that the circumcision of a son by his father represents castration, because the father sees his son as a sexual competitor for the affections of the mother. The father, of course, has no cause for alarm from the birth of a daughter and no need to circumcise her.

These, then, are some of the ways by which 'we' might answer the questions raised by the circumcision of Jewish men and the non-circumcision of Jewish women. All of these approaches have some utility, and in a future book-length study of this topic I hope to avail myself of them. In this essay my goal is more modest. I am writing as a historian; I would like to understand when and why the non-circumcision of Jewish women became a question that required answers, and what answers were advanced by the Jews of antiquity. My concern here is not how 'we' might explain the non-circumcision of Jewish women but how 'they', the Jews of antiquity, explained it. No women's voices will be heard in this essay; no sources tell us how ancient Jewish women explained the absence of a covenantal mark from their bodies. I deal here with male constructions of men and maleness, and of women and femaleness.[3]

First a note on terminology. 'Circumcision' means literally 'cutting around'; when men are circumcised, an incision is made around the shaft of the penis and the foreskin is removed. The clitoris of women does protrude somewhat from the surrounding tissues and consequently can be said to be capable of 'circumcision', but the more accurate term to use in connection with women is 'excision', the 'cutting out' or 'cutting off' of the skin covering the clitoris, and/or some or all of the clitoris, and/or the labia minora, and/or the labia majora (the labia are the folds of skin around the vaginal opening). In this essay I use the term 'circumcision' even with reference to women because I want to contrast the presence of a bodily marker for Jewish men with the absence of an equivalent bodily marker for Jewish women, and I do not want to be distracted by distinctive terminology for each. I realize that this usage may in turn cause some confusion, because the circumcision of men is not equivalent to the excision of women (except perhaps for the mildest forms of female excision). The male equivalent to the excision of a woman's clitoris and labia would be the cutting off of the entire penis, not just the foreskin. With reason, then, many contemporary feminists and activists use the term 'Female Genital Mutilation' or FGM, because they do not want to dignify the maiming of women with the neutral and scientific-sounding term 'excision'. Nevertheless, I hope I may be permitted in this essay to refer to the circumcision of women; my focus is not on circumcision but on the absence of circumcision, the absence of any women's ritual in Judaism that approximates the circumcision of men.

Were, in fact, Jewish women in antiquity uncircumcised? In contemporary times circumcision (excision) of women is practised primarily across northern and central Africa (from Mauritania, Senegal and Guinea in the west, to Sudan, Ethiopia and Somalia in the east, and virtually everywhere in between, from Egypt in the north to Kenya and Tanzania in the south), on the perimeter of the Arabian peninsula (Yemen, Oman, United Arab Emirates and Bahrain), and among various (Muslim) groups in Pakistan, Malaysia, Indonesia and the Philippines. The origins of the practice, how and why it became so widespread, are unknown. The only sure points are two: first, although it pre-dates Islam and is practised also by non-Islamic peoples (Egyptian Copts, Ethiopian Christians, African animists, for example), it is widely associated with Islam and seen as an Islamic custom; second, while many societies practise male circumcision but not female circumcision, the vast majority of the societies that practise female circumcision also practise male circumcision. This suggests that at some point female circumcision was introduced in imitation of the male ritual.[4]

Numerous societies in the ancient Near East practised male circumcision: Israel, Egypt, Ethiopia, Syria, Phoenicia, Edom (Idumaea), Ammon, Moab and Arabia. All of these societies (except the Phoenician) maintained the practice to one extent or another well into the Roman period. Of these societies the only one known to have practised female circumcision is Egypt.[5] The earliest evidence is a papyrus document from 163 BCE, written in Greek by an Egyptian monk at the temple of Serapis in Memphis.[6] In the petition, an Egyptian woman claims that her daughter 'is of the age to be circumcised' since she is about to be married; the monk in turn explains to the Greek governor that such circumcision 'is the custom among the Egyptians'. The verb used is *peritemnein*, the standard Greek verb for the circumcision of men, here applied to the circumcision of a woman. This document shows that the circumcision of women just before marriage was an established custom, at least in Memphis (middle Egypt), not later than the middle of the second century BCE. The absence of any reference to female circumcision in any Egyptian document of the preceding two thousand years, suggests that this practice was a relatively recent importation into Egypt, even if we cannot be sure when it was imported, why, or whence (Ethiopia? Arabia?).[7]

The next piece of evidence brings us to our theme. Strabo, a Greek geographer of the last part of the first century BCE, writes as follows:[8]

> One of the customs most zealously observed among the Egyptians is this, that they rear every child that is born, and circumcise the males, and excise the females, as is also customary among the Jews, who are also Egyptian in origin, as I have already stated in my account of them.

Strabo comments on three remarkable characteristics of the Egyptians: they rear all their children, they circumcise the males (the verb is *peritemnein*), and they excise the females (the verb is *ektemnein*). Strabo notes that the same three remarkable characteristics can be found among the Jews 'who are Egyptian in origin'. In another passage Strabo remarks that the successors of Moses instituted the practice of 'circumcisions and excisions'.[9] In yet a third passage, part of his description of Ethiopia, Strabo mentions the excision of Jewish women:[10]

> And then to the harbor of Antiphilus, and, above this, to the Creophagi [lit. Meat-Eaters]; they are mutilated in their sexual organs and the women are excised in the Jewish manner.

Two points are striking about this passage: first, the excision of the women (the verb again is *ektemnein*) is said to be done 'Jewishly' or 'in the Jewish manner' (*Ioudaïkôs*); second, the mutilation of the male genitals is not said to be done in the Jewish manner. The males are not 'circumcised' but 'mutilated' (the Greek noun is *koloboi*). Elsewhere, when describing another Ethiopian tribe, Strabo explains that 'not only are they mutilated in their sexual organs, but some of them are also circumcised, just as the Egyptians'.[11] Whatever it is that one has to cut or cut off in order to become 'mutilated' (*kolobos*) clearly is less, in Strabo's opinion, than whatever it is that one has to cut or cut off in order to be 'circumcised' (from the verb peritemnein).[12] Egyptians, like Jews, are circumcised; the Meat-Eaters of Ethiopia are not. But their women are excised in the Jewish manner.

What are we to make of Strabo's thrice-told statement that Jewish women are excised? We have two possibilities: either Strabo is correct, or he is not. If he is correct, this will mean that some Jewish community somewhere in the ancient world practised female circumcision, and that Strabo somehow discovered this fact which otherwise is completely hidden from us. There is nothing impossible about this scenario; given the great diversity of ancient Judaism, it is hard to identify a practice that some Jews could not have observed, and given the paucity of our historical documentation, it is not impossible that a stray document (Strabo, for example) may preserve information not found anywhere else. We might perhaps seek to confirm Strabo's statement by appeal to the 'black Jews' of Ethiopia, the Falashas, who do (or did) practise female circumcision, but this will not work, because surely the Falasha practice is to be explained as a manifestation of their Ethiopianness, and not of their Jewishness. (Falashas today are Jews, but their origins are most obscure and the degree of their connection with Judaism in pre-modern times is disputed; it is most unlikely that a 'Jewish' Falasha community existed in the time of Strabo.) Falasha practice is simply part of general Ethiopian culture, in which female circumcision is widely practised, and is not a relic of some long-lost Jewish tradition.[13] Even if Strabo is correct, his statement remains uncorroborated.

The alternative possibility seems far more likely: Strabo simply is wrong.[14] Falashas aside, no Jewish community, in ancient, medieval, or modern times, is known to have practised female circumcision.[15] Various medical writers of the Roman and Byzantine periods, not to mention the physicians of nineteenth-century Europe and America, recommended clitoridectomy if a woman's clitoris grew too large, thereby constituting 'a deformity' and leading 'to a feeling of shame'. The Egyptians were regularly cited as wise precedents — Egyptians yes, Jews no.[16] The best evidence against Strabo is provided by Philo of Alexandria, a Jewish philosopher, exegete and apologist, who flourished in the first half of the first century CE. Philo devotes two long passages to circumcision. The first is the introduction to his *On the Special Laws*, a book that discusses the meaning of the commandments of the Torah; the second is the commentary on Genesis 17 in his *Questions and Answers on Genesis*. The latter contains the following:[17]

> Why does he [God] command that only the males be circumcised?
>
> In the first place, the Egyptians by the custom of their country circumcise the marriageable youth and maid in the fourteenth year of their age, when the male begins to get seed, and the female to have a menstrual flow. But the divine legislator ordained circumcision for males alone for many reasons.
>
> The first of these is that the male has more pleasure in, and desire for, mating than does the female, and he is more ready for it. Therefore He rightly leaves out the female and suppresses the undue impulses of the male by the sign of circumcision.

The second is that the matter of the female in the remains of the menstrual fluids produces the fetus. But the male provides the skill and the cause. And so, since the male provides the greater and more necessary part in the process of generation, it was proper that his pride should be checked by the sign of circumcision, but the material element, being inanimate, does not admit of arrogance ...

Philo begins by contrasting the Jewish practice with the Egyptian: Jews circumcise only the males, while Egyptians circumcise both males and females.[18] Philo thus confirms the joint testimony of Strabo and the Greek papyrus that Egyptian women were, in fact, circumcised, but refutes Strabo's claim that Jewish women were too. The source of Strabo's error is easy to see. Strabo, a geographer, historian and anthropologist, believed that the Jews were originally and 'really' Egyptians,[19] and since he knew that Egyptians circumcised both males and females, he naturally concluded that the Jews did the same. Strabo was the victim of his own anthropological theory; modern anthropologists do not always do better.

The Philonic passage is the earliest evidence for Jewish concern about the imbalance between the circumcision of men and the non-circumcision of women. Why do Jews circumcise only the males? Philo gives two answers. First, circumcision serves to check male lust which is much stronger than the female's, in fact, a little too strong. Second, circumcision serves to check male pride, which has its origin in the fact that males contribute the more important part in the process of generation.[20] Each of these two explanations recurs in Philo's discussions of the meaning of circumcision. In his introduction to *On the Special Laws* Philo says that circumcision both symbolizes 'the excision of pleasures which bewitch the mind' and teaches that 'a man should know himself and banish from the soul the grievous malady of conceit'.[21] Philo has four additional explanations for the practice of circumcision, but only these two explanations are pressed into service to answer the question 'Why only the males?' and they are pressed into service only in this passage. Since males have more pleasure than females in intercourse, their lust needs to be checked, but not the lust of women; since males take greater pride than females in their role in procreation, their pride needs to be checked, but not the pride of women.

No doubt Philo would have argued that Jewish women, no less than Jewish men, need to suppress their lust and their pride, and that this suppression is an essential ingredient in righteousness for both sexes alike. Females, for Philo, are inferior to males, but even they, within their limited capacity, are capable of righteousness.[22] Only males need physical circumcision, while both males and females need the lesson taught by circumcision (what Christians would call 'spiritual circumcision'). Since Philo nowhere says that circumcision is an essential criterion for membership in the people of Israel—in only one exceptional passage does Philo even mention the 'covenantal' value of physical circumcision—he is not troubled by the fact that one half of all Jews are not circumcised. The status of women within the people of Israel is not affected by the absence of circumcision, since circumcision does not determine status.[23]

'Why does he [God] command that only the males be circumcised?' was only one of a series of questions about circumcision that Philo answered. In the first century of our era the practice of circumcision seems to have been widely debated by Greek-speaking Jews. The historian Josephus promised to write an essay on the subject, but apparently did not succeed in fulfilling his promise (or, if he did, his work is lost). Some Jews abandoned the practice, or at least argued that the practice should be abandoned; others actually attempted to conceal their circumcision through epispasm.[24] This passage of Philo suggests that the opponents of circumcision used the non-circumcision of women as one of their arguments. Perhaps they argued that circumcision could not be essential in God's eyes, because women were not circumcised, or perhaps they objected that Jewish circumcision was illogical because it was not practised on Jewish women, even though in other respects it closely resembled Egyptian practice. Philo had to respond.

The most outspoken Jewish critic of circumcision in the first century was Paul. In his letters Paul argued that God did not want circumcision in the flesh because true circumcision was spiritual, not physical (Romans 2:28–9); that Abraham and his descendants occupy a special place in the unfolding of sacred history not because of circumcision but because of faith (Romans 4:11–13); that the law, which somehow is synonymous with circumcision, is antithetical to Christ (Galatians 5:2–6); that Christians are circumcised spiritually through the circumcision of Christ (Colossians 2:11, a passage that also implicitly associates circumcision with baptism); and that the circumcision of the Jews is (merely) a physical circumcision made in the flesh by human hands (Ephesians 2:11).[25]

For all of Paul's opposition to circumcision, one argument that he might have used but did not use is the argument from the non-circumcision of women. According to Paul, in the new dispensation 'there is no longer Jew or Greek, there is no longer slave or free, there is no longer male and female; for all of you are one in Christ Jesus' (Galatians 3:28). According to Paul circumcision is intolerable because it invidiously discriminates between Jew and Greek.[26] But Paul fails to observe that circumcision also invidiously discriminates between male and female—this too should have been a powerful argument against the Jewish ritual. If there is no longer male and female in Christ, then circumcision can play no role in Christ. Here is a good argument against circumcision that Paul might have used, but did not.

The obvious explanation for the absence of this argument from Paul is that Paul did not really believe that there was no longer male and female in Christ. Paul believed that men and women had separate functions in the new order, as in the old, and that the place of women was decidedly below that of men. 'Man is the image and reflection of God; but woman is the reflection of man' (1 Corinthians 11:7). 'Women should be silent in the churches. For they are not permitted to speak, but they should be subordinate ... If there is anything they desire to know, let them ask their husbands at home' (1 Corinthians 14:34–5). Indeed, the resounding proclamation that 'there is no longer Jew or Greek, there is no longer slave or free, there is no longer male and female' recurs in somewhat different form in three other Pauline passages. Only the verse quoted above, Galatians 3:28, includes 'there is no longer male and female'. The other versions read: 'There is no distinction between Jew and Greek' (Romans 10:12); 'For in the one spirit we were all baptized into one body—Jews or Greeks, slaves or free' (1 Corinthians 12:13); and 'There is no longer Greek and Jew, circumcised and uncircumcised, barbarian, Scythian, slave and free' (Colossians 3:11). 'There is no longer male and female' seems to have been a rhetorical outburst (or, as is usually argued, a pre-Pauline formula), nothing more; even in the absence of circumcision females were to keep their separate—and inferior—position according to Paul.[27]

The successors of Paul developed the argument that he had not. The *Dialogue with Trypho the Jew*, written in Greek by Justin Martyr, a Christian apologist of the middle of the second century CE, depicts a dialogue—whether real or imagined does not much matter for our purposes—between Justin himself and a Jew named Trypho. Justin, of course, represents the (winning) Christian side, and Trypho the (losing) Jewish. One of the central concerns of the work is the interpretation of the Hebrew Bible; Justin is determined to show that Christians, who accept Jesus as God and Christ but ignore the laws of the Torah, interpret the Bible correctly, while the Jews, who deny Christ but observe the laws, do not. Thus Justin devotes a good many paragraphs to the ritual observances of the law, especially circumcision. His fundamental thesis is that the ritual requirements in general, and circumcision in particular, are not universal timeless commandments, but were intended for a specific people (the Jews) for specific times and for specific reasons. God never intended them to be observed by his true worshippers, the Christians. Justin argues in the Pauline manner (but without citing Paul) that circumcision cannot be a requirement for salvation:[28]

> The Scriptures and the facts of the case force us to admit that Abraham received circumcision for a sign, not for righteousness itself. Thus was it justly said of your people, 'That soul which shall not be circumcised on the eighth day shall be destroyed out of his people' (Genesis 17:14). Moreover, the fact that females cannot receive circumcision of the flesh shows that circumcision was given as a sign, not as an act of righteousness. For God also bestowed upon women the capability of performing every good and virtuous act. We see that the physical formation of male and female is different, but it is equally evident that the bodily form is not what makes either of them good or evil. Their righteousness is determined by their acts of piety and justice.

That Abraham's circumcision is a 'sign', and not a function of righteousness, is an argument with which Paul would certainly have agreed; the same point is made by Romans 4:11, cited above. No doubt Justin, like Paul, has Genesis 15:6 in mind: 'And Abraham believed in the Lord; and the Lord reckoned it to him as righteousness'. The verse demonstrates that Abraham was righteous even without circumcision. After this Pauline beginning Justin strikes out on his own. Since Genesis 17:11 says that he who is not circumcised is cut off from his people, Justin argues that circumcision is just a 'sign', that is, a sign of belonging to the people. This point refers back to Justin's earlier assertion that circumcision was to serve as a 'sign' that would make the Jews conspicuous and identifiable. Thus, so far, Justin has established that circumcision is a sign not of righteousness, but of belonging to the Jewish people. As further proof that circumcision cannot have anything to do with righteousness, Justin adduces women. Clearly women, like men, are deemed righteous or wicked by their actions; their circumcision—or lack of it—is irrelevant. Since women's uncircumcision is not a function of their righteousness (or lack of it), the same must be true for men.

Justin's argument clearly implies that the Jewish people consists only of men, since circumcision is a sign of membership and distinctiveness, and only men are so signed. Women lack the sign and therefore membership. Justin does not notice the implication of his own argument. It does not occur to him to ask how (or if) women become members of the Jewish people, or to observe that baptism is superior to circumcision because it is practised on males and females alike. The inability of women to be signed as members of the Jewish people is not, for Justin, an argument against Jewish circumcision. We shall have to wait for Justin's successors to develop the potential of his argument. Justin's point simply is that circumcision cannot be a function of righteousness. One can be righteous before the Lord even if one is uncircumcised. Women are proof.

It is likely, I think, that Justin derived the basis of his argument from Jewish circles of the sort combated by Philo. Scholars have long argued that much of the early Christian polemic against the Jewish law ultimately derives from 'radical' or 'radically Hellenized' Jewish circles; similarly, scholars have long argued that Justin is much indebted to Hellenistic Judaism, perhaps even to Philo directly.[29] It is reasonable to suggest, therefore, that Justin, in arguing that the non-circumcision of women demonstrates that God does not demand the circumcision of men, may be echoing the arguments of Jewish opponents of circumcision whom Philo had combated a century earlier.

Much of what Justin says about the observance of 'the Law' in general, and about the observance of circumcision in particular, became common stock in subsequent Christian anti-Jewish polemic. Thus, Justin argues that true circumcision is not carnal but spiritual; God wants the (spiritual) circumcision of the heart, not the (physical) circumcision of the penis; God created Adam uncircumcised; Abel, Enoch, Noah, Melchizedeq, and Abraham all pleased God even though they were not circumcised; God heaped numerous commandments (including circumcision) on the Jews because, recognizing their hardness of heart, God knew that without constant reminders and controls, they would inevitably lapse into idolatry, a danger which Christians need not fear; the blood of the crucifixion has replaced the blood of circumcision. All these arguments recur with some regularity in the Christian anti-Jewish polemics of antiquity and the Middle Ages.

The only one of Justin's anti-circumcision arguments that does not become a staple in subsequent Christian polemic is the argument that interests us, the argument from the non-circumcision of women. As far as I have been able to determine, this argument nowhere recurs in the subsequent anti-Jewish literature written in Greek. There are numerous polemics against Judaism, numerous attacks on Jewish circumcision, but the argument drawn from the non-circumcision of women does not recur again—or, if it does, I have not found it, and the standard handbooks do not record it.[30]

On the Latin side, the argument makes two significant appearances in antiquity. I doubt whether either of these authors read Justin, but each, perhaps independently, has hit upon Justin's argument and developed it further than Justin had himself. Cyprian, a bishop in Carthage in the mid-third century CE, gathered a collection of biblical citations to prove the truth of Christianity, by showing (among other things) the concordance of the Old Testament with the New. Under the heading 'That the first circumcision, the carnal, has been made void, and that a second, a spiritual, has been promised instead', Cyprian briefly marshals some verses demonstrating the Christian position, already familiar to us from Justin, and then tacks on at the end the following line: 'That sign [that is, the sign of physical circumcision] is of no use to women, while all [Christians] are signed with the sign of the Lord [that is, the sign of the cross applied in baptism]'. The superiority of baptism to circumcision consists, in part, in the fact that the former is performed on all adherents of the faith community, men and women alike, while the latter is performed only on men.[31]

The next occurrence of the argument is even richer and more interesting. The *De Altercatione Ecclesiae et Synagogae*, 'Concerning the Dispute between the Church and the Synagogue: A Dialogue', was written probably in the middle of the fifth century CE and came to be ascribed (falsely) to Augustine (hence I shall refer to the author of this work as [Augustine]). This work is one of the first to present the conflict between Judaism and Christianity as a debate between two women, Lady Synagogue (*Synagoga*) and Lady Church (*Ecclesia*), a conceit that will become popular in medieval Christian art and drama. The two women argue in court, each one disputing the claims of the other. In large part the ground covered in this dispute is familiar, even if the literary form is novel. After Lady Synagogue has prided herself on her possession of the Law and circumcision, her 'sign', Lady Church responds:[32]

> For if you say that your people is to be saved through the sign of your passion
> —what shall your virgins do, what shall your widows do, what shall even the
> Mothers of the Synagogue do, if you testify that the sign of circumcision gives

to the people the benefit of eternal life? Therefore it is fair to conclude that you do not have Jewish women: men are circumcised; women, however, cannot have a foreskin; therefore they are not able to be saved, if you are saved by circumcision. You see, therefore, that you are able to have men, that is, the circumcised, as Jews. Women, however, who are not able to be circumcised, I declare are neither Jews nor Christians, but pagans.

The argument of the first sentence is fundamentally the same as Justin's. Circumcision cannot be an agent or 'sign' of salvation, because in that case women would be excluded from salvation. The author calls circumcision a 'passion', that is, a suffering, because from the Christian perspective the blood of Christ has replaced the blood of circumcision, an argument that appears explicitly in Justin.

The author highlights three categories of women who would not be saved if circumcision were an agent of salvation: virgins, widows, and Mothers of the Synagogue. Jewish inscriptions from Italy commemorate three women each of whom was a 'Mother of the Synagogue'. Whether the title was merely honorific, or whether it also brought with it communal responsibility and leadership, is unknown.[33] In any case, I am not sure how to interpret this list of three. Perhaps the author simply means 'all Jewish women': from the young and undistinguished (virgins), to the old (widows) and the distinguished (Mothers of the Synagogue). Or perhaps the author is deliberately choosing as his examples women who are not married: virgins, widows and Mothers of the Synagogue (a title that seems to have been bestowed most often on elderly widows—not one of the three attested 'Mothers of the Synagogue' had a husband at the time of her death). We shall see below that one possible Jewish response to the Christian argument is that Jewish women do not need circumcision because they fulfill their Judaism by facilitating the Jewish observances of their husbands and sons. Perhaps to forestall this response, the author chose to highlight women who do not have husbands. The question must be left open.

If the first sentence is still within Justin's framework, the following sentences go well beyond it. Justin had argued that circumcision was a sign of membership in the people, not a sign of righteousness, and therefore of no consequence to Christians who, like women, could be righteous even without circumcision. As I mentioned above, Justin seems not to have noticed that this argument implies that women are not members of the people of Israel, since they lack circumcision, the sign of membership in the people. [Augustine] takes this argument and develops it. If circumcision is a sign of membership in the people, then Jewish women are excluded not only from salvation but even from the name 'Jew' altogether. If Jewish men are Jews by virtue of their circumcision, then Jewish women cannot be Jews. Not circumcised, they are not Jews. Not baptized, they are not Christians. Therefore, concludes the author in a wonderful *reductio ad absurdum*, they must be pagans.

This argument is especially effective in its literary context. There is something odd about having a woman, in this case Lady Synagogue, defend the importance of circumcision, when women are excluded from membership in the synagogue because of their lack of circumcision. Similarly, in the following sentences the author goes on to mock circumcision as an agent of salvation, and again uses women as proof. Jewish women who have committed adultery, he says, ought not to be punished or condemned, since their only sin is to have played with the circumcised male organ, the sign of salvation. The organ on which circumcision is performed is normally kept hidden and private, to be seen only by a wife. Circumcision is thus a sign not of salvation but of sin, shame and lust.[34] In contrast, the Christian sign is borne publicly on the forehead by men and women alike ([Augustine] seems to be referring to the chrism that is applied right after baptism), an argument we have already seen in Cyprian.

After [Augustine] the argument that the circumcision of men denies women membership in the Jewish community seems not to recur in Christian Latin literature until the Middle Ages—I say 'seems' because, again, I am relying on our handbooks and indexes to supplement my own very imperfect knowledge.[35] Perhaps the argument never became widespread because most Christians intuitively realized that they were no less guilty than the Jews in excluding women from equal membership in their religious community. An argument against Judaism constructed on the premise that there ought to be equality between men and women was too radical not just for Paul but also for his successors. The status enjoyed by Christian women in Christian society was hardly any better than that enjoyed by Jewish women in Jewish society, even if baptism was (and is) indeed performed on men and women alike, and circumcision was (and is) performed only on men. Anti-Jewish arguments based on women's non-membership could not become popular, and they did not.

We have seen that the non-circumcision of women provided Christian anti-Jewish polemicists with three good arguments against Judaism. First, Justin's argument: if righteousness before God requires circumcision, why are women not circumcised? Second, Cyprian's argument: Christian baptism is superior to Jewish circumcision, since baptism applies to both men and women while circumcision applies only to men. Third, [Augustine]'s argument: since Jewish women are not circumcised, are they Jews at all? Philo's moralizing allegory (circumcision serves to reduce lust and pride) does not really answer any of these arguments, since all three Christian authors assume that circumcision affects one's status both in the community of Israel and in the eyes of God, while Philo makes no such assumption.

It is remarkable that the rabbis of antiquity ignore the questions raised by Justin, Cyprian and [Augustine].[36] A few passages indicate that the rabbis were fully aware of the gender implications of circumcision. They emphasize the fact that circumcision is to be performed on the male procreative organ, the place on the body where an infant is recognized to be male or female.[37] In one passage of the Babylonian Talmud women are cited as proof for the view that a gentile who has been immersed for the purpose of conversion but has not been circumcised is nevertheless to be regarded as a valid proselyte, because 'thus have we found to be the case in connection with the matriarchs, that they immersed but were not circumcised'. And how do we know that our matriarchs immersed? 'Logic demands it; for otherwise how did they enter under the wings of the divine presence.' Here, then, women, represented by the matriarchs of old, are paradigms of uncircumcised Jews.[38] In contrast, another passage of the Babylonian Talmud says that, because a woman resembles a man who has already been circumcised, she may perform the ritual of circumcision on an infant (since she is 'circumcised' herself). Here, then, women are paradigms of circumcised Jews.[39] These and related passages do not amount to much; the rabbis of antiquity were aware of the gender implications of circumcision but were not concerned by the absence of circumcision for women.

Why were the rabbis so unconcerned? Whether in general the rabbis concerned themselves with Christianity and Christian polemics against Judaism is a much debated question.[40] No matter how we answer that question, were there any specific values or concepts within rabbinic culture that would explain the rabbinic indifference to the absence of female circumcision? I suggest that there were; in the rabbinic reflections about Israel, women and circumcision, we find the answers that the rabbis could have given to the Christian polemicists, had they chosen to do so.

First, Christianity is a faith community while Judaism is an ethnic community. 'Christians are made, not born.' That is, Christianness is achieved by an individual through faith in Christ, while Jewishness, in contrast, is ascribed to an individual through birth (I leave aside proselytes). As a Church writer of the late fourth century says, 'from a Jew a Jew is born'.[41] The Mishnah, the core document of the canon of rabbinic writings, conceives of the Jews ('Israel') primarily in genealogical terms: they are the lineal descendants of Abraham, Isaac and Jacob. Within the people of Israel, one's status, especially one's marriageability, is determined in large part by birth. The Mishnah does permit gentiles to convert to Judaism and thereby become part of the people of Israel, but they remain anomalous and unequal, precisely because their fathers are not 'our' fathers. Post-mishnaic documents partly redress this imbalance, improving the lot of proselytes and emphasizing Judaism's 'religious' character, but the fundamental point remains. Israel is primarily a descent group which one joins at birth.[42] If so, Jewish women too are Jewish by virtue of their birth. Christian women need to be baptized in order to become Christian, but Jewish women do not need circumcision or any other ritual by which to become Jewish.

Second, although Jewish women are Jews, they are Jews of a peculiar kind. The 'normal' Jew for the rabbis, as the 'normal' Israelite for the Torah, was the free adult male. The exclusion of women from circumcision typifies their exclusion from the observance of numerous commandments. In classical Athens, as in classical Judaism, women of citizen status could not participate in the activities of the public sphere. The term 'Athenians' means men; Athenian women were not 'Athenian' but 'Attic'. The term 'Jews' means men; Jewish women are the wives, sisters, mothers and daughters of men, the real Jews.[43] As the Talmud says, women attain merit (that is, a share in the world to come) by bringing their sons to school and awaiting their husbands' return from the academy. A woman's place is to facilitate acts of piety by her menfolk, acts of piety from which she herself is excluded.[44] Therefore it should occasion no surprise if only men are marked by circumcision—only men are real Jews in all respects.

Third, although the rabbis of the Talmud magnify the importance of circumcision and invest it with cosmic significance ('Great is circumcision; were it not for circumcision the Holy One, Blessed be He, would not have created the world'), the rabbis do not see it as synonymous with Judaism.[45] The rabbis, for example, admit the Jewishness of a born Jew who, for health reasons, is unable to be circumcised.[46] According to one view, at least in theory, a conversion can be valid even without circumcision (see above). Thus, for the rabbis of antiquity, circumcision is an important and distinctive part of Jewishness, but it does not, in and of itself, confer or encapsulate Jewishness. (Circumcised gentiles are not Jews.) Hence Jewish women, like Jewish men, can be Jewish even if they are not circumcised. In contrast, Justin, Cyprian and [Augustine] understand Jewish circumcision in terms of Christian baptism, an understanding that recurs regularly in ancient and medieval Christianity.[47] If circumcision is supposed to play the role for Jews that baptism does for Christians, the questions of Justin, Cyprian and [Augustine] are powerful indeed. But if circumcision is not analogous to baptism, the questions collapse of their own accord. For the rabbis of antiquity, circumcision was not analogous to baptism.

In the high Middle Ages in Europe (1100–1400), Jewish apologists and polemicists turned to the questions that had been posed by Justin, Cyprian and [Augustine]. Since the ancient rabbinic texts did not provide them with ready-made answers, they had to invent new ones.[48] Questions once ignored as insignificant now became worthy of discussion, no doubt because Christian polemic once again made use of the non-circumcision of women as an anti-Jewish argument.[49] But internal developments within Jewish thought meant that answers that once had been obvious were no longer self-evident. Rabbinic reflections on Israel, women and circumcision had developed substantially since antiquity, and new answers were needed. Judaism remained an ethnic community, to be sure, but the growth of Jewish philosophy meant that a religious or philosophical definition became more pronounced during these centuries. If Jews were Jews not only, or not primarily, through birth, but through belief and practice, as most medieval Jews believed ('Our nation of the children of Israel is a nation only by virtue of its laws', one philosopher remarked)[50], then how should women be understood, since they are excluded from so many of the delights of the Torah. The rabbis could no longer simply assume that the Jewishness of Jewish women was simply a function of birth as Jews. Further, whether or not under Christian influence, many Jews began to see circumcision as analogous to Christian baptism, a sacrament conferring spiritual gifts and changing the nature of the person receiving it. It was circumcision that protected a (male) Jew from the fires of Gehenna; Jewish women would circumcise their babies who had died before the eighth day, so that the infant could partake of the eternal life guaranteed by circumcision. In mystical circles an entire theology of circumcision was elaborated, which explained how circumcision allowed a (male) Jew to penetrate the inner mysteries of the Torah. The more that circumcision and its significance were magnified, the more problematic the non-circumcision of women became. As a result of these changes, perhaps, the questions that had been posed but ignored in antiquity now gained force and required attention.[51] One thousand years after Justin, rabbinic Jews finally took his question seriously.

Even if these internal developments within rabbinic society facilitated the emergence of the question, without the external stimulus of Christian polemic rabbinic Judaism would probably not have been troubled by the non-circumcision of women. Similarly I have conjectured above that Philo's treatment of the question was prompted by the objections of some free-thinking Jews who were opposed to the practice of circumcision and based their opposition, in part, on the non-circumcision of women. For both Philo and the rabbis the fundamental inferiority, marginality and Otherness of women were so self-evident that the presence of a covenantal mark on the bodies of men, and its absence from the bodies of women, seemed natural and inevitable. In a sense, both Philo and the rabbis conceded [Augustine]'s fundamental point: women are inferior to men, and therefore their Jewishness is inferior to that of men.

Notes

This article treats a wide variety of topics and I have therefore kept bibliographical annotation to a minimum. The material of this essay will be discussed at greater length in my book *Why Aren't Jewish Women Circumcised?*, currently in preparation. Earlier versions of this article were read by Saul Olyan, David Biale and Lynn Davidman, and I am grateful to them for their comments. I have learned much from Judith Lieu, 'Circumcision, Women, and Salvation', *New Testament Studies*, 40 (1994), pp. 358–370.

   1. See the fine discussion by Joel Marcus, 'The Circumcision and the Uncircumcision in Rome', *New Testament Studies*, 35 (1989), pp. 67–81. It is likely that Ephesians is not by Paul but by a later writer.
   2. For gender-sensitive analyses of Jewish circumcision, see Howard Eilberg Schwartz, *The Savage in Judaism* (Indiana University Press, Bloomington, 1990), pp. 141–76, and Lawrence Hoffman, *Covenant of Blood, Circumcision and Gender in Rabbinic Judaism*

(University of Chicago Press, Chicago, 1995), neither of which deals with the questions and texts I am treating here. For rabbinic views of circumcision, see Sacha Stern, *Jewish Identity in Early Rabbinic Writings* (Brill, Leiden, 1994), pp. 63–7 and pp. 229–32, and David Kraemer, *Reading the Rabbis* (New York, Oxford University Press, 1996), pp. 109–23 ('The Problem with Foreskin: Circumcision, Gender, Impurity, and Death').

3. Since I am a male, this essay too is a male construction.

4. The fullest survey of (and sharpest polemic against) contemporary practice is Fran Hosken, *The Hosken Report, Genital and Sexual Mutilation of Females,* 4th edn (Women's Information Network, Lexington, MA, 1993). On the connection with Islam, see *Encyclopaedia of Islam*, vol. 4, pp. 913–14, s.v. *khafd.*

5. On circumcision in the ancient Near East, see Robert G. Hall, 'Circumcision', *The Anchor Bible Dictionary* (Doubleday, New York, 1992), vol. 1, pp. 1025–31 (introduction and part A, with good bibliography). On the persistence of circumcision in the Hellenistic and Roman periods, see Shaye J. D. Cohen, "Those Who Say They Are Jews And Are Not": How Do You Know a Jew in Antiquity When You See One?', *Diasporas in Antiquity*, ed. Shaye J. D. Cohen and Ernest Frerichs (Scholars Press for Brown Judaic Studies, Atlanta, GA, 1993), pp. 1–45, at pp. 18–20. Circumcision of males in Old Kingdom Egypt: Frans Jonckheere, 'La circoncision des anciens Egyptiens', *Centaurus,* 1 (1951), pp. 212–34; Constant de Wit, 'La circoncision chez les anciens Egyptiens', *Zeitschrift für ägyptische Sprache und Altertumskunde,* 99 (1972), pp. 41–48; Rosalind M. and Jac J. Janssen, *Growing Up in Ancient Egypt* (Rubicon Press, London, 1990), pp. 90–8. Circumcision (excision) of females is nowhere mentioned in Gay Robins, *Women in Ancient Egypt* (Harvard University Press, Cambridge, MA, 1993), or Barbara Watterson, *Women in Ancient Egypt* (St Martin's Press, New York, 1991) or Sarah Pomeroy, *Women in Hellenistic Egypt* (Wayne State University Press, Detroit, MI, 1990).

6. *Greek Papyri of the British Museum*, vol. I, ed. F. G. Kenyon (British Museum, London, 1893), no. XXIV, pp. 31–3; the text is re-edited in Ulrich Wilcken, *Urkunden der Ptolemäerzeit* (Walter de Gruyter, Berlin, 1927) vol. 1, pp. 116–19, no. 2. I cite lines 11–13.

7. That female circumcision is a relatively late importation into Egypt is suggested by Dominic Montserrat, '*Mallocouria* and *Therapeuteria*: Rituals of Transition in a Mixed Society?', *Bulletin of the American Society of Papyrologists* ,28 (1991), pp. 43–9, at pp. 47–8. (At p. 48, n. 19 he quotes Xanthus of Lydia as claiming that the Lydians were the first to 'circumcise' their women, but this translation is probably not correct; Xanthus uses the verb *eunuchizein*, 'to make into a eunuch', which should mean sterilization, not circumcision. Indeed, the context in Athenaeus 12.515d–e demands sterilization, and the word is properly translated in the Loeb edition.)

8. Strabo 17.2.5 p. 824 = Menahem Stern, *Greek and Latin Authors on Jews and Judaism* (3 vols; Israel Academy of Sciences, Jerusalem, 1974–84), no. 124.

9. Strabo 17.2.5 p. 824 = Stern, *Authors*, no. 124; Strabo 16.2.37 p. 761 = Stern, *Authors,* no. 115.

10. Strabo 16.4.9 p. 771 = Stern, *Authors*, no. 118.

11. Strabo 16.4.17 p. 776.

12. Contrast Diodorus of Sicily 3.32.4 (cited in the Loeb edition of Strabo at 16.4.10) who clearly implies that more skin is removed from one who is *kolobos* than from one who is merely circumcised (the opposite of Strabo): *Koloboi* 'have all the part that is merely circumcised by the others cut off with razors in infancy'.

13. 'Falasha circumcision takes place on the eighth day, and since the Falashas also practise female excision it is virtually certain that their circumcision rites are part of the

general Ethiopian heritage and not the result of any separate Jewish inspiration', writes Edward Ullendorff, *Ethiopia and the Bible* (British Academy/Oxford University Press, London, 1968), p. 108. Female excision by Falashas is also mentioned by A. Z. Aescoly, *Sefer ha Falashim* (R. Mass, Jerusalem, 1943), p. 39, as cited by Daniel Sperber, *Minhagê Yisrael*, vol. 4 (Mossad Harav Kook, Jerusalem, 1995), p. 9 (Hebrew), and by Wolf Leslau, *Falasha Anthology* (Yale University Press, New Haven, CT, 1951), p. xvii.

14. Lieu, 'Circumcision', p. 360, and Lawrence Schiffman, *Who was a Jew?* (Ktav, New York, 1985), p. 84, n. 35, simply dismiss Strabo as erroneous.

15. S. D. Goitein, *A Mediterranean Society*, vol. III: *The Family* (University of California Press, Berkeley, 1978), p. 233: 'Female circumcision, practiced among Copts, is unknown in Judaism.' In a note to his translation of *The Book of the Thousand Nights and a Night*, vol. 5 (printed by the Kamashastra Society for the Burton Club, Benares, 1885; frequently reprinted), p. 279, Richard F. Burton argues that 'Female circumcision … is I believe the rule amongst some outlying tribes of Jews'. Burton has no evidence whatsoever for this assertion beyond his own prurient and overactive imagination.

16. Aetios of Amida (sixth century CE), *Gynaecology*, ch. ciii, as translated by James V. Ricci (Blakiston, Philadelphia, 1950), p. 107; substantially the same information is imparted by Paulus of Aigenta (quoted by Ricci in his note on p. 163). Both are probably drawing on Soranus (whose relevant chapter has been lost); see Owsei Temkin, *Soranus' Gynecology* (1956; Johns Hopkins University Press, Baltimore, MD, 1991), p. 200. On clitoridectomy as a standard medical procedure in nineteenth-century Europe and America, see Thomas Laqueur, 'Amor Veneris, vel Dulcedo Appeletur', *Zone: Fragments for a History of the Human Body*, ed. Michel Feher *et al.*, part 3 (Urzone, New York, 1989), pp. 90–131, esp. pp. 113–120 ('The Clitoris as a Social Problem'); and the chapter on clitoridectomy in Edward Wallerstein, *Circumcision: An American Health Fallacy* (Springer, New York, 1980).

17. Philo, *Questions and Answers on Genesis* 3.47, tr. Ralph Marcus in the Loeb Classical Library edition of Philo, supplement volume 1, pp. 241–42. Circumcision is the topic of *Questions and Answers on Genesis* 3.46–52.

18. Similarly, in his other major discussion of circumcision (*On the Special Laws* 1.1–11), Philo compares and contrasts Egyptian with Jewish circumcision; see Richard D. Hecht, 'The Exegetical Contexts of Philo's Interpretation of Circumcision', in *Nourished with Peace: Studies in Hellenisic Judaism*, ed. F. Greenspahn *et al.* (Scholars Press, Chico, CA, 1984), pp. 51–79.

19. In addition to the passage cited above, see Strabo *apud* Josephus, *Jewish Antiquities* 14.118 = Stern, *Authors*, no. 105.

20. Philo follows the common Greek view that menstrual fluid is the stuff out of which the fetus is created; see Marcus' note 'c' on p. 242. On this view see Lesley A. Dean-Jones, *Women's Bodies in Classical Greek Science* (Oxford: Clarendon, 1994), pp. 200–9.

21. Philo, *On the Special Laws* 1.9–10 (trans. Colson, Loeb Classical Library edition of Philo, vol. 7); cf. *Questions on Genesis* 3.48 (pp. 245–6, trans. Marcus). See too *On the Migration of Abraham* 92.

22. Dorothy Sly, *Philo's Perception of Women*, Brown Judaic Studies no. 209 (Scholars Press, Atlanta, GA, 1990).

23. The only Philonic passage that associates circumcision with the election of Israel is *Questions on Genesis* 3.49 (p. 249, trans. Marcus); this association is not typical of Philo's thought. See Ellen Birnbaum, *The Place of Judaism in Philo's Thought: Israel, Jews, and Proselytes*, Brown Judaic Studies no. 290 (Scholars Press, Atlanta, GA, 1996),

pp. 125–6, 155–6 and 158. In *Questions on Exodus* 2.2, a passage often cited by modern scholars, Philo says that the 'proselyte' is the one 'who circumcises not his uncircumcision but his desires and sensual pleasures' (trans. Marcus); the intent of this remark is not clear and is widely debated. See Birnbaum, *Place of Judaism*, p. 200.

24. Josephus, *Jewish Antiquities* 1.192; Philo, *On the Migration of Abraham* 92; Robert G. Hall, 'Epispasm and the Dating of Ancient Jewish Writings', *Journal for the Study of the Pseudepigrapha*, 2 (1988), pp. 71–86. Epispasm is the drawing down or stretching of penile skin so as to give the appearance of a foreskin.

25. For a good introductory discussion of these passages see Hall, *Anchor Bible Dictionary*, s.v. Circumcision, part C, and Otto Betz, *Theologische Realenzyklopädie*, 5 (1980), pp. 719–22, s.v. *Beschneidung*. It is likely that Colossians, like Ephesians, is not by Paul but by a later writer.

26. This point is the centerpiece of Daniel Boyarin, *A Radical Jew: Paul and the Politics of Identity* (University of California Press, Berkeley, 1994).

27. See Lieu, 'Circumcision', pp. 368–9, for a good critique of some modern scholars who see Paul as a crusader for women's equality.

28. Justin Martyr, *Dialogue with Trypho the Jew* 23.5, as translated by Thomas Falls, *Writings of Saint Justin Martyr* (Christian Heritage, New York, 1948), p. 183 (except that I have substituted 'righteousness' for 'justification'). Justin's arguments against circumcision appear chiefly in sections 16–24; see also 29, 41, 46.

29. For Justin's connections with Hellenistic Judaism and Philo, see David T. Runia, *Philo in Early Christian Literature: A Survey* (Van Gorcum, Assen, 1993), pp. 97–105.

30. For surveys of Christian polemic against Judaism (including circumcision), see A. Lukyn Williams, *Adversus Judaeos* (Cambridge University Press, Cambridge, 1935), and Heinz Schreckenberg, *Die Christlichen Adversus-Judaeos-Texte* (3 vols; Peter Lang, Frankfurt, 1982–94). Lieu, 'Circumcision', p. 359, notes the absence of this argument from subsequent Christian thinking about the Law.

31. Cyprian, *Ad Quirinum* 1.8, in *Sancti Cypriani Episcopi Opera* (Corpus Christianorum Series Latina 3,1), ed. R. Weber and M. Bévenot (Brepols, Turnholt, 1972), p. 12. The Latin is *tunc quod illud signaculum feminis non proficit, signo autem Domini omnes signantur*; some testimonia read not *feminis* but *seminis*, which would yield: 'That sign [that is, the sign of physical circumcision] is of no use to the seed [that is, the infant].' If this is the correct reading, I do not understand Cyprian's argument. I owe my knowledge of this text to Lieu, 'Circumcision', p. 359, n. 5 (even if her citation is inaccurate).

32. *De Altercatione Ecclesiae et Synagogae*: text in J.-P. Migne (ed.) *Patrologia Latina* 42.1131–1140; our excerpt is on 1134. On this text see Jean Juster, *Les juifs dans l'empire romain* (P. Geuthner, Paris, 1914), vol. 1, pp. 73–4; Williams, *Adversus Judaeos*, pp. 321–38 (our excerpt is paraphrased on p. 329); Bernhard Blumenkranz, *Les auteurs chrétiens latins du moyen age sur les juifs et le judaïsme* (Mouton, Paris, 1963), pp. 39–42; Schreckenberg, *Adversus-Judaeos-Texte*, vol. 1, p. 354; S. Krauss and W. Horbury, *The Jewish Christian Controversy*, vol. I: *History* (Mohr-Siebeck, Tübingen, 1995), pp. 49–50.

33. Bernadette Brooten, *Women Leaders in the Ancient Synagogue*, Brown Judaic Studies 36 (Scholars Press, Chico, CA, 1982), pp. 57–72. Only three 'mothers of the synagogue' are attested (if we ignore conjectural restorations and the use of 'mother' without 'of the synagogue'), and the epitaphs for all three omit any reference to a husband. I presume that they were widows.

34. The same argument appears in Zeno of Verona, as cited by Lieu, 'Circumcision', pp. 359–60, n. 5.

35. For the anti-Jewish polemic in the Latin Church, see the handbooks of Williams, Blumenkranz and Schreckenberg cited above; on the polemic against circumcision see B. Blumenkranz, *Die Judenpredigt Augustins* (Helbing & Lichtenhain, Basel, 1946), pp. 145–8.

36. In his rabbinic commentary on Philo's *Questions on Genesis*, Belkin transcribes 3.47 and offers no parallel from rabbinic sources; see Samuel Belkin, *The Midrash of Philo ...*, vol. I: *Genesis II–XVII*, ed. E. Hurvitz (New York, Yeshiva University Press, 1989), p. 280 (Hebrew).

37. Male procreative organ: Tosefta Shabbat 15.9, p. 71, ed. S. Lieberman (Jewish Theological Seminary, New York, 1962) = Genesis Rabbah 46.4, p. 461, ed. J. Theodor and H. Albeck (Itzkowski, Berlin, 1912). The place where an infant is recognized to be male or female: Genesis Rabbah 46.5, p. 463 = Genesis Rabbah 46.13, p. 470.

38. Babylonian Talmud, Yevamot 46a–b. On this passage see Gary Porton, *The Stranger within your Gates* (University of Chicago Press, Chicago, 1994), pp. 94–6.

39. Babylonian Talmud, Avodah Zarah 27a.

40. Johann Maier, *Jüdische Auseinandersetzung mit dem Christentum in der Antike* (Wissenschaftliche Buchgesellschaft, Darmstadt, 1982).

41. *fiunt non nascuntur Christiani*: Tertullian, *Apology* 3.1, 3.3, and esp. 18. *de Iudaeo Iudaeus nascitur*: Ambrosiaster ([Augustine]), *Quaestiones veteris et novi testamenti* 81, ed. A. Souter (Corpus Scriptorum Ecclesiasticorum Latinorum 50), p. 137.

42. M. Qiddushin 4:1; M. Bikkurim 1:4, as analysed by Shaye J. D. Cohen, 'Can a Convert to Judaism say "God of our Fathers"?', *Judaism,* 40 (1991), pp. 419–28. The tension within rabbinic Judaism between Israel as a descent group and Israel as a 'religion' is a major focus of Porton, *Stranger.*

43. On classical Athens, see Cynthia B. Patterson, 'Attikai', *Helios,* 13.2 (1986), pp. 49–67, and Nicole Loraux, *The Children of Athena*, tr. C. Levine (Princeton University Press, Princeton, NJ, 1993), pp. 116–23, esp. p. 119 ('there is no such thing as a "female citizen", any more than there is a "female Athenian"'). Similarly the Mishnah regularly refers to an individual Jewish woman as *bat yisra'el* ('daughter of an Israelite'); see Judith Wegner, *Chattel or Person? The Status of Women in the Mishnah* (Oxford University Press, New York, 1988), p. 167.

44. Babylonian Talmud, Berakhot 17a and Sotah 21a.

45. Mishnah, Nedarim 3.11.

46. Mishnah, Yevamot 8.1; Babylonian Talmud, Hulin 4b; and elsewhere.

47. J. P. T. Hunt, '*Colossians* 2:11–12, The Circumcision/Baptism Analogy, and Infant Baptism', *Tyndale Bulletin* 41 (1990), pp. 227–244.

48. See, for example, David Berger (ed.) *The Jewish–Christian Debate in the High Middle Ages: The Nizzahon Vetus* (Jewish Publication Society, Philadelphia, PA, 1979), p. 224, no. 237.

49. Anna Sapir Abulafia, *Christians and Jews in the Twelfth-Century Renaissance* (Routledge, London, 1995), pp. 125–6.

50. Saadia Gaon, *The Book of Beliefs and Opinions* 3.7, trans. Samuel Rosenblatt (Yale University Press, New Haven, CT, 1948), p. 158.

51. In my forthcoming book I hope to study and document this conjecture.

Creation, Virginity and Diet in Fourth-Century Christianity: Basil of Ancyra's *On the True Purity of Virginity*

TERESA M. SHAW

Ascetic behavior and theories on the ascetic life are not unique to Christianity in the late ancient Mediterranean, nor did Christian asceticism develop in isolation. On the contrary, recent scholarship has identified a general intensifying of attention to moral theory, bodily training (*askesis*), regimen and diet, the interdependence of body and soul, and the 'care of the self' in the period.[1] Nevertheless in Christianity certain practices became distinctive, and the theological and ethical reflection and instruction surrounding these practices became elaborate. In this paper I will explore one particular facet of ascetic expression, that is, the relationship between arguments for the value of dietary restriction or fasting and the ideology of female virginity, especially as they reflect and instill concepts of gender.[2] The principal source for this study, a Greek treatise on virginity, represents a type of literature typical in the fourth century, when the theory, institutions and visibility of asceticism developed dramatically. Along with the forms and practices of monastic institutions and communities, a large body of literature was produced, including hagiographical records and accounts, monastic rules and epistolary advice concerning the daily life of male and female renouncers.

In particular, the praise and regulation of *female* virginity became the subject of a proliferation of treatises and sermons written by men; although advocates of the ascetic life encouraged sexual abstinence for both men and women, female chastity and the intact virginal body represented the ideal of Christian perfection. The motivations and social impact of female asceticism in early Christianity have been the subject of intense scholarly discussion in recent years. One must begin with the recognition that our understanding is limited by the fact that the extant sources are almost exclusively male-authored, and by the fact that we know the most about a few aristocratic women. A central question is the extent to which the ascetic life encouraged women to reject traditional familial social roles and allowed them to cultivate increased authority, influence and mobility. On the one hand, the attraction of new arenas for female self-definition seems plausible; on the other hand, scholars also agree that the glowing rhetoric of virginity and female renunciation may tell us very little about the women in question and more about male ideals, fears and pious self-presentation. Further, it is increasingly unacceptable to make broad claims about women's reality as if social, geographical, or class differences did not matter.[3]

In this paper I will examine some of the nuances of the discourse on virginity in order to make connections between its ideology and ancient physiological models. Among the numerous texts written in praise of virginity and offering practical instructions for the virginal way of life, the mid-fourth-century treatise by Basil, bishop of Ancyra in Galatia from 336 CE, is striking for its intense and relentless focus on the physical body of the virgin and her femaleness.[4] Indeed, theories of the creation and 'nature' of male and female bodies form the basis of Basil's arguments concerning the need for sexual renunciation and strict ascetic regimen as well as his theological and eschatological interpretation of virginity. The treatise, entitled 'On the True Purity of Virginity' and addressed to Letoios, bishop of Melitene, features all of the themes and rhetorical topoi that became standard in fourth-century treatments of virginity—including arguments from creation and paradise, the pain and suffering of earthly marriage compared with betrothal to Christ as the heavenly bridegroom, warnings against associations with men and with married women, restrictions on movements and daily regimen, and praise of the freedom and angelic nature of virginity. Like most other works of its type from the late fourth and early fifth centuries, its focus is almost exclusively on female virgins and their lifestyle, while male celibates figure in Basil's discussion as counterparts and associates of the virgins, and the virgins' relations with male celibates is one of the key areas for caution and advice from the bishop.[5]

Basil's treatise is distinctive for its graphic descriptions of the physiology of nutrition and sexual desire, the passions of the body, male and female attraction, and the sexual aggression of eunuchs. These features have been called disconcerting,[6] shocking,[7] astonishing, crude[8] and lamentable[9] by modern scholars. One suspects that such pious reactions have tended to limit scholarly attention to the text until recently.[10] However disconcerting, Basil's attention to the physical realities of the virginal life is essential to his stated task of describing not only the beauties of virginity but especially the dangers awaiting one who has determined to pursue this virtue. All of the virgin's bodily training (*askesis*) is useful not only to bring her body and its passions under control, Basil says, but also, and primarily, in order to protect her 'true' virginity, that is, the virginity of her soul.[11] To do so wisely, the virgin must understand the nature, functions and desires of female and male bodies. Thus Basil begins with creation itself and the origin of gender differentiation, and proceeds to advise the virgin concerning all aspects of her lifestyle (including diet, clothing, appearance, associations, and activities in the church and in the community) and concerning the theological links between that lifestyle, paradise and her role as the bride of Christ.

He relies heavily on physiological, philosophical and mythical categories derived from 'the Greeks', as he refers to non-Christians,[12] and his style of argumentation seems to support the evidence that Basil himself had medical training.[13]

The treatise thus presents a particularly dramatic example of the extent to which the early Christian discourse on virginity weaves together medical and ethical theories, social and theological models of gender, physiognomic interpretation and eschatological vision. Throughout, rigorous physical discipline and ascetic training provide the essential foundation for enabling and protecting virginity. Basil's language is wildly metaphorical: bodily asceticism is sacrifice, castration, dying, cauterizing; it is a cutting off, a closing up, a stamping down, a reining in; the ascetic body is a temple, a nuptial chamber, an unfeeling sculpture, a dead stump. But the virgin's body is also the image of God, a glimpse of angelic purity; it is free, brilliant, sparkling, noble and pleasing. The intensity and variety of these images reflect the paradoxical role of the female and of the body in the treatise.

The creation of bodies and gender, and the origin of procreation, are at the heart of Basil's instruction. In fact, Basil provides two separate accounts of creation, one based on the myth of the androgyne and sprinkled lightly with scriptural references, and one based more firmly on the biblical narrative.[14] Taken together, they constitute a view of creation that provides the physiological and theological rationale for ascetic practice. Basil takes up his first discussion of the origins of humanity early in the treatise, immediately after his introduction. Appealing to the image of an originally androgynous or genderless creation (found in Plato and common in Graeco-Roman literature), he writes that the creator fashioned the corporeal form of each living species, rational and irrational, and divided each form into male and female fragments. The creator 'placed in the nature of each fragment a hidden longing for embrace with the other'. Instructing the first beings to 'be fruitful and multiply' (Genesis 1:28), the creator made the act of sexual intercourse pleasurable to bodies and implanted affection for offspring. By these devices, then, the increase of living species through procreation was ensured.[15]

Although Basil posits a 'root' of bodily being that was not differentiated into male and female, gender hierarchy quickly and definitively intrudes into the picture. Not only is the female a fragment of the male, a fragment which is regained and restored into male wholeness in sexual union, but in all animal species the female is subordinate to the male, while male power is 'tamed' by his desire for the female.[16] Not wanting her to be completely vulnerable in her passive position, the creator endowed the female with the power to attract the male by making the shape, touch, movements and image of her body delicate, soft and pleasing. But this tenderness and beauty irresistibly assault the male's senses, so that he is imprisoned by the pleasure of her body and dragged toward it like iron to a magnet.[17] The force of physical attraction and the natural, created condition of sexual function are fundamental to Basil's understanding of the ascetic project and the specific difficulties and dangers awaiting the celibate woman. For although the virgin must resist the desires and pleasures that she herself might experience, she also battles to subdue and negate the power to draw and enslave the male—a power implanted in the female body itself. Thus the virgin's ascetic struggle is profoundly a struggle against her own nature.[18]

Basil's second account of creation, which appears much later in the treatise,[19] returns to the theme of procreation and desire, but in a more theological framework. As before, Basil affirms that bodily desire serves the procreative purpose of populating the earth with various species. But here the clever work of the creator is discussed in the context of the Genesis story of paradise, Adam and Eve, and the fall from immortality and incorruptibility into death and corruption.[20] Basil notes, as did many other ascetic interpreters, that before the first transgression and its consequences of death and expulsion from paradise, Adam did not have sexual relations with Eve (Genesis 4:1). After the fall, marriage and procreation are methods for restoring a form of 'immortality by posterity',[21] and the bearing of successive generations of children is a kind of 'consolation' for the loss of immortality. It is God who mercifully devised this secondary immortality, and who contrived the physical attraction between male and female in order to encourage marriage, 'so restoring the succession of their race to those who became mortal out of immortals ... and saying on account of this: "Be fruitful and multiply."'[22]

Basil's argument that there was no sex in paradise before the fall must be considered along with his assertion, here and in the earlier description of the separation of the androgyne, that God implanted sexual *desire* before the first sin, in conjunction with the command to 'be fruitful and multiply' (Genesis 1:28). Basil does not discuss the implications of this timetable, where physical sexual attraction seems to have been created before the actual need for marriage, and perhaps it was not a concern. But it is interesting that Gregory of Nyssa (whose treatise 'On Virginity' shows the strong influence of Basil's work)[23] subsequently argued explicitly, in a treatise 'On the Making of Humanity' (written in the 380s), that God created the desire for intercourse and gave the command to be fruitful because of God's divine *foreknowledge* of the fall and mortality. Further, Gregory asserts that the original, genderless creation was in the image of God (Genesis 1:26–7a), while the division into male and female (Genesis 1:27b) was 'apart from the prototype', a kind of second creation devised by God—again in foreknowledge—in order to populate the earth by less than angelic means. Sexual activity, nevertheless, was unknown before the fall.[24] Arguments like Basil's and Gregory's, which assert the essential goodness of marriage while elevating virginity as the superior life, are typical in Christian ascetic discourse of the period. They reflect a concern to affirm the biblical account of creation and a good creator God, and thus to avoid the charge often made against 'heretics' (such as gnostics, Manichaeans and Marcion), that they denigrated material creation.

In Basil's descriptions of creation, then, sexual desire and marriage have their origins in a good creator and serve a noble purpose. But in the latter account it is also clear that, if marriage and procreation are not evils but the accommodations of a merciful God, they nevertheless are alien to the original condition of immortality and incorruptibility and came into being only as a consequence of or in anticipation of the fall. Why, then, should virginity be a goal now? Why resist the force of nature and spurn the gift of God? For Basil, as for other advocates of the virginal life, the answer is clear: first, if procreation had been a necessary means of multiplying the species, the earth was now fully populated.[25] Further, Christ (as a kind of second Adam) had reintroduced virginity and incorruptibility as features of the coming kingdom of God, which is, after all, a restoration of paradise. Just as Adam 'became the seed of the present life through the pleasure of marriages', so the 'seed of the coming age' is planted and comes into being through 'the incorruptibility of virginity'. While preceding generations followed Adam out of paradise and into marriages, the virgin now follows Christ back into paradise.[26] What is more, by her virginity and detachment from worldly passions and affairs, she already lives the life of the angels and anticipates the final resurrection of all flesh. Citing gospel passages that link the resurrection and the coming kingdom to the absence of death and marriage, Basil writes:

> For if in the resurrection they neither marry nor are given in marriage, but are as angels [Matthew 22:30], and will become the children of God [Luke 20:36], those who practice virginity are angels, going about through human life in incorruptible flesh—and not some obscure angels, but exceedingly distinguished.[27]

Basil insists that one of the greatest virtues of virginity is that it is a completely free choice, not commanded by God, by the law of Moses, or by the gospel.[28] If marriage exists because of nature and natural processes and if the law governs or orders nature, Basil writes, virginity surpasses both nature and the law.[29] Thus the one pursuing virginity faces enormous obstacles, whether the sheer force of physical attraction, emphasized in Basil's first discussion of creation, or the heavy weight of tradition, law and social habit, emphasized in the second discussion. In order to succeed, the virgin carefully employs methods and observes regimens that address both these physical and social challenges. Basil intends his treatise to educate the virgin and provide her with the tools, or, more appropriate to Basil's language, the weapons for success.

As mentioned above, Basil's treatise is rather notorious for its frank depiction of sexual physiology. Although Basil more than once excuses himself for 'plunging' into topics that seem unsuitable to the virginal character, he argues that only by an understanding of nature, specifically the nature of male and female bodies, can the purity of virginity be protected.[30] In this Basil seems very much the physician, detailing symptoms and conditions, and prescribing remedies and regimens. Thus the virgin who understands the natural attraction of bodies will be better able to separate her soul and keep it undefiled by passion. She understands that her soul may be drowned in the waves churned up by the force of the pleasure that courses through the five streams of the senses.[31] She understands that bodily passion is a horrific monster like the mythical hydra, growing three new heads for every one cut off: try to end one desire by satiety, and multiple new desires spring up through other senses.[32] And she understands that the different parts or members of the body naturally *know* their use and role in erotic affairs, as can be seen both in the fact that irrational animals manage to have sex without instructions, as well as in the behavior of pre-pubescent boys who 'imitate manly intercourse with their immature parts'.[33]

Using images of soul and body familiar from moral and ascetic discourse, Basil notes that the five senses act as the channels, windows, or gateways to the soul, allowing entry to the sensual experience that can lead to lustful fantasies and propel one toward sexual contact. This is why the virgin very carefully exercises and moderates the use of her sight, hearing, smell, touch and taste. In vivid images, Basil describes the virgin's control of her senses as closing all of the windows and doors in order to keep out dangerous soldiers intent on occupying a house, or as stopping up eyes and ears and placing the horse's 'bit of rationality' in the mouth.[34] Touch, which is active on the whole surface of the body, is according to Basil the most 'slavish' of the senses, and lures the others to pleasure by means of the smoothness of skin.[35] Thus, in Basil's image, the body is permeable by the invasion of lust, charged with the energy of pleasure, and primed for sexual activity and the procreative impulse. It is no wonder that Basil seems particularly concerned that the virgin should avoid touching not only men (including continent males and eunuchs), but also other women and even her own body.

Touch exercises its great power most definitively through taste and through the 'procreative parts'.[36] The pleasure of taste and sexual desire are bound up with each other as mutual slaves, writes Basil, and both eating and intercourse are stimulated by and enjoyable because of the sensual power of touch.[37] Basil writes: 'through the sense of touch in tasting—which is always seducing toward gluttony by swallowing—the body, fattened up and titillated by the soft humors bubbling uncontrollably inside, is carried in a frenzy towards the touch of sexual intercourse.'[38] He here acknowledges a psychological and physiological connection between eating and the need for sexual activity, an argument common in ancient medical and ethical discourse and the source of the popular caricature of the lustful and shameful glutton found in Hellenistic and early Christian literature.

Much of Basil's advice concerning diet and sexual function thus builds on concepts and models that would be familiar to his educated contemporaries, while his clear reliance on physiological analysis and his medical sensibilities regarding these practical issues seem to confirm his own specialized training. His specific warnings and prescriptions reflect the influence especially of Galen (*c.* 129–200) and the Galenic tradition of dietary theory and sexual physiology.[39] To summarize briefly, Galen taught that foods have different faculties, effects, or powers in the body, and specific foods stimulate the production of different fluids or humors. The four main humors in the body are blood, black bile, yellow bile and phlegm. Other humors are produced out of these; for example, semen, breast milk and menstrual fluid all originate in blood which is processed or 'concocted' to different degrees in the body. Foods can be classified by their faculties (usually cooling, heating, drying, moistening, or a combina-tion of these) and by the humors they produce, taking into consideration the condition of the individual body. Honey, for example, tends to produce blood in elderly persons, whose bodies tend to be colder, but yellow bile in younger persons with warmer constitutions.[40] Galen applies these principles when discussing the effects of diet on sexual function and sexual desire, noting that foods that are warming and moistening and full of nutrition (such as meat, beans and chickpeas) tend to produce semen—in male as well as female bodies—while foods that are drying, cooling, or drying and warming at the same time (such as lettuce, rue, and seeds or fruit of the *agnus castus* or 'chaste tree') tend to reduce the level of semen produced. Thus the physician is able to recommend dietary regimens to treat conditions in which the excess or lack of semen is problematic. Further, diet is directly related not only to fertility (since like menstrual blood semen is a product of nutrition), but also to sexual desire and the need for sexual activity.[41] As Basil describes the process, the stomach provides the matter necessary for the sexual organs to operate: 'As the stomach grows heavy with food, it becomes necessary for the organs underneath it, which are overflowing with humors bubbling inside, to move toward their natural function.'[42] It is a straightforward conclusion, then, that the person who has renounced sexual relations and procreation will observe a regimen that hinders the production of sexual humors and therefore the intensity of desire.

Having chosen to live her life in virginity, the celibate female must be careful not to fornicate in regard to food and foolishly 'betray her virginity'. As such, the virgin's very first line of defense is to control her diet and her sense of taste.[43] She will eat only with careful consideration of the faculties of foods as well as the needs of her own body. Her dietary goal is 'to take into account both the condition … of the body and the qualities of foods and to keep in check the thriving body and the increasing of natural heat besides, and by means of diet to drive out heat'. Eating foods that warm a body already sizzling with natural heat (as is the body of a young man or woman in youthful prime) is like throwing wine on fire. Basil instructs the wise virgin therefore to follow a cooling diet that will reduce the danger of sexual desire.[44] But she will eat as needed so as not to weaken the body, which is after all the servant of the soul.[45] Thus if her general rule is to follow a cooling regimen, she nevertheless will not dangerously add more coldness to a body that has already grown cold and dried up on account of weakness, sickness, or old age, but will aid these conditions by proper nutrition.[46]

Regarding specific foods, Basil instructs the virgin not simply to consider their external appearance or reputation but to discern their real faculties and effects. He warns that

> there are not only quite a few seeds and legumes, but even vegetables which, in spite of their common reputation, are not completely useful as nourishment to the ascetic for the purpose of smooth [digestive] management, but tearing at the depths of the internal organs [lit.: the flesh] and producing irritating gurgles—no less than is the case with those foods that are unquestionably avoided—they unexpectedly upset and stir up bodies.[47]

One can assume that 'the foods that are unquestionably avoided' would include meat, wine and the 'seeds and legumes' known for heating, moistening, or otherwise fueling the sexual system. Basil's language suggests that these would be commonly known, especially among ascetic practitioners. He does not offer names of dangerous vegetables and legumes, but gives more details concerning seasonings and condiments that should be avoided because they secretly lure one toward sexual pleasure. He notes for example that salt itself is 'naturally fertile' and is even more potent than other seasonings, causing 'irritations' that incite the body toward copulation. Yet many of the most fervent ascetics unknowingly use salt freely with bread (a standard ascetic diet) while avoiding other seasonings. The virgin must think twice before using it, lest she be 'outwitted' by her sense of taste and suddenly find herself 'chasing after that which she [currently] flees by means of asceticism' (that is, sexual pleasure).[48]

Basil's dietary advice, clearly based in the nutritional and physiological wisdom of his time, is one of the most explicit early Christian treatments of the connection between food and sexual desire or fasting and the repression of desire.[49] Basil's practical approach to daily regimen for virgins may be usefully compared to the dietary prescriptions offered to women in late ancient medical texts, where long-term virginity is not necessarily expected, but where diet is also linked to sexual desire and reproductive goals. As noted above, medical wisdom recognized reproductive fluids as the products of nutrition. Galen and others argued that semen, menses and milk were 'concocted' from blood, which is one of the four main bodily humors. The abundance or lack of reproductive matter, and therefore the procreative health of the body and the intensity of sexual desire, are in part dependent on dietary regimen.

The writings of Rufus of Ephesus (c. 110–80) and Aetios of Amida (sixth century) will serve as just two examples of how these theories are applied in regimens for women and girls in late antiquity. Though Aetios lived several hundred years after Galen and his contemporary Rufus, his *Tetrabiblion* is essentially a compilation of previous medical learning, in which he quotes and paraphrases extensively from Galen, Rufus, the gynaecological writer Soranus (1st–2nd centuries), and others. His writing thus preserves earlier tradition and offers some sense of the continuities in late ancient medicine. Rufus of Ephesus addresses the topic of food and sexuality in different contexts, and regarding both male and female subjects. When discussing the treatment of two conditions in which semen is overabundant (satyriasis and gonorrhea), he prescribes—in addition to blood-letting, cooling ointments, and the avoidance of erotic talk and dreams—a thin and light diet. One should avoid meat and foods that are flatulent or difficult to digest (such as milk, cheese and beans). Instead, the light diet will include rue (as a food or ointment), lettuce and thin porridges. Likewise, in a treatise 'On Sexual Relations', Rufus observes that the best regimen for those who are sexually active is of the warming and moistening type, thus emphasizing meats, certain vegetables and legumes such as chickpeas and beans, and flatulent and filling pods.[50] Rufus also devotes a treatise to the regimen proper for virgin girls, which focuses on techniques for reducing sexual desire and the impetus for sexual intercourse at the time of puberty (when the young body is full of heat), with the intention of protecting virginity until the time of marriage. Not surprisingly, he recommends that the virgin follow a cooling diet, avoiding meat and wine, or at least adding water to her wine (since water is more conducive to self-control).[51]

Aetios of Amida devotes the sixteenth book of the *Tetrabiblion* to female fertility, sexual health and diet. In his dietary advice he classifies foods according to their 'faculties' or powers in relation to various conditions and prescriptions. He discusses regimens for both women and men who wish to maintain or increase fertility, suggesting for healthy men and women 'a way of life' that includes moderate exercise, baths and 'food and drink that stimulate sex drive and generate semen, and such are those that produce heat and elate'.[52] Diets will vary according to whether the individual bodily constitution tends to be hot, cold, dry, or moist. Further, female fertility is linked closely to regular and healthy menstrual flow. Aetios observes that menstrual regularity can be hindered as much by excessive heat (and therefore dryness) as by excessive chill.[53] What is more, Aetios notes (following Soranus), some women naturally do not have menstrual periods, on account of lifestyle or body type. These include dancers and singers as well as those who exercise or work vigorously and those with 'mannish' bodies (broad shoulders, thick thighs, deep voices and abundant body hair).[54] In an interesting aside, Aetios acknowledges that not only is amenorrhea not necessarily a dangerous condition, it may be better for women's health:

> It would be preferable indeed to prescribe a way of living (leading) to a complete preservation of health by which (means) the body of a woman may

become so dry that it is not necessary (for her) to have menstrual periods. This of course would be harmful to conception; for those who do not have their menses do not conceive. Therefore for the sake of conception, and because almost all women live with that purpose, monthly periods are necessary.[55]

I would argue that the regimen prescribed in Basil of Ancyra's treatise on virginity must be considered as analogous to these and other medical discussions, not simply because the specific foods and categories are parallel. More significant, I think, is the shared understanding of the procreative *role* of the female body and the procreative *goal* of diets. Just as Rufus and Aetios write for those who are sexually active or who desire to conceive or who are young but intending to marry and procreate, Basil writes for the one who desires to keep her body sexually *inactive*, to avoid procreation. Although Basil does not specify the cessation of menstruation as a goal, and his diet does not seem to be particularly harsh, he states that the virgin, by her food abstinence, dries and cools her body and reduces lust.[56] He seems to assume a certain level of common knowledge concerning what foods the celibate one should avoid. And he makes the same connections between bodily fluids, heat, food and lust. Indeed, Basil's virgin and others like her are the noteworthy exceptions to Aetios' assertion that 'almost all women' live with the purpose of procreation.

Moreover, in rejecting a role in sexual pleasure and childbearing that is synonymous with female nature and identity, the Christian virgin takes on a social as well as a physical regimen or *askesis*.[57] This is manifest in Basil's directives concerning her daily lifestyle, demeanor, associations and appearance. For in all these areas, the virgin's life is controlled and scrutinized, with the explicit purpose of weeding out all that is associated with the female. Basil's instructions on daily conduct are, to a certain extent, familiar in the context of late ancient discourse on Christian virginity, but his physical and physiological models again distinguish his treatment. Like other writers on virginity, Basil argues that worldly activities and associations are dangerous. The virgin should avoid any sensual contact or outside stimulation that will distract her and threaten the purity of her soul with the corruption of passion. To do this, however, requires both withdrawal from social entanglements and a carefully crafted bodily image. Basil's virgin signifies in every activity, word, gesture, thought and glance that she is the bride of Christ and an image of angelic purity, not a woman of this world and its corruptions. So not only does the virgin not marry, she should not attend weddings nor involve herself in anything associated with marriage. Indeed, the scriptural affirmation that marriage is honorable (Hebrews 13:4), Basil asserts, 'relates to others, not to the virgin'.[58] Moreover, even going out of the house and visiting can be 'licentious' behaviors, for the virgin is exposed to uncontrolled sights and sounds, and may herself speak and listen without discretion, thus violating the sanctity of her senses and the purity of her thoughts.[59] Basil likens virgins who socialize indiscriminately to the young widows in I Timothy (5:13) who flit about, spreading idle gossip and speaking on unseemly matters.[60]

While Basil finds the dangers of most associations alarming, it is important to note that he also assumes that virgins *will* visit regularly with certain men, to whom he refers as the 'servants of the bridegroom' and 'brothers in Christ'. Curiously enough, Basil does not rule out these associations, but rather offers guidelines for keeping the visits as harmless as possible. Specifically, the virgin should keep her body covered, conduct herself carefully and speak to them chastely, take care when kissing or touching them, and do nothing to scandalize her 'brothers'.[61] The identity of the male 'servants of the bridegroom' is a tantalizing puzzle. They appear to be ascetics who keep close company with virgins and engage in conversation or teaching.[62] They may be clerics and/or monks living in the area, or—as Susanna Elm has suggested—they may actually live in ascetic community with the virgins.[63] Their relationship is familiar enough that Basil encourages virgins to love them as brothers 'of the same womb', while warning that even such intimacy and confidence as exists between siblings can be dangerous. Indeed, he notes, the touches and kisses between a sister and brother by birth can lead to excitement and passion, even if they try to repress the impulse by rational thoughts. The reason, again, is the natural power of sexual attraction lodged in bodies.[64]

Basil seems to have cause for alarm, as he reports that some virgins and ascetic men have succumbed to their desires and married, an arrangement he likens to an adulterous offense against Christ.[65] He pictures derisively the 'servant of the Lord' climbing into bed with his master's bride, the virgin.[66] But if the virgin must be careful in her contacts with male associates, she must also exercise caution around her female companions and housemates. Basil's argument here is intriguing: he observes than even when young women sleep entwined on the same bed, because of the heat of their youth and the touch of flesh against flesh their imaginations may be aroused toward that relation which their bodies were 'formed in order to experience', that is, heterosexual intercourse. The enemy (Satan) is thus able to intrude secretly and turn the 'friendly' pleasure of female companionship into the 'carnal' pleasure of the male.[67] Thus what concerns Basil seems to be not so much the possibility of a lesbian relationship, but the desire for sensual contact with a male that may arise from innocent contact with female flesh.

In a world charged with such dangers, the virgin's entire lifestyle and daily regimen must be oriented to neutralizing the attraction between male and female bodies. This is the motive behind Basil's graphic warnings and instructions, and the assumption underlying the idea that virginity goes against nature or does 'violence' to nature.[68] The beginning of this effort Basil identifies as a strict dietary abstinence, as we have seen. But if by 'fasts and training' one is able to reduce the passions associated with the body, the 'effort toward virtue is incomplete' unless one also perfects and purifies the soul.[69] Here Basil shares the concept, common in late ancient moral theory, that some of the passions are primarily linked to the body while others belong more properly to the soul, or to the soul's rational part. Thus gluttony and lust are bodily passions, while Basil identifies irrationality, anger, contentiousness and envy as passions of the soul, infecting and spreading primarily by means of thoughts and imagination.[70] Basil's ideal is a kind of 'peace' between body and soul, with each perfected according to its own 'nature'. The virgin displays both a soul undisturbed by vices and a body unmuddied by lust.[71]

If the virgin protects her soul by closing up her senses, she also takes practical steps to change the external appearance of her body. Of course, all ornamentation, jewelry, and makeup are rejected out of hand. Worldly cosmetics, intended to please men and enhance the attractiveness of the female form, are of no use to the one who is anxious to please only Christ.[72] But Basil goes beyond the usual warnings to suggest that the virgin should not only shun makeup and elaborate dress, but also 'obscure her natural beauty'.[73] If her female form, softness and movements attract males like iron to a magnet,[74] she must 'make her look masculine and her voice hard, and in her walk and generally in every movement of her body, constrain the enticements of pleasure'.[75] By taking on a masculine demeanor she works toward her goal of 'destroying the pleasure of the female in herself, and cutting off the habit of the male' towards the female.[76] Thus her ascetic techniques apply both to the internal workings of nutrition and desire and to the external form and perception of her female body.

Basil's use of physiognomic categories and arguments makes manifest again the bodily basis of his analysis.[77] He not only argues that the virgin should affect a kind of masculinity in order to make herself less attractive by worldly standards, he also understands that a person's character may be read in her or his demeanor and movements. Indeed, Basil writes, because the soul is enclosed by the body and is not able to show its own virtue and beauty, the soul must use the body's voice and look to make itself seen and heard, and the quality of the soul is revealed in the body's movements and clothing, even in one's laugh and walk.[78] The implication for the virgin is that her soul's health and character show in everything she says and does. In Basil's treatise, then, the ideal virginal form is *displayed*—both to her associates and to Basil's readers. He describes her as an 'image of God', painted 'in precise features from her head to her feet'. When she visits with the servants of the bridegroom, she shows herself to be the true bride of the Lord, 'both in her appearance and in her word'.[79]

The ascetic body is, in Basil's treatment, the locus of both sensual dangers and eschatological hopes. Although the body—especially the female body —and its physiological processes and desires are ever-present reminders of human corruptibility and mortality, nevertheless the virginal body, transformed by a correctly prescribed ascetic regimen, becomes an image of God, a 'temple' and 'nuptial chamber' of the Lord,[80] a vision of complete harmony and repose.[81] Indeed, it is possible for the virgin to achieve such absence of passion (*apatheia*)[82] in this life that the lustful attraction between male and female is 'inactive' in her. Basil goes so far as to say that her body becomes 'dead'; only her soul lives in her 'without corruption on account of virtue'.[83] In this angelic condition, the virgin is able to touch the servants of the bridegroom—as Christ washed the feet of his disciples and as Mary kissed the Lord's feet—because she touches with dead hands, and the bodies she touches are also dead to pleasure. The physical touches therefore do not incite images and fantasies in the soul, and the flames of passion remain cold.[84] In an equally stunning image, Basil writes, 'like an image of God, the virgin is molded on earth from her soul and body'. She stands firmly before others 'as an excellent sculpture of God, unmoved towards every mental image and every touch', with her soul thus protected from corrupting influences creeping in through the senses. The virgin therefore earns the honors promised (in Isaiah 56:4–5) to the eunuchs who 'keep the Lord's sabbath', for her very body and passionless soul represent a 'complete day of rest'.[85]

At the same time, Basil warns, even the virgin's 'dead' body, if subject to too many touches, may secretly come alive with desire. And even if one were to be literally castrated as are male eunuchs, even if one were to cut off all limbs and members and stop up all the bodily organs so that the body became like the useless 'stump' of a tree, one is nevertheless able to sin in thoughts and imagination.[86] Within Basil's framework of creation and the physiological basis of desire, then, the virgin's achievement is on the one hand profound, on the other hand limited. Against all of the forces of her own nature as well as the demands of fourth-century society and family, she has by means of her own virtue withdrawn from the cycle of marriage, corruption and death and instead lives already in paradise. And if the goal of chastity is itself praiseworthy, in Basil's analysis *female* virginity is truly spectacular. He writes:

> Although clothed in the female body, they have by means of asceticism beaten off the form engendered from it [i.e. the body] in the soul, and they have shown themselves through virtue to be equal to men, just as their souls have been created equal. And just as men, through asceticism, pass from men to the rank of angels, so also these women, through asceticism, pass from women to the same rank as men.[87]

Basil's lofty praises of virginity are here tempered by his understanding of gender and hierarchy: while men have passed into the rank of angels, women can only be said to equal their rank or dignity in terms of the soul. Their equality is therefore imperfect, with females 'being lame in that equality because of the garment of the female [body]; [but] in the coming age they will be found equal in all ways, through virtue, to those [males] who have been made into angels'.[88] All of the virgin's efforts to destroy the sexual attraction of her female nature—through harsh diet, control of thoughts, masculine guise, and limited movements and associations—are successful only to a point. In the present life she can only limp along, her female flesh making her defective in equality with male ascetics.

The body thus stands at the center of Basil's analysis and praise of virginity. It is at the same time the gift of God and the arena of sin. It is the companion of the soul in the present life and the training ground and visible proof of progress in virtue, but it threatens to destroy the soul as surely as any disease, fire, or stormy sea. In the case of female virginity in particular, it is striking that the transformation of the body is the visible proof of progress while at the same time the inevitability of pleasure implanted in the female body puts firm limits on that progress. And Basil's assurance, that by a correct diagnosis of the 'condition' or 'habit' affecting male and female bodies and an appropriately prescribed ascetic regimen one may hope to overcome corruption and death, is matched by an ever-present fear of infection by passionate thoughts and pleasures.

Finally, in Basil's physiological and naturalistic understanding of the virginal life as well as in his theological and eschatological interpretation of the role of virginity in creation and paradise, it is clear that femaleness is the problem, as the overcoming of femaleness—both in an imperfect sense in this life and completely in the world to come—is the solution. One is left to wonder, then, which body is saved? For in spite of his lofty visions of perfection and his metaphorical images of angelic union with Christ, in Basil's text the 'literal'[89] flesh-and-blood body of the female (that is, the body that eats and digests), and the 'social' body of the woman (that is, the body that is fertile, procreative, dangerous and pleasurable) always intrude, thus inhibiting the full realization of perfection and the possibility of pure love between male and female. Still, the text itself indicates that some men and women understood themselves to be creating together a new reality, a new family and a new body.

Notes

1. The literature is extensive. Representative recent studies include Michel Foucault, *The History of Sexuality*, vol. 3: *The Care of the Self*, tr. Robert Hurley (Pantheon, New York, 1986); James A. Francis, *Subversive Virtue: Asceticism and Authority in the Second-Century Pagan World* (Pennsylvania State University Press, University Park, PA, 1995); Judith Perkins, *The Suffering Self: Pain and Narrative Representation in the Early Christian Era* (Routledge, New York, 1995); Peter Brown, *The Body and Society: Men, Women, and Sexual Renunciation in Early Christianity*, Lectures on the History of Religions, no. 13 (Columbia University Press, New York, 1988).

2. Much of the material in this paper is based on a fuller treatment in my forthcoming book, *The Burden of the Flesh: Fasting, Gender, and Embodiment in Early Christian Ascetic Theory* (Fortress Press, Minneapolis, forthcoming 1998).

3. On these issues see Kate Cooper, *The Virgin and the Bride: Idealized Womanhood in Late Antiquity* (Harvard University Press, Cambridge, MA, 1996). On the

development of female monasticism and the ideology of virginity see in particular Susanna Elm, *Virgins of God: The Making of Asceticism in Late Antiquity*, Oxford Classical Monographs (Clarendon Press, Oxford, 1994); Brown, *The Body and Society*; Thomas Camelot, 'Les traités "de virginitate" au IVe siècle', in *Mystique et Continence: Travaux scientifiques du VIIe Congrès international d'Avon*, Etudes Carmélitaines (Desclée de Brouwer, Brugge, 1952), pp. 273–92; Elizabeth A. Castelli, 'Virginity and Its Meaning for Women's Sexuality in Early Christianity', *Journal of Feminist Studies in Religion*, 2 (1986), pp. 61–88; and Elizabeth A. Clark, 'Ascetic Renunciation and Feminine Advancement: A Paradox of Late Ancient Christianity', *Anglican Theological Review*, 63 (1981), pp. 240–57.

4. *De vera virginitatis integritate* in *Patrologia Graeca* [hereafter *PG*], ed. J.-P. Migne, 30.669–810). The text is included in the *PG* among the spurious works of Basil of Caesarea, but Ferdinand Cavallera has identified Basil of Ancyra as the author ('Le "De Virginitate" de Basile d'Ancyre', *Revue d'histoire ecclésiastique*, 6 [1905], pp. 5–14). There is, to my knowledge, no translation of the Greek into a modern language, although the tenth-century Old Slavonic version (which has large lacunae) has been translated into French by A. Vaillant (*De virginitate de Saint Basile: Text vieux-Slave et traduction française* [Institut d'Etudes Slaves, Paris, 1943]). Susanna Elm discusses the treatise at length in the context of the forms of female monasticism and the ascetic vision of the 'homoiousion' adherents in the Arian controversy of the fourth century (*Virgins of God*, pp. 113–24).

5. Useful discussions of the principal sources on virginity, and of elements of the genre and its ideology, include Camelot, 'Les traités "de virginitate"', and Michel Aubineau's introduction to *Grégoire de Nysse: Traité de la virginité*, Sources Chrétiennes [hereafter *SC*], 119 (Editions du Cerf, Paris, 1971).

6. Cavallera, 'Le "De Virginitate" de Basile d'Ancyre', p. 5.

7. Camelot, 'Les traités "De virginitate"', p. 291.

8. F. J. Leroy, 'La tradition manuscrite du "de virginitate" de Basile d'Ancyre', *Orientalia Christiania Periodica*, 38 (1972), p. 195.

9. José Janini Cuesta, 'Dieta y virginidad: Basilio de Ancira y San Gregorio de Nisa', *Miscelánea Comillas*, 14 (1950), pp. 190–3.

10. Aubineau, *Grégoire de Nysse*, pp. 137–8; Vaillant, *De virginitate de Saint Basile*, pp. i–ii.

11. *De virg.* 1–2 (*PG* 30.669A–73B).

12. *De virg.* e.g. 7; 8; 36; 67 (*PG* 30.681D; 685C; 741C; 805B).

13. Jerome, *De viris illustribus* 89 (in *Patrologia Latina* [hereafter *PL*], ed. J.-P. Migne, 23.731C). Jerome also notes that Basil of Ancyra wrote a treatise on virginity.

14. *De virg.* 3; 54–5 (*PG* 30.673B–6C; 776C–81A).

15. *De virg.* 3 (*PG* 30.673B–6A); see also Plato, *Symposium* 189d–93b (*Plato: Lysis, Symposium, Gorgias*, ed. W. R. M. Lamb, Loeb Classical Library [Harvard University Press, Cambridge, MA, 1967], pp. 134–46); Galen, *De usu partium corporis humani* XIV.2 (*Galeni Opera Omnia*, ed. C. G. Kühn [K. Knobloch, Leipzig, 1821–33; reprint, Georg Olms, Hildesheim, 1964–5], IV:144).

16. *De virg.* 3 (*PG* 30.673C–6A).

17. *De virg.* 3 (*PG* 30.676A–C).

18. *De virg.* 4 (*PG* 30.677A–B).

19. *De virg.* 54–5 (*PG* 30.776C–81A).

20. On these themes in Basil and other early Christian writers see especially Ton H. C. Van Eijk, 'Marriage and Virginity, Death and Immortality', in *Epektasis: Mélanges*

Patristiques offerts au Cardinal Jean Daniélou, ed. Jacques Fontaine and Charles Kannengiesser (Beauchesne, Paris, 1972), pp. 209–35.

21. Van Eijk discusses this Platonic concept and its use in Christian interpretations of the fall in 'Marriage and Virginity', passim.

22. *De virg.* 55 (*PG* 30.780A).

23. Aubineau, *Grégoire de Nysse,* SC, 119:137–42.

24. *De hominis opificio* 16–17; 22 (*PG* 44.181A–9D; 205A–B). On the idea of 'double creation' in early Christian thought see Giulia Sfameni Gasparro, 'Asceticism and Anthropology: *Enkrateia* and "Double Creation" in Early Christianity', in *Asceticism,* ed. Vincent L. Wimbush and Richard Valantasis (Oxford University Press, New York, 1995), pp. 127–46.

25. *De virg.* 55 (*PG* 30.780B).

26. *De virg.* 54 (*PG* 30.777B–C).

27. *De virg.* 51 (*PG* 30.772A–B).

28. *De virg.* 55–6 (*PG* 30.777D–84B).

29. *De virg.* 55 (*PG* 30.780D–1A).

30. *De virg.* 62; 65 (*PG* 30.797A; 801B).

31. *De virg.* 4 (*PG* 30.677B–C).

32. *De virg.* 67 (*PG* 30.805B–8A).

33. *De virg.* 65 (*PG* 30.801C–D).

34. *De virg.* 5; 15 (*PG* 30.680A–B; 700C–4A).

35. *De virg.* 5 (*PG* 30.680B).

36. *De virg.* 6 (*PG* 30.681B).

37. Aristotle also argues that it is the sense of touch that gives pleasure in eating, drinking and sexual relations. See *Nichomachean Ethics,* III.10.8-9 (*Aristotle: The Nichomachean Ethics,* ed. Harris Racham, Loeb Classical Library [Harvard University Press, Cambridge, MA, 1956], pp. 174–6.

38. *De virg.* 6 (*PG* 30.681C).

39. Aline Rousselle has examined monastic diet (as recorded in Jerome and John Cassian), specifically in relation to late ancient medical theory and the link between diet and sexual desire, in 'Abstinence et continence dans les monastères de Gaule méridionale à la fin de l'Antiquité et au début du Moyen Age: Etude d'un régime alimentaire et de sa fonction', in *Hommages à André Dupont, Etudes médiévales langue-dociennes* (Fédération historique du Languedoc méditerranéen et du Roussillon, Montpellier, 1974), pp. 239–54.

40. *De naturalibus facultatibus* II,8 (Kühn, II:107–25).

41. Key texts for Galen's theories of diet, the powers of foods, and the theory of the humors and sexual health include *De alimentorum facultatibus* (Kühn, VI:453–748); *De locis affectis* (Kühn, VIII:1–452); *De naturalibus facultatibus* (Kühn, II:1–214); *De sanitate tuenda* (Kühn, VI:1–452); and *De usu partium* (Kühn, III:1–939 and IV: 1–366).

42. *De virg.* 7 (*PG* 30.684B).

43. *De virg.* 7 (*PG* 30.684B).

44. *De virg.* 8 (*PG* 30.685B–C). Basil follows the widely held view that the young body approaching its prime contains greater innate heat than older bodies. This would be true for both young men and women. At the same time, the male body was generally regarded as hotter than the female body, although there was some debate on this. See G. E. R. Lloyd, 'The Hot and the Cold, the Dry and the Wet in Greek Philosophy', *Journal of Hellenic Studies,* 84 (1964), pp. 102–6.

45. *De virg.* 8; 10-11 (*PG* 30.684C–5B; 688C–92D).

46. *De virg.* 12 (*PG* 30.693B).

47. *De virg.* 8 (*PG* 30.685C–D).

48. *De virg.* 9 (*PG* 30.685D–8B).

49. Two other writers notable for this argument are Jerome (*c.* 342–420), who writes to both male and female ascetics and may have been influenced by Basil's treatise, and John Cassian (*c.* 365–c. 433), whose writings addressed to Western male monastics offer dietary regimens for the reduction of the frequency of wet dreams. On Jerome and Cassian see Shaw, *The Burden of the Flesh* and Rousselle, 'Abstinence et continence'; on Cassian see also David Brakke, 'The Problematization of Nocturnal Emissions in Early Christian Syria, Egypt, and Gaul', *Journal of Early Christian Studies,* 3 (1995), pp. 419–60.

50. C. Daremberg and C. E. Ruelle (eds) *Oeuvres de Rufus d'Ephèse* (Paris, 1897; reprint, Adolf M. Hakkert, Amsterdam, 1963), pp. 64–84; 318–23.

51. In Oribasius, *Libri Incerti,* 18.10–17 (*Oribasius: Collectionum medicarum reliquiae,* ed. Ioannes Raeder [Adolf M. Hakkert, Amsterdam, 1964], vol. IV, pp. 107–8).

52. *Tetrabiblion* XVI.26 (*Aetios of Amida: The Gynaecology and Obstetrics of the VIth Century, A.D.,* ed. and tr. James V. Ricci [Blakiston, Philadelphia, 1950], pp. 36–7.

53. *Tetrabiblion,* XVI.26; 53–54 (Ricci, pp. 37; 56–8).

54. *Tetrabiblion,* XVI.51 (Ricci, pp. 54–5); Soranus, *Gynaikeia* I.27–9 (*Soranus' Gynecology,* tr. Owsei Temkin (Johns Hopkins University Press, Baltimore, MD, 1956), pp. 23–7. On Soranus see Jody Rubin Pinault, 'The Medical Case for Virginity in the Early Second Century C.E.: Soranus of Ephesus, *Gynecology* 1.32', *Helios,* 19 (1992), pp. 128–9.

55. *Tetrabiblion,* XVI.53 (Ricci, p. 56). Ann Ellis Hanson discusses the shift from the Hippocratic view that menstruation, sexual intercourse and childbirth were essential for women's health to the view, represented by Soranus, that menstruation is not necessary for good health ('The Medical Writers' Woman', in *Before Sexuality: The Construction of Erotic Experience in the Ancient Greek World,* ed. David M. Halperin *et al.* [Princeton University Press, Princeton, NJ, 1990], pp. 330–4).

56. See my discussion of these topics in *The Burden of the Flesh,* forthcoming.

57. On this see especially Aline Rousselle, *Porneia: De la maîtrise du corps à la privation sensorielle IIe-IVe siècles de l'ère chrétienne* (Presses Universitaires de France, Paris, 1983), pp. 167–250, especially p. 177; Brown, *The Body and Society*; and Peter Brown, 'The Notion of Virginity in the Early Church', in *Christian Spirituality: Origins to the Twelfth Century,* ed, Bernard McGinn *et al.* (Crossroad, New York, 1985), pp. 427–43.

58. *De virg.* 21 (*PG* 30.712C–3C).

59. *De virg.* 19–20 (*PG* 30.708B–12C).

60. *De virg.* 19 (*PG* 30.709B–C).

61. *De virg.* 35–45 (*PG* 30.740B–60B).

62. *De virg.* 36–7 (*PG* 30.740C–5C).

63. Elm, *Virgins of God,* pp. 118–25.

64. *De virg.* 44–5 (*PG* 30.756C–60B).

65. *De virg.* 37–42 (*PG* 30.743B–53B).

66. *De virg.* 39 (*PG* 30.749A).

67. *De virg.* 62 (*PG* 30.797B–C); see also 66 (*PG* 30.804B).

68. *De virg.* 4 (*PG* 30.677B).

69. *De virg.* 47 (*PG* 30.761A–D).

70. *De virg.* 46–8 (*PG* 30.760B–5B).

71. *De virg.* 47 (*PG* 30.761A).

72. I Corinthians 7:34; *De virg.* 17 (*PG* 30.705A–8A).

73. *De virg.* 18 (*PG* 30.708A).

74. *De virg.* 3 (*PG* 30.676B).

75. *De virg.* 18 (*PG* 30.708B).

76. *De virg.* 19 (*PG* 30.708B).

77. On physiognomy in ancient literature, philosophy and medicine see Elizabeth C. Evans, *Physiognomics in the Ancient World*, Transactions of the American Philosophical Society, 59, 5 (American Philosophical Society, Philadelphia, PA, 1969); Maud Gleason, *Making Men: Sophists and Self-Presentation in Ancient Rome* (Princeton University Press, Princeton, NJ, 1995); and Tamsyn S. Barton, *Power and Knowledge: Astrology, Physiognomy, and Medicine under the Roman Empire*, (University of Michigan Press, Ann Arbor, MI, 1994).

78. *De virg.* 36 (*PG* 30.741A–B).

79. *De virg.* 36 (*PG* 30.740D–1A).

80. *De virg.* 27; 41 (*PG* 30.725B; 749D).

81. *De virg.* 47 (*PG* 30.761A).

82. *De virg.* 50 (*PG* 30.769A).

83. *De virg.* 51 (*PG* 30.772D).

84. *De virg.* 52 (*PG* 30.773A–6A).

85. *De virg.* 58 (*PG* 30.785B–8A).

86. *De virg.* 53; 64 (*PG* 30.776A; 800C).

87. *De virg.* 51 (*PG* 30.772B–C).

88. *De virg.* 51 (*PG* 30.772C).

89. Patricia Cox Miller makes a useful distinction between the 'literal' and 'metaphorical' female body in Jerome's *Epistle* 22 ('The Blazing Body: Ascetic Desire in Jerome's Letter to Eustochium', *Journal of Early Christian Studies*, 1 [1993], p. 24).

THEMATIC REVIEWS

Engendering Egypt

LYNN MESKELL

Ancient Egypt is once again being Orientalized and feminized—not as a result of androcentric colonialist discourses, but through the new spate of studies devoted to the women in ancient Egypt. Egypt is being defined through the constructed category of *women*, so that studies that focus upon women and sexuality are now in vogue. In mainstream archaeology it is now axiomatic that gender studies are an integral part of social analyses and that they have gone beyond the famous *add women and stir* phase. Studies of women as an undifferentiated group do not, in themselves, constitute a gendered analysis and, moreover, gender is not commensurate with the category *women*: men, children, the aged and so on must all be considered. Age, sex, class, status sexual orientation, ethnicity, marital status and religion all intersect to produce variability and hierarchies of difference which must be addressed. Sex cannot be isolated out as a structuring principle, given the significant other factors at play. Moreover, current debates concerning the categories of sex and gender must be addressed, drawing on feminist, masculinist and queer theory (Meskell 1996). Like our Mediterranean neighbours (see Cullen 1996), scholars of Egypt have been slow to take up the feminist challenge and somewhat slower to acknowledge a position of reflexivity in their constructions of Egypt. Integration of theory, either archaeological or sociological, remains a low priority. From this perspective, a handful of writers have engaged with contextual constructions of sex, gender and the body, using the rich suite of data Egypt provides (see Meskell 1996, 1997, 1998; Montserrat 1997; contributions in Wilfong and Jones (1998). The archaeological, iconographic and textual data Egypt yields, for a host of time periods, offers an invaluable opportunity to contribute to contemporary debates— a realization soon to be capitalized upon.

This article considers only recent volumes on the topic of women and gender, though it should be pointed out that an array of interesting papers has recently appeared (Roth 1993; Robins 1994a, 1994–5, 1996; Parkinson 1995; Wilfong 1998) and volumes in related areas (see the important contributions by Pinch 1993, 1994). The four volumes under review are of uneven value and reflect the state of sex-based studies in Egyptology. Two are indicative of simply finding *women* (Tyldesley,

Watterson), another offers a sound study of women accompanied by innovative research (Robins) and the last focuses on gender and the body from a more theoretical perspective (Montserrat). To date, these four represent the most current Egyptological works at the nexus of academia and mainstream readerships since the groundbreaking *Sexual Life in Ancient Egypt* (Manniche 1987). Many Egyptologists have been critical of Manniche's book, yet no single study has yet replaced it in terms of the Pharaonic material. Having said that, each of the books under review is in some way a response to her work.

The first two volumes (Tyldesley, Watterson) can be treated together, since they are mirror images of each other in many respects. To begin with, they both take an *everything you need to know about Egyptian women* approach. Taking women to be a uniform category, each author compartmentalizes their lives into inherently Western categories: economic roles, legal positions, love and marriage, the family, dress and adornment and so on (a quick glance at each table of contents will verify this). These problematic taxonomies are left untheorized, so that etic and emic models of sexed difference are conflated (i.e. Western and indigenous systems are collapsed together). This says more about our own concepts of social structure than the ancient Egyptian system. In fact, Tyldesley's volume suffers most from an explicitly Eurocentric perspective, presenting a scenario where the Egyptians are *just like us*. They are subjected to Western suburbanization: housewives go about their dusting, they suffer from lack of 'personal space', and people do the odd 'DIY alterations'. This colonization of the past makes it a more habitable place for many, yet is a poor substitute for the rich cultural and social variability we know exists between ancients and moderns.

As is often the case in Mediterranean studies, *woman* becomes the signifier for concepts revolving around the body—most often seen in studies of iconography, dress, adornment, posture and hairstyles. However, neither author has considered the body in any nuanced sense, opting instead to focus on female exteriority in the most literal manner. Body and sexuality are thus read straight from the iconographic sources with little consideration of the social construction, much less the embodied reality, of specific groups. So if the body is an absent area of analysis, then embodiment and experience are similarly overlooked. Woman is reduced to visual spectacle, and female sexuality is construed normatively through male-oriented artistic representations or literature (such as love poetry). For example, Tyldesley downplays the possibilities of homosexual practices, even though they do appear in textual sources. There are no individuals in these works, no embodied men, women or children, and no exploration of difference. This *lack* highlights the general reticence by many within the field to incorporate developments from feminism, anthropology, or the social sciences.

Whilst the theoretical underpinnings of *Daughters of Isis* and *Women in Ancient Egypt* are open to criticism, so too is their contribution to the field in terms of new research. Each offers a synthetic overview aimed presumably at the popular reader, with negligible fresh research material. The same ground is covered in both and references are somewhat scarce and outdated, indicating that Pestman's original volume on women and marriage has yet to be superseded . No new translations of texts are on offer, and no additional archaeological analyses have been conducted. The original sources themselves are decontextualized and it is common to discuss Cleopatra and Hatshepsut in the same section, or to use Pharaonic and

Graeco-Roman material interchangeably. The result is that a continuous, uninterrupted narrative is produced, which may prove comforting for a general reader. However, in my opinion, this work coheres falsely and thus undermines the competence and scope of most readers. In sum, these works fall into the category of *wonderful women in ancient Egypt*, an ever burgeoning list of publications (see Lesko 1994, 1994–5), which seek to stress the high status, and wonderful lives, women enjoyed in Egypt without ever unequivocally demonstrating this position. A perspective one could describe only as fictional, utopian, or even colonialist.

A recent challenge to the status quo can be found in Robins's work *Women in Ancient Egypt* and amongst her many books and articles (Robins 1993, 1994a, 1994b, 1994–5, 1996), which seek to explore representations and cultural constructions of women, and subsequently men. Her volume is by far the most scholarly publication devoted to the women of Egypt, covering the extant data and offering important new material. Robins's examination is also a more holistic view of the realities of life for the majority of Egyptian women, taking into account factors such as age, class and status. Her book offers a profile of women across a range of social strata from royal and elite to the middle and lower classes, although there is still a paucity of work devoted to peasants, servants, slaves and prostitutes, which would enhance a gendered perspective. Though Robins takes no overt theoretical standpoint, she implicitly adopts a contextual approach by interweaving textual, iconographic and archaeological evidence. This triple, dialectic use of sources provides an alternative perspective to text-based analyses. The principal textual sources suggest an all-pervasive government and corresponding ideology. However, much of the social, economic and religious life of the ordinary classes may have been self-regulating. Text-based discourse is even more problematic for those interested in issues of sex, since women were largely denied access to literacy along with the middle and lower classes in general. In fact Robins claims that only 1 per cent of the Egyptian population was literate. Yet the prevailing historical picture of Egypt is constituted via its texts, which were written for and by the all-male higher echelons of Egyptian society, with little recognition of this intertextuality (Meskell 1994). Where this volume further departs from those described above is through Robins's expertise in iconographic analysis (see also Robins 1994b), and her research potentially offers scholars working in the Near East and Mediterranean a valuable comparative corpus. Although the lived body is not explicitly at issue here, her analyses represent the most comprehensive argument for the cultural construction of social bodies (male, female and children's) through their corresponding representations. The application of current social theories *on the body* to such rich data could open up promising new horizons.

The realization that contemporary theory and evocative, new data can combine in challenging, informative ways has been demonstrated in Montserrat's new volume, *Sex and Society in Graeco-Roman Egypt*. This work represents the first to consider the body, plus the wider spectrum of gender and sexuality, from both theoretical and Egyptological perspectives. Social history is interpolated with individual histories, and these personalized accounts offer avenues to embodied persons in antiquity. While many might complain that this enterprise is more difficult for the earlier Pharaonic period, an attempt must be made to reinstate the individual and to consider social variability more generally. Taking a Foucauldian perspective, Montserrat problematizes the whole categorization of sex and sexuality, suggesting that they are highly culturally contingent and, if Foucault is correct, a very recent phenomenon indeed. Rather than being seen as monolithic taxonomies, bodies, sexualities and selves are treated from individualistic, contextualized perspectives. Discursive twentieth-century sexual practices and binary gender dichotomies are not simply overlain upon the ancient data. Montserrat also presents the current debates between essentialists and constructionists, though he reaches no definitive position himself other than the realization that we should not conflate modern and ancient constructions of sexuality. This is one of the few volumes to discuss sexuality, in all its manifestations, in a straightforward manner rather than ignoring this integral aspect of social life with its concomitant facets of difference. As Foucault himself said, it is also possible to write the history of feelings, behaviour and the body' (Foucault 1988:112).

In sum, the body has provided a critical site for theorizing society and self within the social sciences in the past few decades, prompting new constellations of meaning for concepts from sex to science, the individual to the institution, domination to *différance*, and from power to the body politic. In archaeology, the body has recently become a central analytic, most notably in European and Mediterranean studies, though Montserrat's volume marks Egyptology's first serious engagement with it. Of particular interest to this discussion are chapters 2 and 3, which are devoted to the social and sensual body in Graeco-Roman Egypt. Montserrat draws upon the works of Freud, Mauss, Douglas, Foucault and Turner to examine bodily experience, the nature/culture dualism, rites of passage and life stages. The conceptualizations of the experience of the lived body and of the body in death differ from the textual representations, since each source can invoke a set of images and practices that do not mesh with each other. Sexed differences between bodies are also demonstrated, as are those based on social status. Of particular note is the section in chapter 3, 'The Sensual Body', which deals extensively with technologies of the body and medico-magical documentation. This example documents the social construction of knowledges surrounding the biological bodies of men and women with all their specificities, and illustrates Montserrat's innovative approach to the data. Throughout the body is perceived as a lived experience where the interplay of irreducible natural, social, cultural and psychical phenomena is brought to fruition through each individual's resolution of external structures, embodied experience and choice. Text and archaeology illustrate that individual bodies represent a particular site of interface between several different irreducible domains: the biological and the social, the collective and the individual, structure and agent, constraint and free will. My only concern here is inherent problems with the uncritical adoption of extreme forms of social constructionism that privilege impersonal forces such as culture, discourse, or power—and Foucault has been widely critiqued for just such a stance (McNay 1992; Foxhall 1994; Goldhill 1995; Meskell 1996, 1997).

Montserrat's work represents a theoretical shift, in that he considers the cultural milieu in which our modern texts on Egypt were created, and continue to be, reflecting on the construction of the discipline itself. In this respect it represents a self-reflexive Egyptology. Finally, this volume offers much new information on the lives of individual men, women and children of varying social status in Graeco-Roman Egypt. It considers their respective life experiences, rites of passage, life stages, and how they perceived themselves and their own embodied sexuality. The data presented are not simply relevant to ancient sexualities, rather they relate to the social realities of individuals and this, in my opinion, is currently our way forward in ancient world studies.

In this review I hope I have shown that it is not enough simply to highlight the category *woman* as a monolithic group since it can never be a representative sample in itself—too many other intersections of difference come into play, whether it be economic or marital status, nationality, or ethnic group, and, more generally, life experience itself. We need to think beyond these initial subjectivities—commitment to a single 'master signifier', whether it be class, race, or sexuality, is always going to prove an inadequate paradigm for these reasons. The shift away from single categories has been made primarily by third wave feminists like Judith Butler or Elizabeth Grosz, and postcolonialists like Homi Bhabha. He sensibly argues that 'the move away from the singularities of "class" or "gender" as primary conceptual and organizational categories, has resulted in an awareness of the subject positions —of race, gender, generation, institutional location, geopolitical locale, sexual orientation—that inhabit any claim to identity in the modern world' (Bhabha 1994:1). Although his position seeks to describe the contemporary scene, it is also applicable to ancient contexts, potentially bringing both fields of inquiry together. This pragmatic approach could truly stimulate archaeology to engage in current issues of cultural difference and thereby position itself as a necessary field within the social sciences.

Barbara Watterson, *Women in Ancient Egypt* (Alan Sutton Publishing, Stroud, 1991), pp. ix + 201, £9.99. ISBN 0 7509 0680 4 (pb).

Joyce Tyldesley, *Daughters of Isis: Women of Ancient Egypt* (Penguin, Harmondsworth, 1994), pp. xvii + 318, £7.99. ISBN 0 14 017596 2 (pb).

Gay Robins, *Women in Ancient Egypt* (British Museum Press, London, 1993), pp. 205, £14.95. ISBN 0 7141 0956 8 (pb).

Dominic Montserrat, *Sex and Society in Graeco-Roman Egypt* (Kegan Paul International, London, 1996), pp. xix + 238, £45. ISBN 0 7103 0530 3 (hb).

Bibliography

Bhabha, Homi (1994) *The Location of Culture*. London: Routledge.

Cullen, Tracey (1996) 'Contributions to Feminism in Archaeology'. *American Journal of Archaeology*, 100: 409–14.

Foucault, Michel (1988) *Politics, Philosophy, Culture: Interviews and Other Writings 1977–1984*. London: Routledge.

Foxhall, Lin (1994) 'Pandora Unbound: a Feminist Critique of Foucault's *History of Sexuality*', in *Dislocating Masculinity: Comparative Ethnographies*. Eds A. Cornwall and N. Lindisfarne. London: Routledge, pp. 133–46.

Goldhill, Simon (1995) *Foucault's Virginity: Ancient Erotic Fiction and the History of Sexuality*. Cambridge: Cambridge University Press.

Lesko, Barbara (1994) 'Ranks, Roles and Rights', in *Pharaoh's Workers: The Villagers of Deir el Medina*. Ed. L. H. Lesko. New York: Cornell University Press, pp. 15–39.

Lesko, Barbara (1994–5) 'Researching the Role of Women in Ancient Egypt'. *KMT*, 5(4): 14–23.

McNay, Lois (1992) *Foucault and Feminism*. Cambridge: Polity Press.

Manniche, Lise (1987) *Sexual Life in Ancient Egypt*. London and New York: Kegan Paul Inc.

Meskell, Lynn M. (1994) 'Desperately Seeking Gender: A Review Article'. *Archaeological Review from Cambridge*, 13(1): 105–11.
Meskell, Lynn M. (1996) 'The Somatisation of Archaeology: Institutions, Discourses, Corporeality'. *Norwegian Archaeological Review*, 1997 29(1): 1–16.
Meskell, Lynn M. (1997a) 'The Irresistible Body and the Seduction of Archaeology', in Changing Bodies, *Changing Meanings: Studies of the Human Body in Antiquity*. Ed. D. Montserrat. London: Routledge, 139–61.
Meskell, Lynn M. (1998) 'Embodying Archaeology: Theory and Praxis', in *The Human Body in the Ancient Near East*. Eds T. G. Wilfong and C. E. Jones. Groeningen: Styx (in press).
Montserrat, Dominic (ed.) (1997) *Changing Bodies, Changing Meanings: Studies of the Human Body in Antiquity*. London: Routledge.
Parkinson, Richard B. (1995) '"Homosexual" Desire and Middle Kingdom Literature'. *Journal of Egyptian Archaeology* 81: 57–76.
Pestman, Pieter W. (1961) *Marriage and Matrimonial Property in Ancient Egypt: A Contribution to Establishing the Legal Position of the Women*. Leiden: NINO.
Pinch, Geraldine (1993) *Votive Offerings to Hathor*. Oxford: Griffith Institute, Ashmolean Museum.
Pinch, Geraldine (1994) *Magic in Ancient Egypt*. London: British Museum Press.
Robins, Gay (1993) 'The God's Wife of Amun in the 18th Dynasty in Egypt', in *Images of Women in Antiquity*. Eds A. Cameron and A. Kuhrt. Revised edition. London: Routledge, pp. 65–78.
Robins, Gay (1994a) 'Some Principles of Compositional Dominance and Gender Hierarchy in Egyptian Art'. *Journal of the American Research Center in Egypt*, 31: 33–40.
Robins, Gay (1994b) *Proportion and Style in Ancient Egyptian Art*. Austin: Texas University Press.
Robins, Gay (1994–5) 'Women and Children in Peril: Pregnancy, Birth and Infant Mortality in Ancient Egypt'. *KMT*, 5(4): 24–35.
Robins, Gay (1996) 'Dress, Undress, and the Representation of Fertility and Potency in New Kingdom Egyptian Art', in *Sexuality in Ancient Art*. Ed. N. B. Kampen. Cambridge: Cambridge University Press, pp. 27–40.
Roth, Ann Macy (1993) 'Fingers, Stars, and the "Opening of the Mouth": the Nature and Function of the Ntrwj-blades'. *Journal of Egyptian Archaeology*, 79: 57–79.
Wilfong, Terry G. (1998) Synchronous menstruation and the 'Place of Women' in ancient Egypt (Hieratic Ostracon Oriental Institute Museum 13512), in *Gold of Praise: Studies on Ancient Egypt in Honor of Edward F. Wente*. Eds E. Teeter and J. Larson. Chicago: Oriental Institute Press (in press).
Wilfong, Terry G. and Jones, Charles E. (eds) (1998) *The Human Body in the Ancient Near East*. Research Archives Bibliographies and Informational Documents. Groeningen: STYX (in press).

Re(ge)ndering Gender(ed) Studies

ALISON SHARROCK

The six books which I was asked to consider for this review article are all multi-authored, and in some cases also multi-edited, collections of essays.[1] The majority of the contributors are women, with a significant minority being men: it seems to me that at this stage in 'the struggle' that is as it should be. The 'collection of essays' has much to recommend it as a forum for the publication of gender-sensitive re-search. As well as allowing a multiplicity of voices, which must be integral to the project of gendersight, it displays in its medium the deconstruction of the Author-Father which it expresses and engenders in its message.

A second effect of the medium is, perhaps inevitably, that there is considerable variety in the quality of the contributions. While most of the essays are helpful, in-sightful, stimulating and exciting, a few, it seemed to me, are slight, unhelpful, or even (arguably) wrong. Do I thus undermine my celebration of 'multiple voices' and 'enabling scholarship' in the previous paragraph? If feminist scholarship means what it says, it should be renewing not only what we say about the (ancient) world, but perhaps also how we say it, and what we say (and do) *about* what we say. We should be listening to voices which have been silenced for centuries. We should be rebelling against the author-itarian strategies of the patriarchal Institution and Discipline. We should be reviewing the criteria by which we make judgements about what is said. Some would say we should not even be making judgements at all ... At the same time, however, there is also a pressing need for gender-sensitive scholarship of the highest level, by whatsoever standard that is measured. While there is indeed a need for a gender-sensitive development and a collective examina-tion of values as regards criteria of excellence, and while *any* (even a deconstructionist-feminist) monolithic view of 'what is excellent' is likely to be constricting, it is es-sential that we do not fall into the trap of thinking that because there are problems about making judgements then no judgements can be made. That way lies the kind of cacophony that we are already seeing on the Internet.

My six books cover quite a wide chronological range: the publication dates of the books range from 1992 to 1996; McAuslan and Walcot is overtly a collection of essays from twenty years of scholarship on women; the essays in Archer et al. have their origins over a period of about ten years. The six fall roughly into two categories. I might characterize them, very broadly, as English and American. Even more broadly, those two categories map on to another pair: 'women's history' and 'feminist theory'.[2] There are moments of cross-over, of course, along each axis, but the general point stands. This reflects something which, as many people know, has

been happening in gender-sighted studies over the last twenty-five years, something which might be called 'from women's studies to gender studies'.[3] To present
a simplification: in the beginning we started to study women, then we realized that
we (1) needed a theory and (2) wanted to avoid ghettoization (amongst other
things). The result was gender studies, which incorporated also masculinity and the
history of sexuality.

Two of the books under consideration (Archer *et al.* and Hawley and Levick)
found their creative origins in the Oxford Women in Antiquity Seminar, now
retitled 'Gender Studies: the Ancient World'. The seminar continues to flourish, as
(I believe) the only regular forum in Britain for the examination of gender-sensitive
issues in the ancient world. It has tended, as these books also tend, to be more
historical than literary, artistic, or philosophical (with notable exceptions): it would,
I suggest, be a creative move if the literary angles were to be further developed.[4]
I wonder, however, whether the movement to gender studies is really the best way
forward now. If everything to do not only with the constructions of gender and
identity, with sexuality, masculinity, femininity, and so on (all very proper subjects
of inquiry), but also with women's lives, children, the family, women writers, the
recuperative strategies of reading as a woman, the whole of feminist literary (and
other) theory are put together; if all that is to come under the aegis of 'gender', then
it seems to me to beg as many questions as it answers. This way women (and children) become carriers of gender as 'others' against which the 'type' (man) is defined.
This may always have been the case in the societies we study: it does not mean we
have to perpetuate it. I am unconvinced of the value of placing all types of family
studies, for instance, under the umbrella of 'gender', as seems to be the suggestion
of Rawson in Hawley and Levick. Of course gender constructs and is constructed
by the arrangements of domestic space, but if all we say about domestic space
becomes saying something about gender we are likely to lose some important
insights into the lives of ancient people who were not 'men' (Roman or Athenian
citizens). If 'women' says 'gender' then 'men' remain(s) as the prototype. At this
stage in the proceedings, there probably does still need to be an umbrella-term,
and a focus for considering these issues. I would suggest that 'gender studies' is
not the right one, but that 'gender-sensitive studies', or perhaps 'gendered studies',
would be more appropriate. These may not sound as good, but they may more
accurately reflect, and *so more helpfully shape*, the nature of the activities under
their wing. I would add, further, my vision for the next stage. There should be space
in all forms of classical scholarship for an awareness of gendered issues, for a woman's
perspective, and for a sensitivity towards gender-difference (and sameness) in
ancient culture. This needs to be underpinned by some theory, which is likely to
remain specialist for a while, but the theory should feed into mainstream activities
in all areas of ancient study.

There are in these books many signs of an opposition, even a tension, between
the 'optimists' and the 'pessimists', as Richlin rightly puts it in her contribution to
Rabinowitz and Richlin. Do we celebrate heroic women? Or expose and decry the
wrongs they suffered? I would commend on this particularly the paper by Helen
King in Hawley and Levick, as nicely balanced between the celebration of ancient
women's knowledge and effectiveness in medical matters, and a quite unromantic
sensitivity not only to the sufferings they endured in the name of therapy, but
also to the gendered relationship which both constructs and is constructed by the

interactions of doctor and patient. Some papers seemed to fall into some rather naive traps, caused by the refusal to hold multiple elements in tension. For example, Richlin (in Richlin and Rabinowitz, p. 292) expresses surprise and distress that rich Roman women oppressed poor Roman women, while a number of papers argued that women's lives were not so bad, and importantly that they were quite happy, and that's all all right. I would say, rather, that of course many were happy, but it's not all right. We should be able to do a double-take: to read ancient culture at multiple levels. Yes, they were happy, yes, they were oppressed: and that is not just a matter of lack of consciousness. This leads me to two other observations: there is a paucity of 'reader response' approaches among these essays, despite a well-heralded prevalence of 'situatedness'.[5] This stems, I think, from a tendency in many of the essays to be monolithic, both as regards gendered categories and the kinds of meanings which might arise out of them. The Americans, in particular, if I may generalize, are inclined to a kind of moral absolutism. It is largely, I suspect, because of the American emphasis on political activism that American scholars are inclined to view the (ancient) world in univocal ways. Furthermore, while there is a significant (although not absolute) English/American split, there is not a great deal of evidence of the French feminist theory which is influential on the European side of the Atlantic in particular, and which informs the kind of construction of 'woman' followed in Henderson (1989). Gold (in Richlin and Rabinowitz) is perhaps the most sympathetic of the Americans to French theory. British scholars should be well placed to take advantage of both sides here: we need to develop our activism (for example, the academic system and the discipline in the UK need to work out how better to enable mothers), but we are, I hope, sensitive to the linguistic force of phallogocentrism. So to the books themselves.

McAuslan and Walcot (eds) arouses mixed feelings in me. It is a collection of papers published in *Greece and Rome* in the last twenty years on 'women's issues': as such, it is a fascinating historical document in its own right. The volume contains some very good papers. I have the slight feeling, on the one hand, of an attempt to get on to the bandwaggon of (at least lip-service to) feminism, and that therefore there had been some rather uncritical inclusion of any essay which mentions women, whether or not it is gender-sensitive.[6] On the other hand, however, if we seek the mainstreaming of gendered study then this is it, I suppose. MacDowell's paper on Menander's *Aspis*, for example, strikes me as being really interested in the legal ramifications of the *epiklerate*. The argument is that Menander is suggesting that the law allowing an uncle to marry the *epikleros* (a woman whose father dies without male heirs) against her will is wrong, and that people should marry for love. My anxiety is that the *epikleros* herself is as much a pawn for MacDowell's discussion of legal niceties as for the characters' manipulation of them.

Thomas Wiedemann's analysis of Thucydides' use of women as a kind of foil to his own ('real man') historiography (because women are irrational and suited to the poets or Herodotus) is a good example of the gendered nuancing of mainstream histor(iograph)y.[7] There are two beautiful pieces of writing by Gillian Clark: first, the accessible but subtle introduction which charts the changes in the study of women in antiquity, in which Clark herself has played so distinguished a role; second, her excellent essay on Roman women, which is and should be compulsory reading for all undergraduates. By the way, despite the fact that so many children never made it through their early years, I do not believe that Roman women did not care about their losses. Personal accounts from women who lived in the end of the last century, when infant mortality was still high, are evidence of the same kind of grief as that expressed in the various funereal items presented by Reeder (for example, entry 54, which shows one such item with a toddler on top of a grave, looking towards the presents his mother and nurse are bringing). There is clearly a development over the twenty years: the papers of Hardwick on the Amazons as outsiders, and of Versnel on the Thesmophoria (not only a fertility festival but also a feast of exception and reversal which gets away with being 'all wrong'), clearly show the development in our understanding of the constructions of gender, and of how gender-constructions themselves contributed to the negotiation of identities and other activities.

There are two papers in this collection which surprise me (in a sense). I did not know what to make of Walcot's paper on 'awful mothers', which seemed to me to come straight out of the same stable as 'mother-in-law' jokes. While no one could deny that there are some dreadful mothers (there are dreadful fathers too), this does not mean that mothers are dreadful. I looked for the irony, but I missed it. Perhaps a change of perspective would help. The other odd paper is Andy Fear's voyeuristic account of Spanish dancing girls. As Gillian Clark says: no comment.[8]

Archer et al. is by-and-large a 'women's lives' volume, although it has important ramifications for theory and for the discipline also (compare Nixon on archaeology as a man's world and the womanufacture[9] of the Neanderthal 'Lucy' with Brown in Rabinowitz and Richlin on 'feminist archaeology'). The range is broad: from the aforementioned Neanderthal to Anglo-Saxon England (Gameson) and to a comparative reading of modern Hindu culture (Leslie), and one of witchifying both ancient and modern (Gibbs-Wichrowska), via Egypt and Israel[10] as well as Greece and Rome. The ethos of most of the essays is optimistic: Depla on the relatively 'good' position of women in ancient Egyptian society,[11] Brock, Herrin and Archer mentioned elsewhere in this review, parts of King (see above), perhaps Hawley on women philosophers,[12] Fischler on the power of some imperial women,[13] Gameson on Anglo-Saxon women as heroes, saints and owners of property. Some of the papers, perhaps, would have benefited from a more sophisticated theoretical underpinning, but nonetheless they are very scholarly articles about many subjects, all with a gendered perspective (rather than a fully developed feminist theory): if we could encourage the spread of gendersight of this nature more widely in the discipline then we would be making progress. But we will always need the theory. One paper which struck me as both scholarly and theoretically sophisticated is that of Maria Wyke. This excellent analysis of how the rhetoric of personal adornment is constructed by and constructs men and women (men as full citizens, women as luxury objects) mixes the best of new historicism and of discourse-theory. Lovibond's essay on the Aristotelian/Pythagorean table of opposites is also theoretically sophisticated, and ends with an interesting discussion of 'why we are doing this'.

Since the collection edited by Hawley and Levick has the explicit aim of assessing developments in women's studies over the last generation, it is *de rigueur* that there should be a contribution from Sarah Pomeroy, whose groundbreaking book, which really started it all, was published twenty years earlier. The programme of revision is more obvious in some places (particularly Rawson, Katz, Beard and Pomeroy) than in others, but many issues traditionally associated with (the study of) women are contained in the other papers: religion, myth, domestic life, medical matters, even a little bit of love (Fantham's entertaining piece on why Apuleius' wife knew what she was doing). The most overtly revisionist paper is Beard, reassessing her own 1980 paper, which argued that the sacrality of the Vestal Virgins stemmed from their ambiguous gendered status. Beard would now see that gender-categories are more complex and fluid, with the Vestal Virgins *contributing* to the construction of Roman gender as much as being constituted by it. Quite so.

Most of the papers in this volume are broadly historical in approach, with literary contributions only from Braund on Juvenal and Zeitlin on Hesiod (which is a paper about 'myth' as much as 'literature', and is as forceful and insightful as ever). Braund studies the way in which Laronia is used in Juvenal *Satire* 2 to attack hypocritical pathic men, inverting the topoi of misogynistic attacks on women. Is this a woman's voice? Laronia seems so reasonable that we cannot help feeling she is being given 'free voice to defend womankind' (p. 213). But, Braund argues, in the end she is a construct, and satire is a male genre. I would add that the bigot who speaks the satires is himself a construct also, but I am inclined to agree that even a determined recuperative reading of Laronia does not stand much chance against the many very strong elements in the reading community of the satires who would hear only the manipulation of the 'woman's' voice to reinforce phallocentric hierarchical attitudes.

Most of the papers are optimistic. Nixon and Foxhall, for example, both read various Athenian festivals not just as agricultural fertility rites used to control women, but also as celebrations which women could use to control their lives. I wondered whether Nixon was perhaps a little over-optimistic on the possibilities of classical Greek women controlling their own fertility through various herbal means and the festival of Thesmophoria, but I am sure that both authors are right to see how these festivals provided opportunities for mutual support between women, which would have helped them cope with their lives. Likewise, Savunen's description of how women played an independent role in the public support of candidates for office in Roman Pompeii (by posters) is an optimistic celebration of women's activity. I would note, however, that the evidence of 2 per cent of posters being female-named, with 21 per cent male-named, does not quite qualify as making women 'equal'. Likewise, again, in Lambropoulou's description of some writers, including female writers, in the Pythagorean tradition, on the virtues proper to women, we hear that in Pythagoreanism women are equal, but it seems to me that their equality is expressed in very traditional (unequal) virtues, like silence.

But perhaps I am being over-critical, both of critics' laudable attempts to recover ancient women and also of the ancient societies themselves. One essay here which is a paragon of historical sensitivity is Anna Wilson on women saints. Wilson is willing to make the kind of 'double-take' on attitudes to the ancient world which seems to me essential if we are to make any progress, for she holds in tension a celebration of the relatively high status of women in martyr acts together with a proper sensitivity to the voyeuristic and pornographic elements in their deaths and their representations. This seems to me to be right. With it should be compared Herrin's generally optimistic discussion (in Archer et al.) of the way in which the possibilities for personal and public devotion on the part of Byzantine women decreased from the sixth or seventh centuries on, and also the two rather pessimistic papers by Cameron. That in McAuslan and Walcot suggests that the prominence of women in early Christianity was accidental (unless I have missed the point), while that in Archer et al. argues that the celebration of virginity in early

Christianity is only misogynistic. The type of multiplicity of reading brought to bear by Wilson might perhaps have seen how the erotic language applied to the soul and God may be recuperated creatively *at the same time* as the misogyny is exposed.

An interesting feature of reviewing books which are a few years old is that one can see already how the academic world has changed. Amy Richlin's *Pornography and Representation*, at 1992 the earliest published of my six books, opens with an introduction containing a number of prophecies. She says, for example, that there has been very little classical scholarship which is interdisciplinary, and which crosses the art-literature interface (p. xii), and that the ancient novel is 'only beginning to be taken seriously' (p. xiii). All these claims are less true now than when they were originally made.[14] The programme of the book—to consider the potentially harmful dynamics of representation (of women, sex, death and other such taboos)—is one which I find fascinating.[15] I would recommend Richlin's introduction as one of the most concerted pieces of feminist writing in my remit, but I should like to make a few points: a plea for less monolithic gender-categories, and for every effort to ensure that feminism develops its multiplicity; and an observation that this book, in keeping with a powerful strand in American classical feminism, displays a kind of moral absolutism which, while laudable in some ways, nevertheless seems somewhat lacking in a sense of history, and somewhat naive in expecting things to be good and beautiful (and unproblematic) in all ways. Richlin's own essay is a case in point: a subtle reading of rape-narratives in Ovid, it nonetheless displays an uncomfortable ambivalence between hate (we should not look at Ovid's text, because it is obscene and damages women, and by looking we are perpetuating that obscenity and damage) and a slightly guilty love of the poem. I do not feel the need to 'approve' of every aspect of Ovid's poetry in order to enjoy it and to study it. One contribution which I thought avoided this pitfall was that of Zweig, who considers whether the female silent characters in Aristophanes are more likely to have been nude *hetairai* (prostitutes) or men in padded costumes (probably nudes). There is a good appreciation here of the tension (for us) between the exuberant, life-affirming, vibrant sexuality of the bawdy games of Old Comedy, and the disturbing way in which such dramatic pornography (for example, the woman's body as map in *Lysistrata*) displays and reinforces unequal social dynamics in a society which 'approves the degradation and oppression of women'. Are we allowed to laugh at this *and* see how it contributes to the oppression of women? I think there is a difference between 'now' and 'then'. The pornographic nature of a (reading of a) particular item depends considerably on the situation of reading. A peephole show is not just the same as a museum, even if they are not completely unconnected either.[16]

A number of the essays deal with material which many readers would not be happy to call pornographic. Each case could be debated: I pick on Montague's paper on *Daphnis and Chloe*. It seems to me oddly judged to include a paper about women and sex in a volume on pornography. Even if we accept the author's view that the violence of the erotic interest in Chloe has something of the pornographic about it, if we follow the line taken here then everything we might say about women and sex becomes tainted with the suspicion of pornography. Surely not many people want that type of sexual repression. Another essay deals with material that the author herself denies to be pornographic: that is Myerowitz's enjoyable and positive reading of erotic pictures in Roman houses, which she sees as non-violent, even expressing a mutuality and equality between the lovers.[17] Fair enough, but if these representations are not pornographic then it is a nice irony that one of them graces the front of the volume.

Shapiro also claims that his material is not pornographic, or rather that homosexual pornography on Greek vases is different from heterosexual versions, being largely non-exploitative, because pederasty is aristocratic and not based on dominance. I am intrigued that the kind of moral absolutism that makes us (sometimes) so hard on ancient men for their behaviour to women does not seem to be carried over to our attitude to their treatment of boys, about which the modern world is almost obsessively concerned. The differences in the dynamics of representation are certainly interesting and telling. But how can it be that his beautiful 'bobbin' (p. 71) does not objectify the men depicted there? Is it because they are both subjects? Are they, then, subjects because we are trained to read them as such? Sutton says, rightly,[18] that it is easier to see nude women as pornographic than nude men: again, I suggest that is because our reading/viewing is constrained by centuries of reading women as sex-objects. Objectification is in the eye of the beholder, but no less active for that.[19]

Perhaps the most challenging book in my remit is Rabinowitz and Richlin's collection *Feminist Theory and the Classics*, which addresses head-on some of the crucial questions behind the entire project of engendering classics, both in content (what we say about the ancient world) and in form (the lives of women students and academics). Although the book is four years old now, and there are more gender-sensitive critical writings on the ancient world in print, and more academic women in post, including senior posts, than there were then (but only marginally more), the issues are still as live as ever. Indeed, the book has not had as much impact on the study of the classical world, at least in Britain, as one might have hoped. This may be in part because quite a lot of it speaks a language alien to that of the British academic world; in part because some of the papers do not seem well grounded in the ancient world; in part because some are simply not very good. As an illustration of my second 'part', perhaps I might take Gold's essay on 'Finding the Female in Roman Poetry', which in my opinion is one of the best in the collection. Gold offers a clear (if somewhat rigid) analysis of the differences between French feminism (language, discourse, 'Woman') and American (political engagement, real women's lives). She argues that the American can learn from the French. Propertius, for example, may be seen to destabilize feminine (and masculine) gender-norms. More explicit readings of Roman elegy would have given more force to this important point.[20] Skinner's essay on Sappho, another of the very good contributions in this volume, is less sympathetic in its engagement with French feminism. The essay is directed towards a plea for a gynocentric curriculum for classical studies: we should read Sappho (of course), and other women's literature. I would certainly agree on the importance of reclaiming any literature by women that we can,[21] but I cannot see much future in valorizing it *above* literature by men (some of which I really rather like, and want to keep reading), and, moreover, we should be informed by the sort of 'discourse'-discourse which in this review is being characterized as 'French' (in fact it is more complex and interactive than that) in order to appreciate the complexities of writing as a woman. Sappho's voice, I submit, is not unproblematically 'a woman's voice', nor (as Gold notes) is Sulpicia's, nor are those of the writers of sex manuals,[22] nor is Skinner's, nor is mine. A 'woman's voice' is a

constantly shifting process of renegotiation. I think the 'American' response would
be to say that it is the voice of 'someone who worries about childcare'. Yes, indeed,
and this should be remembered more often, but it should also be acknowledged
(I believe) that worrying about childcare is not something with a simplistic, constant, unambiguous meaning.

In common with many of the essays in my six books, a significant number of
papers in this volume have something to say about the discipline, and about their
own situation with respect to it and to the wider world. This emphasis on the
situatedness of reading has been given explicit attention recently in Hallett and van
Nortwick (1997), but the issue seems to be a long way from being resolved. Not
just any old personal details matter to 'situate' a reading; the telling of one's own
story does not give an automatic validity to what one says about other stories. One
example will have to serve for analysis of a problem which is by no means re-
stricted to this case: Tina Passman's story of her experiences as a Lesbian classicist
in modern America is her own story. Fine, but it does not prove anything at all
about the value of Jane Harrison's scholarship, nor about myths of matriarchy.
Passman suggests that the myths of a pre-historic time of female dominance could
be used as encouraging ideals for modern feminists. I do not feel confident that she
is arguing this *despite* their non-historicity. I am not a pre-historian, but even I can
tell that the fact that Passman was told not to believe Jane Harrison ('because she
was a Lesbian') does not prove that there actually was a time when women ruled.
Perhaps by accident, this is the implication of the paper. For what it might be worth,
I would note that the time when 'pre-historic matriarchy' was fashionable was a
time of almost exclusive male-dominance of the discipline (the late nineteenth and
early twentieth centuries).[23] This suggests, perhaps, that the relationship between
the situation of reading and the outcome of that process is not something unequivocal and absolute.[24]

Finally: Ellen D. Reeder's *Pandora* is a beautiful book. The project has some
affinities with Fantham et al. (1994), which also seeks to interweave primary
material and responses to it. *Pandora* contains ten essays by well-known scholars
in the field of Greek cultural studies, together with the catalogue of an exhibition,
run by the Walters Art Gallery, showing the artistic representation of women in
ancient Greece. The catalogue itself has fine colour photographs, plus additional
images of different views, technical descriptions of the pieces and their history,
followed by critical analysis of their iconography. I am not competent to judge the
technical aspects of this project, but the iconographic dynamics are excellent. The
very project of presenting visual material according to the dynamics of poetry (if I
may make so bold) is a creative one. The images are arranged in four sections: the
development of the portrayal of women; the image of the container (Lissarague's
essay providing an extensive survey of the association of women with containers,
both in form and in content); and that of the untamed animal; and finally what
happens when the taming process 'goes wrong' (various monsters, witches and
misbehaving goddesses). As well as the much-discussed images of erotic pursuit
(for example), we see here a great many representations of weddings (and quasi-
weddings) and of children. I, personally, was delighted to see space given to the
interactions of mother and child, from the inside. Others will take further the analyses of these images, but everyone interested in the representation of women, in art,
in aesthetics and in women's lives, will want to study and enjoy this magnificent

work. I feel the need, however, to register one slight anxiety about the representational strategies employed here: how far is the work implicated in the kind of 'womanufacture' which feminist literary and art criticism (with which, I presume, it at least moderately aligns itself) are seeking to expose? The constant reference to statues of women as 'she', as is done throughout this book, looks rather uncritical. I would like to see a more self-conscious consideration of the issue. Likewise, Humphreys' 'optimistic' essay on the separateness of women's lives in classical Athens, where she argues that women lived in their own community as 'herding animals', ends by asking whether it is necessarily worse to be a cow than a lap-dog (symbol for the middle-class, twentieth-century housewife). Again, I feel this is implicated in the injustices it exposes.

The essays tend towards the descriptive rather than the analytical, perhaps in part because the book aims at a relatively broad audience. Some are sophisticated pieces, such as Zeitlin's reading of Hesiodic misogyny,[25] and how it makes Perses into a 'woman' (greedy and enervating). Sourvinou-Inwood's contribution to the nuancing of the *oikos–polis* ('house'–'city') opposition[26] shows how women's religious role in the *polis*, although important, was not connected with the *oikos*, on behalf of which only a man could act. Oakley's essay in the collection is a particularly useful discussion of how details from wedding-iconography contribute, even sometimes subversively, to the readings of scenes that are not literally weddings. I felt that this contribution could perhaps be a little more explicit about the impact of the iconography it presents: for example, that the fleeing reticence of the bride is (1) part of the myth of the bride, for the sake of proving her virginity, and (2) produced for the voyeuristic pleasure of the (male) viewer. Stewart's generally sensitive consideration of rape (or rather 'Rape?') seemed to me to suffer similarly. I am sure he is right that the images of erotic pursuit on fifth-century vases have to do with male self-assertion and the power of the citizen, and also with male fears and anxieties about women and sex, but I missed a full sense that what makes an object desirable is (in part) its reticence, and that the backwards look of some victims, which may well be intended to indicate some hint of erotic interest, is itself part of the fantasy of the male viewer/pursuer. A girl must not want it, but she must want it really.[27]

Ian McAuslan and Peter Walcot (eds) *Women in Antiquity*, Greece and Rome Studies (Oxford University Press on behalf of the Classical Association, Oxford, 1996), pp. vii + 216, £11.99/$19.95. ISBN 0 19 920303 2 (pb).

Leonie J. Archer, Susan Fischler and Maria Wyke (eds) *Women in Ancient Societies: 'An Illusion of the Night'* (Macmillan Press, Basingstoke and London, 1994), pp. xx + 308, £16.99/$18.95. ISBN 0 333 52397 0 (pb).

Richard Hawley and Barbara Levick (eds) *Women in Antiquity: New Assessments* (Routledge, London, 1995), pp. xix + 271, £13.99/$18.95. ISBN 0 415 11369 5 (pb).

Amy Richlin (ed.) *Pornography and Representation in Greece and Rome* (Oxford University Press, New York and Oxford, 1992), pp. xxiii + 317, £18.00/$21.95. ISBN 0 19 506723 1 (pb).

Nancy Sorkin Rabinowitz and Amy Richlin (eds) *Feminist Theory and the Classics* (Routledge, New York and London, 1993), pp. viii + 314, £12.99/$19.95. ISBN 0 415 90646 6 (pb).

Ellen D. Reeder, *Pandora: Women in Classical Greece* (Trustees of the Walters Art Gallery, Baltimore, MD, in association with Princeton University Press, Princeton, NJ, 1995), pp. 431, £30.00/$35.00. ISBN 0 691 01124 9 (pb).

Notes

1. The one semi-exception is Reeder, which is an exhibition catalogue published together with a set of essays by different authors. The point remains. There is of course a grand tradition of collections of essays on women: Foley (1981), Cameron and Kuhrt (1983), Peradotto and Sullivan (1984), and the various issues of *Helios* in the late 1980s and 1990s. For a bibliography on women in antiquity see Clark (1993), and see the basic bibliographies on feminism and classics at the end of Rabinowitz and Richlin.

2. Archer *et al.*, Hawley and Levick, and McAuslan and Walcot are based in Britain and are largely on 'women's lives'; Richlin, Rabinowitz and Richlin, and Reeder are based in America. The first two American books are largely theoretical; Reeder does not quite fit comfortably into my dichotomy.

3. See, for example, the critique of this development in Modleski (1991).

4. Cf. Richlin in Rabinowitz and Richlin, p. 286: 'history is a more feminist project than literature'. I do not agree, of course.

5. If we are going to talk about ourselves: I find it surprising and worrying that so few contributors who did so had anything to say about motherhood, to me the most important part of my life as a woman.

6. When I first picked up the volume, and saw in it a paper by my dear, unreconstructed friend and colleague Andy Fear, I thought 'Ah, Not the Women in Antiquity Volume' (on the model of Not the Nine O'clock News). But it is not quite as 'alternative' as that.

7. Only the most pessimistic part of me responds with the accusation of implication.

8. Also in the collection are Marshall on Tacitus and whether women were allowed to accompany generals and other officials in the field; Cameron on early Christianity; an optimistic celebration of marital happiness by Lefkowitz; Walcot, showing how Greek myth expresses Greek men's fears about women and sex; Haley's gender-sensitive description of the quintuple marital adventures of Pompey; Cohen on Athenian women not being secluded in the way we (might have) thought; Gardner on how Aristophanes reflects the anxiety of his male audience about the safety of the city.

9. For this metaphor for the construction of femininity, see Sharrock (1991).

10. I would commend particularly both articles on things Jewish: Archer on the gender-insensitivity in modern writing on ancient Jewish life, and on the richness of Jewish women's history; and Brock on the prominence given to the role of Sarah in some versions of the Sacrifice of Isaac.

11. I am not enough of a specialist to know whether the hint of wishful thinking which I seemed to detect stems only from my own inclination to pessimism.

12. I did feel that the emphasis on the beauty of women philosophers is a very easy sign that they are still considerably womanufactured.

13. This is perhaps a positive recuperation brought about by a confrontation with unjust representations of women's behaviour. The argument is that the behaviour expected of elite Roman matrons took on an uncomfortably political aspect when those women were Imperial. Because that gave them a kind of access to power which was not felt appropriate for women, in literary depictions they tend to be presented as transgressive. What we are really seeing is powerful women.

14. The rise in popularity of interdisciplinarity, together (I do not doubt) with the lessening of linguistic rigour in training, has contributed to the rise of 'cultural studies' (soft or otherwise). This is a move to be welcomed, but I would hope that the more language-based literary criticism and theory will not fall by the wayside, *and that it will be gender-sensitive*. You do not have to do cultural studies to be feminist.

15. See my forthcoming 'Looking at Looking: Can You Resist a Reading?', which will appear in a special issue of *Arethusa* devoted to the Roman Gaze.

16. Cf. Elsom in this collection.

17. But see Wyke in Archer *et al.*

18. This is a survey of the development of erotic imagery on Greek vases, arguing that it becomes more 'romantic' and less 'obscene' as the classical period develops.

19. Also in the volume are Rabinowitz on tragedy (a good feminist reading, although putting some pressure on the term 'pornography'); Parker on erotic handbooks; Joshel on the use of raped and murdered female bodies for political effect in Livy; Brown on mosaic representations of death in the arena; Henry on the commodification (I would have said 'commedification') of woman as food in Athenaeus; and a piece of creative writing by Marsh based on various mythological women.

20. On this type of reading of Roman elegy, see now Wyke (1995) and Sharrock (1995).

21. Snyder (1989) is of course seminal.

22. See Parker in Richlin.

23. Myths of matriarchy appear in various places in my remit. Quite a sane discussion plays a role in Zweig's contribution to Rabinowitz and Richlin, which argues for a higher valorization of women before the classical period. I think many people could accept that.

24. Also in the volume are Haley on Cleopatra as a Black woman; Hallett on going beyond classical Athens and first-century BCE Rome (another prophecy?); Robin on Seneca's tragedies, using film theory but applying it more aurally than visually; Rose on looking for an alliance between Marxism and feminism; Brown on feminist archaeology.

25. This essay comes from the same stable as Zeitlin's contribution in Hawley and Levick, and ultimately from her 1995 study.

26. It is becoming increasingly clear that the opposition *polis*-male-public/*oikos*-female-private will not hold. See, for example, Strauss (1993:36–53).

27. A few details in this book look a bit insecure to me, although I am not an expert. Stewart uses the fact that we have very few records of rape cases in the ancient Greek court to prove that there were very few rapes. This might have more to do with the loss of status of women and the public shame involved than a low incidence of rape itself. To be fair, Stewart does acknowledge this point. Reeder, in her introductory essay, says that the fact that we know of no case of a woman actually being sold into slavery for pre-marital sex is an indication that the law was a powerful deterrent. But this would be like arguing that no football is played on Sundays. And moreover, the evidence for that law is Plutarch saying that Solon did not forbid it (*Life of Solon* 23). Also in the volume are Lefkowitz on *parthenoi* ('maidens'); Shapiro on the daughters of Cecrops; and Schmidt on 'sorceresses'. Carol Benson makes a significant contribution to the catalogue.

Bibliography

Cameron, A. and Kuhrt, A. (eds) (1983) *Images of Women in Antiquity*. Detroit, MI: Wayne State University Press.

Clark, G. (1993) *Women in the Ancient World: Greece & Rome*. New Surveys in the Classics 21. 1989; 2nd edn, Oxford: Oxford University Press.

Fantham, E., Foley, H. P., Kampen, N., Pomeroy, S. and Shapiro, A. (1994), *Women in the Classical World: Image and Text*. New York and Oxford: Oxford University Press.

Foley, H. P. (ed.) (1981), *Reflections of Women in Antiquity*. New York and London: Gordon & Breach Science Publishers.

Hallett, J. P. and van Nortwick, T. (1997), *Compromising Traditions: The Personal Voice in Classical Scholarship*. London: Routledge.

Henderson, J. G. W. (1989) 'When Satire Writes "Woman": Gendersong', *PCPhS* 215: 50–80.

Modleski, T. (1991), *Feminism without Women: Culture and Criticism in a 'Postfeminist Age*. New York and London: Routledge.

Peradotto, J. and Sullivan, J. P. (eds) (1984), *Women in the Ancient World: The Arethusa Papers*. Albany, NY: State University of New York Press.
Pomeroy, S. B. (1975), *Goddesses, Whores, Wives, and Slaves*, New York: Schocken Books.
Sharrock, A. R. (1991), 'Womanufacture', *JRS* 81: 36–49.
Sharrock, A. R. (1995), 'The Drooping Rose: Elegiac Failure in *Amores* 3.7', *Ramus* 24: 152–80.
Sharrock, A. R. (forthcoming), 'Looking at Looking: Can You Resist a Reading?', *Arethusa*.
Snyder, J. M. (1989) *The Woman and the Lyre: Women Writers in Classical Greece and Rome*. Bristol: Bristol Classical Press.
Strauss, B. S. (1993), *Fathers and Sons in Athens: Ideology and Society in the Era of the Peloponnesian War*. London: Routledge.
Wyke, M. (1995), 'Taking the Woman's Part: Engendering Roman Elegy', in *Ramus Essays in Honour of J. P. Sullivan*. Ed. A. J. Boyle. Bentleigh, Vic.: Aureal Publications, pp. 110–28.
Zeitlin, F. I. (1995), *Playing the Other: Gender and Society in Classical Greek Literature*. Chicago and London: University of Chicago Press.

Manhood in the Graeco-Roman World

JONATHAN WALTERS

As was the case with most disciplines, it was the second, modern wave of feminism which provided the impetus for an increased interest in the study of gender in the Graeco-Roman world. At first, as one would expect, the emphasis was on redressing the balance and bringing to light what scholarship had hitherto, for the most part, neglected: information about women. It soon became clear, however, that the overwhelmingly male origin of the literary sources made uncovering the reality of women's lives no easy task. Indeed, the notion of 'reality' itself, it became clear, was a dubious one, for what outside the texts themselves could be recovered from documents written by and for elite men? Investigation shifted to an examination of the discourses within which gender was discussed, and the focus of attention moved from women to the gender-system which underlay whatever was said about women, or about men. Greek and Roman 'manhood' itself, once unexamined and taken for granted (as much by recent scholars as within the texts studied), now came under the spotlight, and revealed itself to be complex, multifarious and far from the seamless whole that Graeco-Roman texts proclaimed or implied. Its bases intertwined in complex ways with other social statuses, such as citizenship, age and occupation, and it was manifestly subject to slippages and contradictions. As became clear, the topic was one fraught with considerable anxiety for the men who wrote the vast majority of the texts that classicists study.

The two books reviewed here are both important contributions to the study of manhood in the Graeco-Roman world, written by scholars at the forefront of their discipline. Though both use as their method the close examination of literary texts emanating from the 'high culture' of the male elite, they deal with very different historical periods and therefore focus on rather different concerns.

Professor Loraux's subject is manhood, and the use of 'femininity' in its construction, in the Greek world of the autonomous city-states of the fifth and fourth centuries BCE, particularly those about which we know most, Athens and Sparta. These city-states were 'men's clubs', in which citizenship and adult manhood were coterminous, and in which, therefore, the formal discourse of what it was to be a man was usually civic. Professor Loraux examines literary texts of the period, and the 'canonical' writings of Homer and Hesiod that were fundamental to education in that culture. She deploys close examination of words and phrases in context and their parallels elsewhere in order to get at the implied, rather than overtly stated, conceptualization in play in each case. Moving forward from the now generally accepted position that 'manhood' (which equalled citizen and soldier) was the conceptual norm and femininity was 'Other', marked either by excess or by lack, she rejects as too facile such a simple disjunction between the two. She looks beneath the 'cardinal opposition of sexual roles' (p. 46) to the less obvious exchanges between masculine and feminine, pointing out that such superficially binary thinking ultimately subverts itself, and she discovers an 'infinitely variable landscape' (p. 42). Her thesis is that, as one would expect, such seemingly total rejection of the 'Other', the feminine, conceals a fascination with it, a desire to incorporate elements of it within the male norm, and that aspects of what were apparently purely 'feminine' were ineluctably—though concealed by linguistic sleight-of-hand—to be found within the masculine ideal of the period. Thus behind an overt emphasis on the manly strength of the warrior she uncovers a fascination with his weakness, and despite the supposed impenetrability of the male body many references to its penetrability by weapons. Her various chapters were originally written separately over a number of years and then revised for this book (which was first published in French in 1990) to form a continuous argument. They cover such topics as the connection in Greek thought between the warrior's death in battle and the wife's death in childbirth, soldiers' wounds and death by strangulation, the rare and anomalous emergence of women into historiographical narrative, and such emblematic figures as Heracles (a curiously gender-ambivalent male) and Tiresias (a man who, legend has it, spent part of his life as a woman).

Though the title of Professor Gleason's book speaks of 'ancient Rome', the author concentrates in the main on the culture of the Greek-speaking elite of the Roman Empire in the second century CE. This elite lived and moved and had its being in a world very different from that discussed in Professor Loraux's book, though they prided themselves on being its heirs and continuers. The autonomous cities of the classical period had become part of the vast Roman Empire, an empire with which the Greek urban elite had by now reached a complex accommodation. The enormous expansion of the Greek-speaking world during and after the conquests of Alexander the Great had changed Greek men's sense of what it was to be Greek. A uniform educational system, based on the maintenance of what was now seen as the 'classical' language and literature of the fifth and fourth centuries BCE, had led to the production of what one might call a standardized Greek gentleman, whose membership of the elite was demonstrated by his command of this classical culture. In particular, this status was demonstrated by the ability to make formal public speeches, an art which was practised by men alone, and thus had become a mark of elite manhood. This 'manhood', however, was a status the attainment and retention of which was never assured once and for all: it was subject to attack by other elite men in the intensely competitive world of the urban elite, and needed periodically to be reaffirmed by successful performance. At this time, speechmaking had become a culturally central, and very popular, art-form, with virtuoso practitioners who travelled from city to city and could win fame, power, prestige and wealth by their performances. Professor Gleason's book deals with such star performers of the manly art of speech-making. She examines the ways in which the making of these formal public speeches was bound up with questions of gender, particularly with the speaker's success or failure in embodying the cultural ideal of manhood. This she does by bringing together an examination of the rules of corporeal and vocal deportment enjoined on public speakers, with the more general rules of bodily deportment by which men were judged, and with the theories of healthcare and bodycare prevalent at the time.

Both authors bring a very wide range of learning to bear on their chosen topics, and cite both primary and secondary sources fully so that the reader is enabled easily to follow up areas of particular interest. Both these books are accessible to the non-specialist reader, at least to the extent that in both cases all Greek (and in the case of Professor Gleason's book Latin) words or passages cited are translated. In the case of both books, however, those readers who do not have a basic grounding in the historical background may find themselves occasionally rather at a loss. Professor Gleason's book is in this respect easier for the non-classicist reader. Her style is also perhaps more easily readable than that of Professor Loraux, though this may be the effect on this reviewer of its being in the English-language academic tradition, while the other is translated from the French. Both, however, are works of impresssive erudition and scholarship. They offer no simple answers to such over-simplified questions as 'What did "manhood" mean then?'; rather, they patiently lay bare the fissures in the seeming monolith, prudently refusing to attempt to draw overarching conclusions. Latest reports from the front line, and well worth reading for those who want to know the current state of play in the study of Graeco-Roman gender.

Maud W. Gleason, *Making Men: Sophists and Self-Presentation in Ancient Rome* (Princeton University Press, Princeton, NJ, 1995), pp. 193 + xxxii, $29.95/ £25.00 (hb). ISBN 0 691 04800 2.

Nicole Loraux, *The Experiences of Tiresias: The Feminine and the Greek Man*, tr. Paula Wissig (Princeton University Press, Princeton, NJ, 1995), pp. 348 + viii, $37.50/£29.95 (hb). ISBN 0 691 02985 7.

Getting/After Foucault: Two Postantique Responses to Postmodern Challenges

PAUL CARTLEDGE

Michel Foucault, late Professor of History of Systems of Thought at the *crème de la crème* Collège de France, was both an enormous inspiration and a huge irritation. If it is significantly thanks to his three-volume *Histoire de la Sexualité* that classics has come to occupy a prominent place in the gender/sexuality studies revolution of the past two decades, yet not all classicists by any means have found themselves equally thrilled by their unsought connection with that uneven and inchoate work. On the one hand, it was a classicist, Paul Veyne, a colleague at the Collège de France and like Foucault a paradoxically self-marginalized scholar at the very epicentre of French and so Western intellectual life, who bluntly and approvingly stated (in the revised 1978 edition of his *Le pain et le cirque*) '*Foucault révolutionne l'histoire*'. On the other hand, those classicists working prominently in gender/sexuality studies who have chosen to engage directly with him—they include Amy Richlin, David Cohen and Richard Saller (all in *Helios* 1991), Lin Foxhall (in Andrea Cornwall and Nancy Lindisfarne's 1994 collection, *Dislocating Masculinity*), and Page duBois (in her *Sappho Is Burning*, 1995)—on the whole end up disapproving more than they approve. (The giant exception is David Halperin, the title of whose *Saint Foucault: Towards a Gay Hagiography*, 1996, says it almost all.)

DuBois offers a particularly neat example of the classicist's—and especially the feminist classicist's or classicist feminist's—double-bind, partly because she is so helpfully up-front about her own theoretical-political and other self-positionings ('a psychoanalytic female subject, a Marxist historicist feminist classicist, split, gender-troubled ...'). She could not, she is sure, have written her Sappho book 'without Michel Foucault'. For the inspiration of his anti-essentialism, his defamiliarization of the past, his notions of episteme, discourse and disciplinary genealogies that allow her to think about history 'otherwise', even for his inconsistency ('exemplary') —for these she has nothing but praise and gratitude. But for his non- or rather antifeminism, exhibited in his positing of a continuity of masculine subjective centrality and in his denial through suppression of female desire, she can summon up nothing but castigation and contumely.

Simon Goldhill does not of course bring with him to his self-appointed task quite the same mental and psycho-physiological equipment as duBois, but he too is attempting the ambitious feat of reading critically and against the grain for the benefit of a wide contemporary audience some densely sophisticated literary texts written in ancient Greek, in a very different, indeed 'other', elsewhere and elsewhen.

Since Foucault eschewed grand theory, or rather—according to his own rhetoric—theory of any sort, and because he was notoriously or famously inconsistent within as well as between his various projects, it is hard to say just what the 'burden' of his scholarly contribution was or should be taken to have been. But any retrospective assessment is unlikely not to make the trinity of discourse, power and knowledge somehow central. The question, therefore, inescapably arises of how Foucault's own discourse stands in relation to the discursive formations it analyses.

At the outset of *L'usage des plaisirs*, the second volume of *l'Histoire de la sexualité*, the one devoted chiefly to ancient Greek sexual thought and practices, Foucault sensibly sought to cover his back, while at the same time enunciating why if we care for our selves we should still care for and about the Greeks:

> I am neither a Hellenist nor a Latinist. But it seemed to me that if I gave enough care, patience, modesty and attention to the task, it would be possible to gain sufficient familiarity with the ancient Greek and Roman texts; that is, a familiarity that would allow me—in keeping with a practice that is doubtless fundamental to Western philosophy—to examine both the difference that keeps us at a remove from a way of thinking in which we recognize the origin of our own, and the proximity that remains in spite of that distance which we never cease to explore.

(The translation is by Robert Hurley, also neither a Hellenist nor a Latinist, but a more than competent *traducteur*.) An Afrocentrist, or anyone seeking a more inclusive geo-cultural framework for the understanding of Western 'roots', might fault Foucault for concentrating only on Greek and Latin texts. A classicist, however, might well fault him rather for his choice of privileged Greek and Latin texts to concentrate on, and that is one—but only one—of the gripes Goldhill has with his somewhat regretfully acknowledged *maître-à-penser*.

Whereas Foucault rather conservatively accorded discursive priority and privilege to Xenophon, Plato and Aristotle, and the more or less canonical writers of later Graeco-Roman pagan and early Christian antiquity who recognizably shared their moral predilections and cultural authority, Goldhill, as a progressive classicist, has warmly embraced what has been described as 'the politically led deprivileging of the subject's traditionally perceived values' and rushed through the door newly opened to the upwards revaluation of the handful of extant ancient Greek novels or romances, 'these non-civic, subversively erotic, above all innovative inhabitants of the canon's chronological and geographical margins' (J. R. Morgan, 'The Ancient Novel at the End of the Century: Scholarship since the Dartmouth Conference', *Classical Philology*, 91 [1996], p. 73). Foucault did not ignore the novels altogether, as with his priorities he might have done, but he did ignore the main body of their narratives. Concentrating instead on the denouements, whereby the more or less wondrously intact heroine marries at last the predestined hero, Foucault inferred that the authors—pagan to a man—shared in the movement towards the promotion of heterosexual self-restraint that was simultaneously and later being embraced by early Christian writers. That is, to say the least, a partial reading.

Yet more telling, though, is Goldhill's critique of Foucault's project as a whole on the grounds of the insufficiency of 'his very understanding of what constitutes the discursive field ... what the constitution of a normative discourse is, and how its boundaries are articulated'. Rather than, or in addition to, (merely) representing and exploring 'the relations between philosophy, sexuality and nature', the novels in Goldhill's readings 'ironize and eroticize' them, in 'a process open to wry self-consciousness, sly manipulations and the duplicitous playfulness of narrative irony'. Foucault was of course primarily a philosopher, or at any rate *philosophe*, and literary criticism was doubtless not his forte, nor main interest, but there is much justice as well as considerable glee in Goldhill's exposures of the reductive one-dimensionality or plain anachronism of Foucault's readings (and not only of the novels, either).

Not that Goldhill necessarily has things all his own way. Foucault rarely replied to his critics, but perhaps he might have been tempted to turn the tables on this attacker and question Goldhill's own role of omniscient narrator, or even to don the mantle of the source-critical historiographer and ask whether Goldhill himself does not in the end make all his sources (not confined to the novels by any means, either) come up looking rather too similar, that is, insufficiently differentiated by genre, epoch, society and individual identity. However that might be, *Foucault's Virginity* in its book form should serve as no less of a 'provocation for the standard methods of producing historical accounts of ancient sexuality' than the lectures given in Dublin (in memory of Bedell Stanford) on which they are based. Goldhill's attempt to reinscribe 'some little-read texts' more centrally in the cultural history of 'a period of great importance in the development of Western attitudes to sexuality' was certainly well worth making and is likely to be adjudged largely successful on his own terms.

Another such period, arguably even more important, was the Victorian, and especially perhaps the late Victorian *fin-de-siècle*. Early on, Goldhill makes a sweeping, too sweeping, reference to 'the Victorians', who allegedly 'found the sexy, violent and sophisticated writing of the novels inappropriate for Classical Study'—this despite their passion for tragedy (not notably non-violent) and Plato (not exactly unsophisticated, nor unsexy). One of the many valuable features of reading Linda Dowling's history of the promiscuous intermingling of classics and homosexuality in Victorian Oxford is to problematize and stigmatize any such broad-brush dismissal of our cultural forebears. Here, moreover, she is self-consciously cultivating an already well-tilled discursive field in which the input and influence of Foucault are surely yet more marked than in classical studies. Indeed, according to one Foucauldian school of thought (represented somewhat unevenly in classics by the contributors to *Before Sexuality*, ed. J. Winkler, D. Halperin and F. Zeitlin [Princeton University Press, Princeton, NJ, 1990]), sexuality itself, as a constructed and self-ascribed identity, was precisely an invention of the later Victorian period, the period of—in Dowling's far from parochial terms—Jowett, Pater and Wilde.

Her scholarly and important monograph forms part of the almost entirely positive revaluation of Wilde that has been practised with especial vigour since the recent gender/sexual literary-historiographical instauration (cf. Ian Small's 1993 *Oscar Wilde Revalued*). Most readers of Linda Dowling's book will therefore be specialists in Victorian literature, society and culture, or specialists in the history and historiography of gender and modern sexual identities, the sorts of reader catered for by Sally Ledger and Scott McCracken's stimulating collection *Cultural Politics at the Fin de Siècle* (1995). But the book demands to be read, also, on its own explicit terms, as a contribution to classical studies: more particularly to the history of the creation, reception and transmission of the classical tradition in its specifically Hellenic variant. For among his many other extraordinary accomplishments Oscar Wilde was, as the late and lamented Bedell Stanford observed in 1976 in his devotedly learned *Ireland and the Classical Tradition*, 'perhaps the best educated in classics of all the major figures in the Anglo-Irish literary tradition'. *Hellenism and Homosexuality in Victorian Oxford* thus also takes its worthy place alongside, for example, Frank Turner's more strait-laced *The Greek Heritage in Victorian Britain* (1981).

Yet the book's chief strength seems to me to lie precisely in its combination of the more traditional, typically male-centred intellectual history with a more supple, interactive cultural history of gender. For, as Dowling amply documents in a study which takes Wilde's pederastic Hellenism as its almost inevitable climax, Wilde remained active to the end of his unnaturally abbreviated life within the culturally constructed formation of that late Victorian intellectual Hellenism which she has herself done so much to explicate and explain, both here and elsewhere (e.g., especially, in her stimulating article 'Ruskin's Pied Beauty and the Constitution of a "Homosexual" Code', in the *Victorian Newsletter*, 75 [Spring 1989], pp. 1–8, in which she sets out her manifesto for any 'future studies of Victorian sexuality').

Dowling's complex series of interlocking theses runs broadly as follows. Victorian Oxford, specifically the reformed and reforming university of the middle decades and second half of the nineteenth century, played a crucial role in 'the modern emergence of homosexuality as a positive social identity'. It did so first by generating, out of a seemingly paradoxical legacy compounded of 'traditions of Tractarian friendship, Socratic education, spiritual procreancy and cultural renewal', what Dowling dubs a new Hellenism. By that she means a controversial, secularizing discourse, formulated by socially aware pedagogic reformers such as, notably, Benjamin Jowett of Balliol. This new discourse was designed to remedy Britain's apparent social, economic and intellectual stagnation and predictable further decay, and to do so by taking the finest impressionable young (male) minds of the day back to the ancient Greek cultural, spiritual and moral fountainhead, above all to the philosophic wisdom of Plato.

Once established, however, as a component or complement of the dominant discourse of martially active manly virtue that had allegedly been formed in significant part by 'the eighteenth-century revision of classical republican discourse', the new liberal Hellenism became available for recuperation or even subversive inversion from within, by adepts of 'Greek love'. The advocates and maybe practitioners of this latterday erotics represented it optimistically as a sublime re-creation of the classical Greek *paiderastia*, a socially useful pedagogic institution as well as purely personal 'sensuous pulsation'. Put differently, Jowett's asexual homosociality had yielded to Walter Pater's and more especially Wilde's homosexuality, 'even as English religious prohibitions on sodomy were simultaneously being made to recede'. Hence the need for and creation of a 'legitimating counterdiscourse of social identity and erotic liberation', which at any rate in retrospect can be seen as 'pointing forward to Anglo-American decriminalization and, ultimately, a fully developed assertion of homosexual rights'.

On balance I find Dowling's picture both 'curious' and 'subtle' (in their positive, Wildean senses), though I do also have some substantial reservations, and questions, both as to her chosen theory of intellectual history and as to its application. Thus I am entirely with her in her treatment of the 1890s as the threshold or gateway of modernism in respect of both literary-aesthetic and psycho-social self-definition, rather than as the doom-laden terminus and nadir of Victorian moral decadence and narcissistic introspection. So too her account of the 'fierce struggle of competing discourses' that underlies the 'Hellenist' reappropriation of Greek literature (especially Plato's *Phaedrus* and *Symposium*) for countercultural ends seems to me exemplary.

On the other hand, I question her privileging of 'discourse', allegedly a far more complex phenomenon, and so far above class as an explanatory theory of intellectual and social change, as to render the latter negligible or forgettable. Nor was it always clear to me just what work her Foucauldian construal of discourse was supposed to be doing: does discourse 'determine' or (rather?) 'foster' non-discursive actualities, and what is the phenomenological or hermeneutic status—discursive? or not?—of 'a mode of feeling'? At all events, however one decides the issue of priority, is not the relationship between them anyway dialectical?

However, such reservations or questions pale beside Linda Dowling's formidable positive achievements. Not least of these is the demonstration that the classicism of the nineteenth century, in its specifically Oxonian local manifestation, was and still is a living discourse. Reviewing a recent collection of essays on *Feminist Theory and the Classics* (ed. Nancy Sorkin Rabinowitz and Amy Richlin, 1993 [reviewed above]), Simon Goldhill rightly observed that 'there is no theory without contest, disagreement, redefinition and debate'. *Pace* Foucault, such theory is of the essence in any worthwhile discourse about the ancients, and if we are to follow his lead in seeking to understand the configuration of multiple discourses about their (and our) social existence, we need critically theory-laden books like these of Goldhill and Dowling.

Simon Goldhill, *Foucault's Virginity: Ancient Erotic Fiction and the History of Sexuality* (Cambridge, Cambridge University Press, 1995), pp. 208, £30.00 and £9.95. ISBN 0 521 473721 (hb) and 0 521 479347 (pb).

Linda Dowling, *Hellenism & Homosexuality in Victorian Oxford* (Ithaca and London, Cornell University Press, 1994), pp. 173, £21.50/$29.95. ISBN 0 801 429609.

Reading the Female Body

HELEN KING

The history of medicine, as Joan Cadden puts it, allows us to examine 'a body of articulated knowledge and a well identified (if not always easily accessible) domain of practice with women as both subjects and objects' (p. 7). The appearance in paperback of Cadden's sensitive and scholarly study of medieval views of sexuality and gender, which won the 1994 Pfizer Award as the Outstanding Book in the History of Science, makes accessible a further chronological section of this domain, and provides an opportunity to compare her work with two recent books on similar issues in the classical world. If we are to deepen our understanding not only of the ways in which medical writing can construct the female body, but also of the impact or lack of impact of scholarly medical texts on women's healthcare, we need to continue to challenge the influential but reductionist models of Michel Foucault and, to a lesser extent, Thomas Laqueur.[1] Both men covered very long periods of time and used very specific types of text; all three books reviewed here draw their strength from detailed study of relatively short time-frames, and Cadden has also performed the valuable service of going far beyond the obvious printed sources to investigate the manuscript Latin tradition for the period from the end of the eleventh to the fourteenth centuries.

Cadden organizes her study around the central questions that preoccupied the writers of her texts. What are the respective contributions of women and men to the process of reproduction? How and why does the embryo become male or female? Which sex is responsible for infertility? Do women and men experience equal desire for, and pleasure from, sexual intercourse? And—particularly important in terms of monasticism—is sex really necessary for health and, if not, then what are the consequences of abstinence? All these questions were addressed, implicitly or explicitly, in the Hippocratic medical texts of fifth- and fourth-century BCE Greece, a mixed bag of case histories, aphorisms, theoretical arguments and lists of remedies, which form the basis for both Nancy Demand's study of the cultural construction of 'giving birth' and Lesley Dean-Jones's comparison of Hippocratic and Aristotelian models of the female body.

Cadden's book is the richest, and also the most difficult to review, because of her determination to resist the temptation to come up with 'the' dominant concept of sexuality for her period; instead, she emphasizes that the contrasting traditions with which medieval physicians worked meant that they too refused to make a decision between the possibilities offered. In the first part of her book she distinguishes three phases of development: the contributions of the classical writers whose works survived into the learned tradition, the work of Constantine the African and Hildegard of Bingen, and the final phase of university-trained philosophers applying 'scholastic' methods in an attempt to organize the disparate elements of their intellectual inheritance. She also emphasizes the lack of any single model of sex-difference in the classical tradition itself. She identifies as the Hippocratic contributions to this emerging tradition the centrality of humoral balance in defining health, the view that the womb is 'a powerful and active organ' with an 'erratic influence' (p. 26) and the two-seed model of generation, in which both the female and the male partner contribute to the constitution of the embryo. In the Hippocratic female body, failure to menstruate with sufficient frequency and regularity played a central role in causing disease. Aristotle, writing at the same time as or a little later than the Hippocratic medical writers, contributed to the tradition the argument that it is only men who can produce seed and who can feel sexual pleasure; he also produced the memorable definition of the female as 'a defective male'.

A year after the first publication of Cadden's book, Lesley Dean-Jones's study of the Hippocratic writers and Aristotle appeared; she interprets Aristotle's woman as 'a substandard man' in contrast to the Hippocratic woman as 'a completely different creature' (p. 85). In both traditions, she shows, woman was seen as inferior, and the crucial factor in the articulation of this inferiority was not the anatomical feature of the womb, but the physiological function of menstruation; in the Hippocratic woman, menstruation allowed the restoration of a bodily balance which could, however, never be any more than precarious, while for Aristotle it was the sign of the essential female coldness which prevented women from producing seed. Dean-Jones's work allows us to recover the history of the Hippocratic theories themselves; these are polemical texts coming at the end of long debates about the nature of the body and of gender which took place between the philosophers of the sixth and fifth centuries BCE. In addition to her focus on physiology rather than anatomy, Dean-Jones has some other points of difference from Cadden on the classical Greek contributions to the medieval tradition. For example, Cadden argues that the Hippocratic use of polarities—such as hot/cold, wet/dry and firm/loose—is, in contrast to Aristotle, non-hierarchical (p. 17). Certainly the use of polarities in Hippocratic medicine is more varied than Aristotle's all-embracing statement of female coldness which makes women unable to 'concoct' or cook their menstrual blood into semen. Dean-Jones, however, shows the range of 'Hippocratic' beliefs; women may be seen as hotter, or colder, than men (p. 45), but in any case the poles are valued in such a way that the end result is the inferiority of women (p. 85).

Cadden's book allows the reader to see the further development of the classical Greek traditions, but her otherwise exemplary summary misses out an important stage: the Hellenistic era, when the conquest of Egypt by Alexander's armies led to a brief period in which a combination of royal patronage of science and the availability of a subject population allowed for human dissection (and, as Dean-Jones reminds us, perhaps also vivisection [p. 22]). Hellenistic anatomy demonstrated that the womb could not, as the Hippocratics had believed, move around the body, and also showed the presence of the Fallopian tubes. Anatomy moved the focus of the medical gaze away from fluids, and on to organs. Cadden also gives too little space to Pliny, whose ideas about the malign power of menstrual blood may give us access to a popular tradition which continued outside the debates of learned men. She picks up the chronological account in the early Roman empire with the Greek writer Soranus, whose allegiance to the medical sect known as 'methodism' entailed a belief that all disorders, in both sexes, are the result of one of the three basic bodily states: constriction, relaxation, or a 'mixed' condition. Soranus played down the necessity of menstruation and, indeed, of sexual intercourse in maintaining female health. The most influential of all the medical writers of Greece and Rome, the second-century CE Galen, tried to reconcile Hippocratic and Aristotelian views; however, in the process he produced a version of Hippocrates in his own image, one that has affected our reading of the Hippocratic texts ever since.[2] Galen resuscitated the idea that the woman, too, produces a seed which contributes to the formation of the embryo, and played down the possible dangers of suppressed menstrual blood, on the grounds that the failure to evacuate female seed was a far more dangerous situation.

In the period of late antiquity the Latin West lost contact with works written in Greek, but these survived in translation elsewhere, particularly in the Arabic world. In the eleventh century, Constantine the African translated Arabic works into Latin, thus returning to the Latin West much of this forgotten Greek material. One of Cadden's most impressive aspects is her use of unpublished Latin collections of medical questions, discussions of sex and conception, and lists of signs of conception. It is often in these that, as Cadden puts it, 'theory (the necessity of female semen) and fact (the pregnancies of rape victims) confront each other directly and vividly' (p. 95). Some at least of those who were accepted as 'the authorities' in the later Middle Ages insisted that conception required a female seed which could not be emitted in the absence of pleasure. Yet pregnancy could occur from an act of rape. Logically, therefore, either female seed must be unnecessary, the emission of such seed must be possible without the woman feeling pleasure, or women must enjoy rape. One answer to the conundrum was that women could enjoy rape, not at the level of 'reason', but at that of 'the flesh'; Cadden points out that, although we may find it worryingly close to the 'modern pornographic commonplace' (p. 96) that women can move from revulsion to enjoyment, this can be seen as a much more sophisticated answer, one which emphasizes the humanity of women, their possession of both rationality and physicality being something that sets them, along with men, apart from the animal world. It is in their discussions of the nature of female sexual pleasure that Cadden regards the medieval writers as having diverged the most from all the classical writers whose works they had inherited.

In the second part of her book, Cadden examines how medical writers and natural philosophers tried to define gender through anatomy, the qualities of the body —such as heat and moisture—and its humoral constitution. Importantly, she includes discussion of the application of the idea of a gendered cosmos to other aspects of the natural world, such as animals, plants and planets. She also looks at those who crossed the boundaries which had been set up, such as viragos or 'masculine women'. Straight eyebrows, for example, are a sign of femininity (p. 169). The book ends with two chapters on sterility and the consequences of abstinence.

Although Cadden is using elite Latin sources, she rightly stresses that these were also owned and used by practitioners who were not trained in the universities, while elite practitioners and those working from popular traditions used the same suppliers for their pharmacological materials and would therefore have come into some sort of contact. Furthermore, she argues that practitioners needed to deliver their explanations and carry out therapy within the framework of 'the expectations and practices of the patient's family' (p. 5), so that there cannot have been an insurmountable gap between the university-trained physician and his patients. This emphasis on the family rather than the individual patient, performs some useful fine tuning to Dean-Jones's assertion that Hippocratic treatment offered to women 'must have been acceptable to them and have squared with their view of their own physiology' (p. 27); in classical Greece, as in medieval Europe, what we know about medical practice and the structure of the household would suggest that treatment needed to be congruent not so much with the beliefs of the female patient, as with those of the male who may have paid the physician.

Work on the classical Greek medical texts has long been divided on the ultimate origin of their contents; should we focus on the amount of remedies included to see this primarily as women's traditional, orally transmitted, knowledge taken over by men (Aline Rousselle),[3] or should we focus on the invasive treatment methods and the more bizarre theories and conclude that what we have represents punitive male fantasies (Paola Manuli)?[4] Demand argues that this is information discovered and then passed on by women, but transmitted to us through Greek men (p. xvi); Dean-Jones goes further, to suggest that the medical texts 'contain privileged information available only from women' (p. 27). But the claim by a male medical writer that 'I learned all this from women' may be a strategy, an attempt by one medical man to trump another. Because she is dealing with the subsequent history of these materials Cadden, although noting the claimed source of some of the material in women's lore, manages to avoid this issue.

For the classical world a further concern is the role of female medical personnel: were men involved in normal childbirth in ancient Greece, or was this an area of practice reserved for midwives? Dean-Jones argues from silence to challenge the established notion that the division between female practitioners for normal births and male practitioners for difficult births can be traced back to antiquity, suggesting (p. 212) that Hippocratic physicians observed normal birth so frequently that they 'did not bother recording those they observed'. Demand argues that the norm in childbirth would be female carers, but she also points out that the texts show male physicians working with women assistants in both normal and abnormal labour (p. 66), and uses this to support her suggestion that the women who worked with men—seen as the up-and-coming healthcare providers in fifth-century Greece—would gain new status in their communities. She also regards the alleged involvement of Hippocratic male physicians in normal labours as the first step in the medicalization of childbirth, a 'crucial point in women's history'.

All three books raise the issue of whether science and medicine support, or challenge, ideas in the rest of society. Cadden shows how the authority of classical medical theories in a Christian society sometimes led to challenges to the broader culture's assumptions about gender; ideas changed in the process of being copied, translated, or compared. In the case of the remedies given in medical texts for the restoration of virginity, however, Cadden shows how such 'counterfeiting' should be understood not as a challenge but as a way of emphasizing the true value of the currency, the social importance of virginity (p. 264). Texts may constrain, but they also stimulate, and the work being done on the textual construction of the medical woman in the Greek and medieval past stimulates new ways of looking at women in history more generally.

Joan Cadden, *The Meanings of Sex Difference in the Middle Ages: Medicine, Natural Philosophy, and Culture* (Cambridge University Press, Cambridge, 1993 [hb] and 1995 [pb]), pp. viii + 310, £37.50/$59.95 and £14.95/$18.95. ISBN 0 521 34363 1 (hb) and 0 521 48378 6 (pb).
Lesley Ann Dean-Jones, *Women's Bodies in Classical Greek Science* (Clarendon Press, Oxford, 1994), pp. ix + 293, £30. ISBN 0 19 814767 8.
Nancy Demand, *Birth, Death, and Motherhood in Classical Greece* (Johns Hopkins University Press, Baltimore, MD and London, 1994), pp. xx + 276, £33.00/$39.95. ISBN 0 8018 4762 1.

Notes

1. Michel Foucault, *Histoire de la sexualité* (3 vols, Gallimard, Paris, 1976–84); T. Laqueur, *Making Sex: Body and Gender from the Greeks to Freud* (Harvard University Press, Cambridge, MA, 1990).
2. On the Galenic 'Hippocrates', see Wesley D. Smith, *The Hippocratic Tradition* (Cornell University Press, Ithaca, NY, 1979).
3. Aline Rousselle, 'Images médicales du corps. Observation féminine et idéologie masculine: le corps de la femme d'après les médecins grecs', *Annales E.S.C.* 35 (1980), 1089–1115 and *Porneia: On Desire and the Body in Antiquity*, tr. F. Pheasant (Blackwell, Oxford, 1988).
4. Paola Manuli, 'Fisiologia e patologia del femminile negli scritti ippocratici dell'antica ginecologia greca', in *Hippocratica. Actes du Colloque hippocratique de Paris 1978*, ed. M. D. Grmek (Eds de CNRS, Paris, 1980), pp. 393–408 and 'Donne mascoline, femmine sterili, vergini perpetue. La ginecologia greca tra Ippocrate e Sorano', in *Madre Materia. Sociologia e biologia della donna greca*, ed. Silvia Campese, Paola Manuli, and Giulia Sissa (Boringhieri, Turin, 1983), pp. 147–92.

Gendered Religions

GILLIAN CLARK

These three books are all concerned with early Christianity in relation to the Graeco-Roman culture within which it developed; Brooten and Sawyer are also concerned with Judaism(s) of the period. All three emphasize cultural continuities across this range and diversity within cultures, all are informed by gender theory, and all (as in all fields of gender history at present) are mostly concerned with women. Early Christianity, whatever your theological beliefs, is an extremely interesting historical phenomenon. How did an eccentric Jewish splinter-group become the dominant religion of the Roman Empire? How did some early Christians convince themselves that what God really wanted them to do was to reject the obligations of family and property and to spend their lives in chastity and poverty, fasting and prayer? What happened to traditional structures of authority and gender when efforts were made to replace paternal authority with the alternative family of the Church, tender to women the new opportunity (or perhaps the new repression) of celibacy, and thereby offer them new spiritual status in a world which refused hierarchical status to women?

Deborah Sawyer's book (to begin with the most general view) is a teaching text which surveys recent scholarship on the religious options for women in the early Christian period. Its introductory sections make clear and sensible use of gender theory, emphasizing that maleness and femaleness are a spectrum with polarities, that 'gender' and 'religion' are fluid not fixed categories, that class and age must also be considered, that gender-roles shape religion and religion modifies gender-roles. Sawyer invites us to regard the diversity of this period as 'pre-traditional', predating monolithic religious systems and therefore of special interest to a post-traditional age. (Christianity, especially in late antiquity, was no more solid a monolith than the former Soviet Union, but there is indeed a contrast.)

The book makes an intelligent selection of examples for discussion from the immense range of possible material. Specialists in the different fields will, inevitably, have doubts, will want to add different material and will make other cross-connections. Here, for their general interest, are three examples from the Graeco-Roman field. First, John Chrysostom (cited p. 150) does not say that women have lost the image of God. He says that Paul, in a passage of I Corinthians which is notoriously difficult to reconcile with the creation-account in Genesis, must be using 'image' to mean something specific, namely 'authority'; and he says this because he thinks Paul cannot have meant that women are not in God's image. Second (it may be a resource for post-traditionalists), the *Homeric Hymn to*

Demeter does not necessarily support Sawyer's interpretation of the Demeter cult as an acknowledgement of, and consolation for, the women victims of patriarchy. The plot-line of this remarkably gynocentric text is that Demeter loses her daughter Persephone, who has been abducted into a forced marriage. So far from passively lamenting, she enlists female help—divine and human—in her search; begins to immortalize a mortal child, and when that fails (because the child's mother panics) teaches humans a ritual that promises them benefits after death; then resorts to world-wide crop failure, which forces Zeus, king of the gods, to negotiate through a female intermediary and to concede that Persephone will spend part of the year with her mother. For the other part of the year Persephone is queen of the underworld. Passive resistance rules.

Third, Sawyer concludes that Christianity engaged in more explicit theorizing about gender-roles than its competitors did, precisely because the earliest churches had provided women with a wider range of options. Among those options was asceticism, and ascetics are useful to think with. They were in a minority, but it was a bigger minority than the Vestal Virgins and eunuch priests of the Great Mother whom Sawyer (following Mary Beard) discusses, and they too challenged gender-roles. Women ascetics were praised for their manly virtue: so were other strong-minded women, but ascetics were (sometimes) encouraged to use physical techniques that aimed to de-sex the female body, making it drier and thinner, non-reproductive and free from desire. But looking more like a man, by cross-dressing and cutting the hair short, remained unacceptable. Similarly, male ascetics were (sometimes) praised for receptivity to the fertilizing word of God and for bearing spiritual children, and were (sometimes) encouraged to use physical techniques that aimed to de-sex the male body, making it smoother and weaker, non-reproductive and free from desire. But looking more like a woman, by wearing softer clothing and growing the hair longer, remained unacceptable. Traditional gender-roles were no excuse for having a female celibate partner to run the house or a male celibate partner to negotiate with the outside world; untraditional communities of women (and, separately, of men) both confronted and were shaped by old anxieties.

Bernadette Brooten's *Love Between Women* is an extremely careful, detailed, learned examination of the evidence for female homoerotic love in the Graeco-Roman world, and of the ways in which that evidence has been interpreted, evaded, or explained away, even by scholars working (as many have since the 1980s) on male homoerotic love. She uses 'homoeroticism' rather than 'homo-sexuality' to avoid the connotations of a fixed homosexual identity, which was not usually acknowledged in Graeco-Roman culture. The sum total of evidence is small, but Brooten deploys a very wide range of expertise. She discusses the reception of Sappho's poetry in the Roman period, and other literary and visual representations of female homoeroticism, including the interpretation of Leviticus in post-biblical Judaism. The only subject not treated in depth, in this section and in the book as a whole, is Plato, who gets half a page and three short footnotes. (The book must have gone to press before the current controversy on whether he ever endorses male homoeroticism.) Brooten mentions the speech of Aristophanes in Plato's *Symposium*, which recognizes among the sundered human wholes seeking reunion in love some that are female-female, and finds it contradictory that in the *Laws* Plato condemns female-female relationships. His most obvious reason for doing so needs a higher profile. Brooten highlights the importance of the categories active/passive, natural/unnatural, in Greek and Roman analysis of sexual relationships. Reproductive/non-reproductive (mentioned later in relation to Philo and Clement) is also important, because the standard philosophical argument about sexual relations was that any sexual intercourse not intended for reproduction is a victory for desire over reason, and therefore damages the soul. This included heterosexual intercourse with non-marital partners, and *a fortiori* homosexual intercourse.

But there is much more to come. Brooten provides a detailed account of ancient dream-analysis, and deals very thoroughly indeed with the two topics on which even specialist readers need technical help, namely the surviving erotic spells (one, perhaps two) in which female seeks to bind female, and the medical texts referring to (partial) clitoridectomy performed on women who were perceived to have an excessively large clitoris—almost a small-scale penis—and pathologically masculine sexual desires. There are, as she points out, many questions we cannot answer. Why do erotic spells identify their target by mother's, not father's, name? (Perhaps because it is the physical being, not the social identity, of the target that matters?) Who asked the doctor to perform the partial clitoridectomy: scandalized husband or parent, concerned midwife? (Perhaps even a woman unable to accept her body and her desires?)

Brooten demonstrates both that Greeks and Romans were aware of female homoerotic relationships and of women whose sexual orientation was towards women, and that female homoeroticism, especially females 'playing the man's part', was generally denounced as unnatural. The final section of her book shows that, even if Christians were exceptionally hostile to male homoeroticism (and that is doubtful), Christian attitudes to female homoeroticism were no different from those of the surrounding culture. She argues (this is a very brief summary of a very full discussion) that in Paul's Letter to the Romans 1.26–7, still used by some Christians as authoritative condemnation of a corrupt society, 'their women exchanged natural intercourse for unnatural' does refer to female homoeroticism, not to bestiality or sodomy, and that it can no longer be authoritative because Paul and subsequent early Christian commentators reflect a general belief in asymmetric gender-relations, female subordinate to male, with gender boundaries clearly marked by behaviour and appearance.

Kate Cooper's book prompts a further question about this rhetoric of condemnation, and more generally about the interpretation of texts as evidence for practice and belief. Classicists have throughout this century used the findings of anthropology, especially Mediterranean social anthropology, to help interpret the cultures they study. One thesis has had a particular influence on classical gender history since the early 1980s: that when men talk about family relationships and about the proper behaviour of women, they are actually engaged in status-competition. Modest, self-controlled women reflect credit on their menfolk and therefore on the family as a whole, and this is also to the advantage of the women (a message understood by the older generations of the British royal family). Family, of birth and of marriage, is for both sexes the source of identity and status, and their effort is directed to advancing the family interest; the distinction made between the masculine public sphere and the feminine private sphere is, again, for public consumption. In a Graeco-Roman social context, cities also benefit, because the prosperity of stable families allows them to compete for political status by civic benefactions. Classical Greeks and imperial Romans naturally did not put it so bluntly: they spoke of their duty to parents, fellow-citizens and the gods, and it was their political enemies who pointed to the family interest. But Greek and Roman education was designed to produce persuasive speakers, and we would miss the point, just as a modern anthropologist would miss the point, if we thought that our sources were telling it how it was.

Cooper applies this thesis, in a concise, lively and very intelligent book, to the behaviour of Christians in the early centuries of the Roman Empire. She accepts the current consensus that there was a sexual morality common to ordinary Christians and decent 'pagans' (no one has yet found a satisfactory alternative to this disparaging Christian label). You could give a Christian or a non-Christian the *Sentences of Sextus* as a wedding present: devotees of *Cold Comfort Farm* will be reminded of the invaluable *Pensées* of the Abbé Fausse-Maigre. Celibate and world-renouncing ascetic Christians were a small minority who often, despite the efforts of Christian publicists, inspired as much doubt and disapproval among conventional married Christians as they did among pagans. Cooper argues that writing about dedicated virgins and about married women who demand celibacy is a status-claim by Christian missionaries and clerics seeking to establish their authority over against families; after Constantine gave Christianity official acceptance, resolutely celibate women also reflected credit on their family of birth. A rhetoric which apparently encourages women to subvert gender expectations continues to use them as tokens of masculine authority.

Cooper is surely right to emphasize that Christian treatises on asceticism were public statements shaped by expectations of rhetoric and genre, and that the debate on marriage and asceticism was interlinked with theological controversy, ecclesiastical power and the disposition of property. But we are also talking about how people chose to live their lives. (Consider academic conversations, in which, to be sure, status is continually being renegotiated, but at least some academics are also interested in the subject and in getting it right.) Some of those engaged in, or influenced by, the ascetic debate committed themselves to extremes of austerity. Thereby they acquired status, but the writings of ascetics profess acute awareness of the dangers of spiritual status-seeking: is that, too, a rhetorical status-claim to be holier (because more aware of sin) than thou? When they said they were not worthy, they may have meant it, because they were thinking not (only) of their fellow-Romans, but of God, who is not a presence in this book.

Again, Cooper is surely right to warn us against assuming that late-antique women wanted autonomy as (celibate) individuals, and to remind us that family and social group were central to the sense of who and what one was. She links this, in her epilogue, with the present-day debate about western individualism in relation to 'traditional' societies: is there really a frustrated heroine trapped within the household? But Graeco-Roman philosophy does not support the grander claim that awareness of oneself as an autonomous individual is a postclassical phenomenon. Most classical Greek philosophy taught that every human being should live by reason and develop virtue, acknowledging duties to family and community but remaining wary of undue attachment to perishable things; Stoics thought particularly carefully about the requirements of social roles, late-antique Platonism tended to minimize the duties and maximize the detachment. The philosophic stance was, of course, also used as rhetorical power-play and status-enhancement, but that does not mean that no philosopher ever seriously tried to live a philosophic life. Novels of the early Christian period, as Cooper says, detach hero and heroine from their families and expose them to trials and wanderings, but the point of it all is the happy ending: they marry and become pillars of society. Philosophy would remind them not to define themselves exclusively by their social or their gender roles; and, as these three books remind us, gender roles, and therefore social roles, were powerful but not unchallengeable.

Bernadette Brooten, *Love Between Women: Early Christian Responses to Female Homoeroticism* (University of Chicago Press, Chicago, 1996), pp. xxii + 412, $34.95. ISBN 0 226 07531 (hb).

Kate Cooper, *The Virgin and the Bride: Idealized Womanhood in Late Antiquity* (Harvard University Press, Cambridge, MA and London, 1996), pp. xii + 180, £24.95. ISBN 0 674 93949 2 (hb).

Deborah F. Sawyer, *Women and Religion in the First Christian Centuries* (London and New York, Routledge, 1996), pp. 186, £12.99 (pb). ISBN 0 415 10748 2 (hb) and 0 415 10749 0 (pb).

Gender and Sexuality on the Internet

JOHN G. YOUNGER

The study of the nature and social constructions of gender and sexuality has become a major tool in analysing society, both modern and ancient. It is not surprising, therefore, to find it on the Internet. What follows is a select review of items of interest in the area of the ancient Mediterranean, both the classical world and the ancient Near East;[1] and in this review I shall define 'gender and sexuality' broadly, using the phrase to enscribe the binary 'central society : other'. What I include here depends, of course, on what I have found out there on the Internet, but its broad range will become clear.

The Internet, in so far as ancient gender and sexuality are concerned, is fairly new. None the less, I hope I am right in assuming that readers will be familiar with its two major components: email discussion groups (both lists and newsgroups); and the various systems for retrieving documents, especially (for our purposes) sites on the World Wide Web (WWW or just the 'web'). Since the vocabulary can often be confusing, I shall try to keep it relatively straightforward.

One web site, *Diotima*, devotes itself entirely to 'Materials for the Study of Women and Gender in the Ancient World', and it lists as its areas of concern (or keywords for search engines) the following: Greece, Rome, the Etruscans, Egypt, the Bible, women, gender, marriage, family, sexuality, homosexuality, bibliography and iconography. The web address (URL or 'Universe Resource Locator') is http://www.uky.edu/ArtsSciences/Classics/gender.html.[2] And the site is maintained by Suzanne Bonefas of Emory University and Ross Scaife of the University of Kentucky (where it is also located).

The home page of *Diotima* acts like a table of contents listing a series of 'hot-linked' documents, which, when you click on them with your mouse, will bring up more sites: a welcome page that gives specific information on how to use *Diotima*, as well as special sites that list new items of interest, announcements (such as calls for papers or new of conferences), images of ancient art, bibliographies, entire essays, short articles and abstracts, and course syllabi.[3] These are all the sorts of linked documents one expects to find in most web sites that try to cover a large area of academic interest.

Diotima's site 'Essays' contains links to other sites in four major areas: the ancient Near East; Greece; Rome; and late antiquity. 'Images' links one not only to sites containing specific images, especially those from the photo-archive *AERIA* (Antikensammlung Erlangen Internet Archive) of the University of Erlangen (e.g. the Crouching Aphrodite of Doidalses),[4] but also to the ancient Greek world, a collection of dictionary-like entries at the University of Pennsylvania Museum of Archaeology and Anthropology (e.g. 'Dress and Toilet Articles').[5] There are also links to special exhibitions and to museum holdings.

Diotima has another feature that makes it especially valuable: its links to search engines—documents that ask you to type in a word or phrase and that then bring up other documents or citations that contain it. One especially valuable search engine is Biblical Studies: Here you can find special documents such as the various *Lives of Hypatia of Alexandria* (mathematician, astronomer and philosopher; died 415 BCE), but you can also search not just the Bible but also the Koran, various Jewish texts, the Latin Vulgate, the Dead Sea Scrolls, and more — to anyone working in late antiquity and in gender and sexuality in early religion, this search engine should rank amongst the primary research tools.

Even more helpful is the link to *Perseus*. As is well known, *Perseus* is the mammoth project at Tufts University designed to place on-line an encyclopaedic range of classical texts (in the original language and in translation), citations and images. In *Diotima* one can browse *Perseus*'s course syllabi, for instance, while, at the same time, one can use it as a gateway to *Perseus* itself to find pertinent ancient passages or dictionary-like descriptions of classical sites and artefacts. Fortunately, too, the introductory page on browsing with *Perseus* is clear, with many examples that tell you how to search for specific items and words (even in the original ancient Greek), as well as phrases and concepts.

Other sites for ancient gender and sexuality also exist, but for these you need to do some surfing; surfing the web casually on your own can take up inordinate amounts of (occasionally enjoyable) time. One way to simplify matters is to use one of the various popular search engines like *Yahoo*, although what you find is often too general to be of much use; type in the keywords 'women, ancient', for example, and you are likely to get a listing of an enormous number of sites that concern both 'women' and something 'ancient' but will have nothing to do with 'women in antiquity'. More helpful will be the subject-specific search engines, and here classics has *Argos*[6] which concerns the ancient and medieval worlds in general. *Argos* is fairly new and growing, but it has been quite useful the few times I have used it.

Otherwise you may find interesting items on web sites devoted to the broader concerns of the ancient world; there are several of these that maintain lists of other web sites, often listed in a random order but searchable within the document with your 'Find' option. *ABZU*[7] handles the ancient Near East, and *Kapatija*[8] the Bronze Age Aegean and the classical worlds. In browsing through both these sites, I found little that had not also been picked up by *Diotima*, but none the less there were a few new items. Through *ABZU* (both NEW and OLD) I found a few more sites by Meir Bar-Ilan on witches, children, monsters, and mysticism and eroticism;[9] an intriguing site on women in Nubia by Tara L. Kneller;[10] and the occasional homoerotic site by Greg Reeder[11] on ancient Egypt. And through *Kapatija*, I found ancient medicine[12] and the Center for the Study of Eurasian Nomads.[13]

Two more important web sites are the home pages for the Women's Classical Caucus[14] and for the Lesbian, Gay, and Bisexual Classical Caucus,[15] two affiliate organizations of the American Philological Association. These sponsor panels at the APA's annual meetings (27–30 December) and represent the interests of women and of Lesbians and gay men in the profession of classical studies.

There are thousands of email discussion lists, both academic and popular. Many of these will be listed, by subject and title, in the *Directory of Electronic Journals, Newsletters and Academic Discussion Lists*[16] and in *The Internet Yellow Pages*[17]— both resources are annually updated and not only list groups and sites but give short descriptions along with Internet addresses. Usenet discussion lists, those whose addresses look something like 'sci.archaeology' or 'soc.something', are very popular with lay members—they can get quite bouncy. The academic lists are usually more stable and vastly more reliable in their information, although here too you need to have common sense, a sense of humour, and a ready finger on the 'delete' button.

I try to maintain an up-to-date web site that catalogues email discussion lists for archaeology of all kinds, technical and cultural, both classical and other.[18] Subscribing to the lists in that web site is free (after paying whatever is the cost for using the Internet in general), and usually follows the format of sending a message like 'subscribe LISTNAME' to a 'majordomo' or 'listserv' address. Upon subscribing you will receive, in most cases, a 'Welcome to Our List' message that describes the list in detail, spells out areas appropriate for discussion and the rules of net-etiquette ('Netiquette'), and gives commands that allow you to perform special functions like finding out the subscriber list and, more importantly, learning how to unsubscribe.

There are a few lists that specifically concern the area of gender and sexuality. For the most part they are not very active, with only a few messages per week. For women's issues, there are two lists: *Anahita* for women and gender in classics and archaeology;[19] and *MedFem-L* for medieval feminist issues.[20] For Lesbian and gay issues, there are two parallel lists: *ClassicsLGB*[21] for classical queer gender, and *MedGay-L* for medieval gay issues.[22] These lists are most useful for their announcements of conferences, calls for papers, and specific responses to questions of bibliography and resources.

The intellectual discussions of ancient gender and sexuality, it seems to me, take place more often on the more general lists where they frequently crop up in the context of other issues. For instance, in the early Fall 1996, a discussion on *ANE* (the Ancient Near East list)[23] concerning women's roles in the ancient Near East turned to modern ways of subordinating women in the same geographical areas, and this included a spirited discussion of body and genital mutilation (female castration, infibulation, scarification), and also male circumcision, both ancient and modern.[24] The discussion spread to its sibling list, *AegeaNet* (the Bronze Age Aegean),[25] where it included references to the evidence of tattooing on Cycladic idols before widening to discuss the meaning of the female iconography on the frescoes from Xeste 3 at Akrotiri, Thera. Similarly, there are frequent discussions of the construction of classical homoeroticism, as well as of homoeroticism in other cultures, on the list *QStudy-L*,[26] which otherwise usually concerns modern queer theory and expressions of homosexuality in the modern world.

Other places to watch out for the occasional piece on ancient gender and sexuality include the more general classics email discussion lists, *Classics*,[27] plus *GreekArch* and *RomeArch* (or their combined *GRomArch*),[28] and the various email review journals and magazines (e-zines). The *Bryn Mawr Classical* and *Medieval Reviews* and *Scholia*[29] often have reviews of interesting books in this area.

In this brief survey it should be obvious that the Internet seems 'made' for discussions of gender and sexuality. The ongoing and expanding definitions, theories and discoveries in this area of study are perfect for presentation in web sites that can be continually updated. Already powerful compilations of web sites and search engines allow Internet users to find the obscure as well as the obvious contribution easily.

Although certain areas of antiquity have, of course, received almost instantaneous treatment, such as women's issues and, to some extent, queer issues, there are many more that remain relatively untouched. Here are a few of my favourite topics that I have yet to see explored in any detail either on the web or in email discussions: in the area of the physical human body, I would cite children, old people, body and genital mutilation, deformity; in the intersection between gender and art, I cite architecture and architectural space, music, vase production, and textiles; and in the antique construction of the political body, I cite citizen, cultural, and ethnic identity and 'otherness'.

No doubt these will appear, for contributors continue to find the Internet the democratic place that it is: a place where all voices can be heard, read and surfed.

Notes

1. I have tried to be attuned to the appearance of gender and sexuality in other ancient areas, but have seen little. For web sites in Pre-Columbian archaeology: http://www.duke.edu/web/classics/Maya.sites/ .

2. In this essay, I have left a space between the end of every web address and any punctuation mark that follows; the address will therefore be complete in and of itself.

3. For instance, my own 'Gender and Sexuality in Ancient Greece': http://www.duke.edu/web/jyounger/gendr.html .

4. A list of sites for this statue exists at: http://www.phil.uni-erlangen.de/~p1altar/photo_html/ plastik/weiblich/sitzend/ebene4.html ; and you may view specific statues (e.g. http://www.phil.uni-erlangen.de/~p1altar/photo_html/plastik/weiblich/sitzend/aphrodite/kauern18.html).

5. http://www.museum.upenn.edu/Greek_World/Daily_life/Women_dress.html . There is also a /Daily_life/Men's_life ; both are sanitized.

6. http://argos.evansville.edu .

7. http://www-oi.uchicago.edu/OI/DEPT/RA/ABZU/ABZU_NEW.HTML (case sensitive); this site will also link you to ABZU_OLD, the first site of sites.

8. http://www.duke.edu/web/jyounger/kapat97.html .

9. http://www.biu.ac.il/~barilm/ .

10. 'Neither Goddesses nor Doormats: The Role of Women in Nubia': http://www.msstate.edu/Archives/History/USA/Afro-Amer/women_in_nubia .

11. E.g. 'The Mysterious Muu and the Dance They Do': http://www.sirius.com/~reeder/muu.html .

12. http://www.ea.pvt.k12.pa.us/medant .

13. http://garnet.berkeley.edu/~jkimball .

14. http://weber.u.washington.edu/~wcc/WCC.html .

15. http://www.duke.edu/web/jyounger/LGBCC.html .

16. Edited by D. Mogge (Association of Research Libraries, Washington, DC, 1996).

17. G. B. Newly, *Mecklermedia's Official Internet World. Internet Yellow Pages* (IDG Books Worldwide Inc., Foster City, CA, 1996). Though both volumes claim to be up-to-date, neither gives a full listing of everything 'out there' even at the time of going to press. I note both have moderately large sections on sexuality, but small sections on archaeology, and virtually nothing on classical studies or on gender.

18. http://www.duke.edu/web/jyounger/archlist.html .

19. Send 'subscribe anahita <Your Name>' to 'listserv@lsv.uky.edu'.

20. Send 'subscribe medfem-l' to 'listproc@uwavm.u.washington.edu' or to 'listproc@vmb.u.washington.edu'.

21. Send 'subscribe classicslgb' to 'majordomo@acpub.duke.edu'; this list offers anonymous posting and a confidential subscription list known only to the list-owner.

22. Send 'subscribe medgay-l' to 'listserv@ksuvm.ksu.edu'.

23. Send to 'majordomo@oi.uchicago.edu' one of these messages: 'subscribe ane' for the regular list; 'subscribe ane-digest' for the digest; 'subscribe anenews' for moderated news; and 'subscribe anenews-digest' for moderated news in a digest form.

24. The Intersex Society of North America (ISNA) offers a support group for people of all cultures who were 'born with anatomy or physiology which differs from cultural ideals of male and female': http://www.isna.org/ .

25. Send 'subscribe aegeanet' to 'majordomo@acpub.duke.edu'.

26. Send 'subscribe qstudy-l Your Name' to 'listserv@ubvm.cc.buffalo.edu'.

27. Send 'subscribe classics Your Name' to 'listproc@u.washington.edu'.

28. For these three lists, mail to 'majordomo@rome.classics.lsa.umich.edu' one of the following: 'subscribe greekarch <your@address>', 'subscribe romarch <your@address>', or 'subscribe gromarch <your@address>'.

29. To receive the *Bryn Mawr Classical* or *Medieval Reviews*, send 'subscribe bmcr-l' or 'sub bmmr-l', respectively, to 'listserv@cc.brynmawr.edu'. To receive *Scholia*, send 'subscribe scholia' to 'majordomo@mtb.und.ac.za'.

30. Available on the web: http://www.shef.ac.uk/uni/union/susoc/assem/ .

NOTES ON CONTRIBUTORS

Julia M. Asher-Greve is the author of *Frauen in altsumerischer Zeit* (1985), and has published a variety of articles in English and German on Mesopotamian as well as women and gender themes. She is president of the Women's Association of Ancient Near Eastern Studies and the editor of a new journal, *NIN, Journal of Ancient Near Eastern Gender Studies*. Currently she is writing a book on gender concepts in ancient Mesopotamia and lecturing at the University of Hamburg (Germany).

Mary Beard teaches Classics at the University of Cambridge and is a Fellow of Newnham College (UK). Among her books is (with John Henderson) *Classics: A Very Short Introduction* (1995).

Paul Cartledge is Reader in Greek History at the University of Cambridge and Fellow of Clare College (UK). He is the author, co-author, and co-editor of eight books, most recently *The Greeks: A Portrait of Self and Others* (1993; rev. edn forthcoming 1997), which includes a chapter on gendering in historiography, and of numerous articles, review articles and reviews on all aspects of ancient Greek history and historiography.

Gillian Clark is Senior Lecturer in Classics at the University of Liverpool (UK). She works on gender history in the third to the sixth centuries CE, with a special interest in the interrelation of Christianity and Graeco-Roman culture. Her books include *Women in Late Antiquity: Pagan and Christian Lifestyles* (1993) and *Augustine: Confessions 1–4* (1995).

Shaye J. D. Cohen is Ungerleider Professor and Director of Judaic Studies at Brown University, Providence (USA). He is author of *Josephus in Galilee and Rome: His Vita and Development as a Historian* (1979), *From the Maccabees to the Mishnah* (1987), *The Beginnings of Jewishness* (forthcoming), and numerous articles and reviews. Boundaries, boundary-crossing, and the definition of status within the Jewish communities of antiquity have long been at the centre of his scholarly interests.

Ann Kessler Guinan is a PhD candidate in Assyriology at the University of Pennsylvania (USA). Her forthcoming dissertation deals with sex omens from Mesopotamia and examines sexuality and gender within a theory of divination. It is part of her larger project to produce a text edition of an unusual and largely unpublished corpus of Akkadian omens, written on cuneiform tablets and preserved in the British Museum.

John Henderson teaches Classics at the University of Cambridge and is a Fellow of King's College (UK). He is preparing (with Mary Beard) a book on Seneca's *Apocolocyntosis*.

Helen King is Wellcome Trust Research Fellow and Lecturer in Classics and History at the University of Reading (UK). She is the writer of numerous articles on the history of gynaecology and, with Sander Gilman, Roy Porter, George Rousseau and Elaine Showalter, wrote *Hysteria Beyond Freud* (1993).

Lynn Meskell is a member of King's College, Cambridge (UK). Her research interests include Egyptian and Mediterranean archaeologies, feminist and queer theory and, specifically, the testing of current theories surrounding sex, gender and the body upon the ancient archaeological sources. She has written widely on these topics and is currently editing a book on sociopolitics and archaeology in the Eastern Mediterranean and Middle East entitled *Archaeology Matters* (forthcoming 1997).

Robin Osborne is Professor of Ancient History in the University of Oxford and Fellow and Tutor at Corpus Christi College (UK). His writing and editing activities range over the fields of Greek history, art and archaeology. He is author of *Greece in the Making 1200–479 B.C.* (1996) and his *Archaic and Classical Greek Art* will appear in the Oxford History of Art series in 1988.

Lynn E. Roller is Professor of Classics at the University of California, Davis (USA). She has been a member of the archaeological term investigating the Phrygian site of Gordion since 1979 and has published a monograph, *Gordion Special Studies I,* and numerous articles on Phrygian epigraphy, history and religion. Her book on the Phrygian Mother Goddess Cybele, entitled *In Search of God the Mother: The Cult of Anatolian Cybele,* will be published by the University of California Press.

Judith Lynn Sebesta is Professor of Classics at the University of South Dakota (USA). She participated in the National Endowment for the Humanities Seminar 'The Social, Religious and Political Significance of Roman Dress' in 1988. She is co-editor, with Larissa Bonfante, of *The World of Roman Costume* (1994).

Alison Sharrock is Senior Lecturer and Head of Department at the University of Keele (UK). She has published on Ovid (including *Seduction and Repetition in Ovid's Ars Amatoria 2,* 1994), on Roman elegy and on Roman comedy. Her next books will be *Fifty Key Classical Authors* and an edited collection entitled *Intratextuality.* Most of her work is informed by a discourse-based feminist theory.

Teresa M. Shaw is Program Co-ordinator and Adjunct Assistant Professor in Religion at the Claremont Graduate School in Claremont, California (USA). She is the director of the research project on 'Models of Piety in Late Antiquity' at the Institute for Antiquity and Christianity in Claremont and the author of *The Burden of the Flesh: Fasting, Gender, and Embodiment in Early Christian Ascetic Theory* (forthcoming 1998).

Jonathan Walters is Mellon Fellow at the University of Southern California, Los Angeles (USA). His research interests include gender and sexuality in the ancient world and, in particular, Roman concepts of manhood. He has written widely on these issues.

Maria Wyke is a member of the editorial collective of *Gender & History* and is Senior Lecturer in Classics at the University of Reading (UK). She has written widely on gender and the representation of women in ancient Rome and has co-edited *Women in Ancient Societies: 'An Illusion of the Night'* (1994). As a companion to this book, she has also edited another collection entitled *Parchments of Gender: Deciphering the Bodies of Antiquity* (1998).

John G. Younger teaches Greek art and archaeology at Duke University, North Carolina (USA). He manages several email discussion lists, maintains several web sites on archaeology and on gender and sexuality, and writes 'Caught in the Web', a continuing column on archaeology on the Internet, for the periodical *Biblical Archaeologist.*

Index

abortion 105
Abraham 142, 143, 144
Acilisene 69
Acro-Corinth 72
Acropolis 86
Adonis 70, 122
Aeneid 127, 128–30, 135n
Aetios of Amida 152n, 162, 163, 164
Africa 138
Akkadian language 23
Akkadian texts 18, 22, 40
Akurgal 13
Alexander the Great 192, 200
Amazons 182
amenorrhea 163
Ammon 138
Anaitis 69
Anaphe *kouros* 88, 89
Anath 65
Anatolia 133n
Andrews, Tamsey 101n
angels 11, 167
Anglo-Saxons 182
Antenor 90
Antiphanes 122
apatheia 167
Aphrodite 56, 57, 58, 68, 69, 71, 72, 73, 127
Aphrodite Paphia 72
Apostolius 78
Arabia 138, 139
Aristion 126, 129
Aristogeiton 90
Aristophanes 82, 184, 188n, 205
Aristophanes (painter) 99
Aristotle 122, 170n, 182, 195, 200
'Armed Aphrodite' 72
Armenia 59, 67, 68, 69
aryballos 86
asceticism 6, 155
Asheras 65
Ashtaroth-Astarte 72
Ashtoreth 65
assinnu 45
Assurbelkala 22
Assyrians 68
Aštar (see also *Ištar*) 33n
Astarte 59, 65, 66–67, 69
Atargatis 70, 72
Athena 86, 114n
Athenaeus 57
Athenaios 122

Athene Nike 81
Athens 57, 81, 82, 90, 96, 114n, 122, 132n, 149, 154n, 187, 188n, 191
Attis 119, 123–24, 127, 132n, 134n
Atraharsis 23, 29
Atys 123
Augustine of Hippo 70, 145, 147, 149, 150
Augustus 56, 100, 105, 106, 107, 108, 109, 110, 113, 114

Baalbec 59, 69, 70
Babylon 58, 59, 60, 61, 63, 64, 69, 70, 73
Babylonia 67
Babylonian Talmud 148, 154n
Basil of Ancyra 155–72
Basilica Aemilia 107
Battakes 134n
battle 19, 20
Beard, Mary 205
beards 14, 96, 99, 109, 120, 132n
Bhabha, Homi 177
black-figure pottery 90
'black Jews' see *Falashas*
Boardman, John 81
Boiotia 87
Bosch, Hieronymus 11
bride-auction 63
Brooten, Bernadette, 205–6
Butler, Judith 2, 177
Byblos 70
Bynum, Caroline 8

Cadden, Joan 199–202
Canaan 65, 66–67, 72
Carthage 65, 70
Cassian, John 170n, 171n
castrato 29, 33n
Catullus 127, 134n, 135n
Celts 120, 133n
Ceres 114n
Charles, HRH 80
Christ 142, 156, 159
Christianity 6, 69, 78n, 143–44, 145, 146, 147, 148, 149, 155–72, 188n, 195, 204–8
Chrysostom, John 204
Chigi Vase 84, 85
Cicero 108, 115n
circumcision 136–54
City of God 70

Clairmont, Christoph 81
Clark, Gillian 181
Clark, Kenneth 80
Clement of Rome 122, 206
Cleopatra 174, 189n
Clouds 82
Cohen, David 194
Comana 59, 71
Constantine 207
Constantine the African 200, 201
Cooper, Kate 206–8
Corinth 4, 56–58, 71, 72, 73
creation 155–72
creation myths 10, 23
curses 28
Cybele 5, 118, 128, 132n, 133n, 135n
  (see also *Great Mother*)
cylinder seals 11, 19
Cyprian of Carthage 145, 147, 149
Cyprus 69, 72
Cyrus the Great 58, 64, 68

D'Ambra, Eve 107
Daphnis and Chloe 184
Dean-Jones, Lesley 199, 200, 202
Delaney, Carol 109
Demand, Nancy 199
Demeter cult 205
Derketo 72
Diderot, Denis 80
diet 155–72
Diodorus of Sicily 151n
Dionysermos 86
Dionysios of Halikarnassos 126
Dionysos 93–95, 96, 99, 102n
Diotima 209–10
divination 39, 40, 49
divorce 38, 105, 136
Douglas, Mary 41
Douris 91, 92
Dowling, Linda 196–98
Downham, Simon 78n
DuBois, Page 119

Edom 138
Egypt 10, 70, 72, 138, 139, 151n, 173–78,
  182, 200, 209
Egyptian women 173–78
Elm, Susanna 165, 169n
En of Uruk 18
Enetoi 60
Enlil 9
Epistle of Jeremias 65, 68, 76n
Erech 63
Eryx 71
Ethiopia 138, 139–40, 152n
ethnography 3
Etruscans 90, 209
eunuch 34n, 118–35
Euripides 93

Falashas 140, 151n, 152n
Festus 115n
figurative art 11
financial profit 43, 44
flaminica Dialis 113
flood myth 19, 23
Forum 107
Foucault, Michel 1, 30n, 175–76, 194–97,
  196
Foxhall, Lin 194
Frazer, J.G. 59–60, 69
Freud, Sigmund, 23, 176

Galen 161, 162, 170, 201
Gallus 123–30, 133n, 134n, 135n
gender studies 179–90
Genucius 125
girsequ 45
Gleason, Maud 192–93
gnostics 159
Goldhill, Simon 194–96, 198
Gombrich, Ernst 88
Great Mother (also *Magna Mater*) 5, 118,
  124, 125, 126, 129, 132n, 133n, 135n, 205
Gregory of Nyssa 158
Grosz, Elizabeth 177
Gudea of Lagash 28
Gyges 116n

Hallpike, Christopher 10, 32n
Halperin, David 119
Hammurapi 9
Harmodios 90
Hathor 72
Hatshepsut 174
Hera 86
Herakles 96, 104n, 192
Hercules 111
Herms 93
Hermes 91
Herodotus 56, 58, 59–60, 61, 64, 66, 68, 69,
  70, 76n
Hesiod 183, 187, 191
Hierodules 64
Hildegard of Bingen 200
Himmelmann, N. 101n, 102n
Hinduism 182
Hipparkhos 90
Hippocrates 122, 199, 200, 201, 202
Hittite texts 18
Holy Trinity, Brompton 78n
Homer 191
Homeric poems 83, 84, 204
Horace 134n

Inanna 18, 65
Internet 6, 209–13
Ishchali 26
Ishtar 65, 72
Islam 138

Išmedagan of Isin 9, 20
Israel 62, 138, 182
Ištar (also Ishtar) 45, 59, 62, 66

Jerome, Saint 170n, 171n, 172n
Jews 5, 136–54, 188n, 204
Johnson, Mark 8
Jowett, Benjamin 196, 197
Judaism, Hellenistic 144
Judaism, rabbinic 5, 136, 137
Justin Martyr 69, 143–44, 145, 146, 149, 150
Juvenal 183

Khairedemos 96, 98, 104n
komos 91, 92
korai 86
kouros 86, 87, 88, 99
Kritios 90
Kudur Mabuk 16
Kuhrt, Amélie 30
Kyzikos 120, 121

Lambert, W.G. 65
Langdon, Susan 101n
Laqueur, Thomas 196
Laronia 183
laws 22, 45, 46
Lenaea 94
Letoios of Melitene 156
Levine, Molly Myerowitz 109
Livia 106, 111
Livy 105, 107, 113, 120, 125
Long, Edwin 63
Loraux, Nicole 191–92
Lucian 70
Lucretia 105, 114
Lucretius 125–26
Lydians 69
Lykeas 96, 98, 103n
Lysippos 104n
Lysistrata 184

Ma 71
Magnesia 132n
Makaria 97
Manichaeans 159
Manuli, Paola 202
Mapplethorpe, Robert 80, 103n
Marcion 159
Mari 14, 15
marital abuse 38, 43
Martial 127
martyrs 183
Marxism 189n
Medes 67, 69
medicine 3
Megalesia 124, 125
Memphis 139
Menander 122, 181
Mesopotamia 3–4, 8–37, 38–55, 62, 65

Meter 118, 120, 122, 123–24, 132n, 133n
metragyrt 120, 122, 123
Michelangelo 13, 103n
Millar, Sandy 78n
Mishnah 148
Moab 138
monasticism 155
Mother Goddess 119, 121, 123
Mylitta 59–60, 61, 63–64, 65, 67

Naramsîn of Agade 35n
Nesiotes 90
Nicolaus Damascenus 67, 68, 77n
Nineveh 22, 24
Ninlil 76
Nintu 23
Nippur 9
Nubia 210
nudity 4, 11, 18, 20, 35n, 36n, 80–104

Odyssey 83, 84
Oltos 94
Olympia 122, 132n
Olympic games 82
Osiris 70
Ovid 126, 184

Panatheaia 90, 99
Parthenon 82, 95–96
Parrot, André 33n
Parthians 68
Pater, Walter 196, 197
Paul, Saint 78n, 142–43, 144, 147, 204, 206
Paulus of Aigenta 152n
Perizoma 90
Perseus 207
Pessinous 120, 123, 133n, 134n
Philistia 72
Philo of Alexandria 18, 35, 140–42, 144, 147, 150, 206
Philodemus 134n
philosophy 3
Phoenicia 65, 70, 138
Phrygia 118, 119, 120, 123, 125, 127, 128, 132n, 133n
pictographs 10–11
Pindar 57, 72
Plato 8, 127, 195, 196, 197, 198, 205
Platonism 28, 207
Pliny 90, 116n, 200
politics 3
Polybios 120, 125
Polykleitos 95, 96, 104n
Pomeroy, Sarah 182
Pompeii 183
Pompeius Trogus 69
Praxiteles 104n
Propertius 184
prostitution 56–79

psykter 91, 92
Pythagoras 182, 183

Qudshu 65
queer theory 173
Quintilian 108

ram 14, 83
rape 43, 184, 189n
red-figure pottery 90, 91, 92, 94
religion 3, 204–8
Rhea 122
Riace Bronzes 88, 95, 99
Richlin, Amy 119
Ridgway, Brunhilde 81
Rimsîn of Larsa 16
Robertson, Martin 82, 86
Roma 106, 107, 114, 114n
Rome 45, 46, 105–17, 119, 189n
Romulus 107
Rousselle, Aline 202
Rufus of Ephesus 162, 163, 164
Ruskin, John 197

Sabazios 122
Sabines 107
saints 11, 183
Saller, Richard 194
Sappho 185, 194, 205
Sardis 123
satyrs 91, 96
Sawyer, Deborah 204
segregation 6
self-castration 118–19, 131n
Seleucids 69
Seneca 189n
Sennacherib 22
Serapis 139
Serdaioi 102n
Sestos 120
sex omens 4, 38–55
sheep 14
Shulgi of Ur 35n
Sibylline oracles 124
Sicily 65, 71
Simonides 57, 72
Sophocles 82
Soranus 152n, 163, 171n
Soterides 120
Soviet Union, former 204
Sparta 57, 191
Spivey, Nigel 81
Stanford, Bedell 196
statuettes 22, 83
Stewart, Andrew 81, 82
Stobaeus, John 68
stola 107, 111, 112, 113, 114
Strabo 56, 57, 65, 67, 68, 69–70, 71, 72,
    139–41, 151n
Suetonius Augustus 105, 110

Sulpicius Gallus 111
Sumerian language 8, 9, 10, 23
Sumerian texts 9, 18, 20, 22, 23
synagogue 136, 145–46
Syria 70, 72, 138

Tacitus 188n
Talmud 149
Tanit 65
Tarpeia 107
Tell Halaf 27
Tellus 106, 107, 114
terracottas 22, 26, 27
Thebes 132n
Thesmophoria 182, 183
Thucydides 90, 181
Thyrsos 93
Tiberios Claudios Deiotarus 132n
Tiberios Claudios Heras 132n
Tiberius 111
Tiresias 192
toga 105, 107, 108–10
Torah 136, 148, 150
Trojans 124
Trygonion 128, 129
Turkey 115n, 116n, 118
Tzvi Abusch 28

Ur III 30, 33n
Uranus 126
Urnanše 14, 15, 33n
Urnanše of Lagaš 13
Uruk vase 14, 17

Valerius Maximus 70, 111
Van Gennep, A. 62
Varro 107, 113
vase-painting 4
Venus 70, 114n
Verrius Flaccus 107, 108, 110,
    111, 113
Vestal Virgins 70, 108, 183,
    205
Veyne, Paul 194
Virgil 127, 128–30
Virginity 155–72

Wasps 82
Western Africa 65
Widows 165
Wilde, Oscar 196–97
Winckelmann, J.J. 81, 82
Winkler, John 44
witches 182, 186, 210

Xanthus of Lydia 151n
Xenophon 99, 195
Xerxes 90

Yamauchi, E.M. 65, 67

CPSIA information can be obtained at www.ICGtesting.com
Printed in the USA
BVOW09s0431241214

380685BV00009B/165/P